Praise for *Kite Strings of the Southern Cross*

Finalist for the Thomas Cook/Daily Telegraph Travel Book Award 2000

Winner of Foreword magazine's Silver Medal for Travel Book of the Year

'Anyone who can persuade a Fijian island community to wear leaves in their sandals for good luck is a poet of the road'

Justine Hardy, author of *Scoop-Wallah*

'The best travel book I've read in years. It's the kind of book you want every traveller you know to read'

Brad Newsham, author

'Gough records everything she sees with a subtle wit, a lyrical turn of phrase, and a remarkably open mind… Her writing is vigorous, sensual and visual… She sweeps the reader into her world'

Globe and Mail (Canada)

'Outer and inner landscape and the poetry of her convictions conspire to create a narrative that is rich and emotional. Whether she is describing the way the angelic translucent bodies of the jellyfish form a gently swaying cathedral near the sea's surface, or the morning ritual of the Giant Aunts in which each woman floats her gorgeous body adrift… Gough is present, vulnerable and delightful'

San Francisco Examiner

'lovely, lyrical… a bittersweet tale, heartfelt and well told… Though she has encountered unhappiness, bewilderment and even terror on the road, her voice is fresh and still full of wonder at what the world still holds'

Trips Magazine

'… an amiable and engaging storyteller, who knows how to bring characters, dialogues and situations to compelling life… Reading this book is like travelling all over again'

Don George, *Salon.com*, editor of *Wanderlust*

'A great page-turner… The image of the "Great Aunts" floating like starfish on the water is one I shall never forget… Her seemingly effortless writing… will no doubt make her a new star in the Southern Cross'

New Zealand Herald

'an arresting account of an individual's odyssey over a ten-year span in which time she explores her own growth as a human being, and how travelling has helped to nourish that growth. One also suspects, however, that Laurie, even without the travels, would still have her say, beautifully and with a gifted poet's vision… Her tone of understated charm, humour, honesty, courage, and resiliency…combine to create tales that readers from any walk of life can relate to simply as human beings… refreshingly renews one's wonder of the world and broadens one's appreciation for it'

The Toronto Star

'Colourful and inspiring… This feisty, sexy, energetic tale… offers the best of memoir and travel narrative combined. Gough chronicles her encounters with both humour and wisdom'

Amazon.com

'A terrific yarn. Highly recommended'

Choice

'Skip this review, head straight to the bookstore, and buy Kite Strings of the Southern Cross'

Spa Magazine (U.S.)

KISS THE SUNSET PIG

An American Road Trip with Exotic Detours

LAURIE GOUGH

PENGUIN CANADA

PENGUIN CANADA

Published by the Penguin Group

Penguin Group (Canada), 90 Eglinton Avenue East, Suite 700, Toronto, Ontario, Canada M4P 2Y3
(a division of Pearson Canada Inc.)

Penguin Group (USA) Inc., 375 Hudson Street, New York, New York 10014, U.S.A.
Penguin Books Ltd, 80 Strand, London WC2R 0RL, England
Penguin Ireland, 25 St Stephen's Green, Dublin 2, Ireland (a division of Penguin Books Ltd)
Penguin Group (Australia), 250 Camberwell Road, Camberwell, Victoria 3124, Australia
(a division of Pearson Australia Group Pty Ltd)
Penguin Books India Pvt Ltd, 11 Community Centre, Panchsheel Park, New Delhi – 110 017, India
Penguin Group (NZ), cnr Airborne and Rosedale Roads, Albany, Auckland 1310, New Zealand
(a division of Pearson New Zealand Ltd)
Penguin Books (South Africa) (Pty) Ltd, 24 Sturdee Avenue, Rosebank, Johannesburg 2196, South Africa

Penguin Books Ltd, Registered Offices: 80 Strand, London WC2R 0RL, England

Published in Penguin Canada paperback by Penguin Group (Canada),
a division of Pearson Canada Inc., 2006. Simultaneously published in the U.K.
by Summersdale Publishers Ltd, 46 West Street, Chichester, West Sussex PO19 1RP.

(WEB) 10 9 8 7 6 5 4 3 2

Manufactured in Canada.

LIBRARY AND ARCHIVES CANADA CATALOGUING IN PUBLICATION

Gough, Laurie, 1964
Kiss the sunset pig : an American road trip (with exotic detours) / Laurie Gough

ISBN-13: 978-0-14-305615-7
ISBN-10: 0-14-305615-8

1. Gough, Laurie, 1964– —Travel—United States. 2. United States—Description and travel. I. Title.

E169.Z83G69 2006 917.304'931 C2006-900917-1

British Library Cataloguing in Publication data available

Visit the Penguin Group (Canada) website at **www.penguin.ca**

Special and corporate bulk purchase rates available; please see
www.penguin.ca/corporatesales or call 1-800-399-6858, ext. 477 or 474

To Joe Fisher,
wherever you are

'It should not be denied that being footloose has always exhilarated us. It is associated in our minds with escape from history and oppression and law and irksome obligations, with absolute freedom, and the road has always led west'

Wallace Stegner, *The American West as Living Space*

'And the climb upward out of the cave into the upper world is the ascent of the mind into the domain of true knowledge'

Plato

'Sometimes she thought she was just trying to have fun in life, and other times she realised she must be terribly confused'

Lorrie Moore, *Like Life*

'Each day at the hour of the highest tide a large white sow would appear at the end of the street in Palestina. With calm, slow dignity, threading her way between the chunks of balsa and the trunks of trees that had been torn away and flung up on the beach by the winter storms, she would stand finally for a moment where the last waves spilled around her feet; then, head held high, staring intently toward the north and oceanic curve of the horizon, she would move out into the water and stand there in profound meditation up to her shoulders in the sea while the breakers crashed over her head. Something deep and awful drove her into the sea; something deep and awful, poetic and unpiggish drew her daily to contemplate the vastness and mystery of the Pacific. Her eyes were drawn to the northern edges of the earth at the limits of her vision as though, the first pig in the history of the world, she were realising the roundness of this globe upon which she was imprisoned. Almost immediately I identified myself with that old white sow, envied her that dignity and that impulse toward transfiguration that drove her into the breakers. I could only give her my own qualities; we were both strangers on a savage coast, both of us burned with longings, an awareness of mortality, a sense of having arrived at that point when we would harvest our own destinies.'

From Moritz Thomsen's unpublished memoirs

Acknowledgements

I offer my deepest thanks to Jennifer Barclay who believed in this book from the beginning and offered invaluable help and advice as a friend long before she became my editor. Thank you also to Carol Baker and everyone else at Summersdale. I'm very grateful for the support of Rob McCart and my parents, Tena and Patrick Gough, who have always encouraged my writing. Thank you to the wonderful friends who read early versions and offered suggestions: Andrea Hossack, Eric Innanen, Kevin Shortt, Dawn Matheson and Joanne Astley. I thank Stephan Johnson, Ann Austin, Lawrence Jaffe and all the others who make appearances in this book and I hope you don't mind that some of your names have changed. I'm also indebted to Linda and Steve Kommrusch for their generous financial gift in my early writing of this book, and I gratefully acknowledge the Canada Council for the Arts for their much needed support. Thanks to the people at Travelers' Tales in San Francisco, thanks to Marty Williams for a line from his song, and thank you to Marney Makridakis in New York and Philip Blazdell in the U.K. who wrote me long letters after reading my first book and continue to write and be my friends today. I am continually amazed at the wealth of support and encouragement I receive from readers around the world. Finally, thanks to all my fellow travellers out there, searching for outer and inner roads to some place new. May we all find what we're looking for.

L.G.

The events in this book all took place before September 11, 2001, when the world was, or seemed to be, a simpler place, certainly less wary, and when it was still OK to have a quarrel with an American border guard.

Chapter 1

June 20, 1998

I just left my life behind and am heading to the other side of it. The other side of it is called California, the land of iced organic defatted decaf soy mochas at every small town street corner, T-shirts any day of the year, taco stands in the desert, orange trees on front lawns and avocado trees in the back; the land of redwoods and palms and palm readings down the road, mountains almost everywhere and a twelve-hundred-mile view of the sea. It's the land of Tom Waits drinking tea in a backwoods café. I saw him once. He ordered the tea with his gravelly voice and when he got up to leave, he turned around to smile at me as if we were in one of his songs.

California, I've wanted you all my life. You're almost on the horizon, although I can still see my hometown of Guelph, Ontario, Canada in the rearview mirror and California is 2,500 miles west of here.

I'm driving a blue, beat-up mini Ford Bronco that I've decided to call Marcia, in honour of Marcia Clark, the prosecuting attorney in the O. J. Simpson trial. I didn't want the Bronco to remind me of O. J. Simpson who tried to escape down the LA freeway in a Ford Bronco with a disguise, ten thousand dollars and a pistol to his head. Next to me sits a woman I've decided to call Morticia, although I call her that only in my mind. She's wearing a black polyester dress draping down to her ankles on one of the hottest days of the year and her long hair is dyed the colour of slick tar. Enough black make-up is painted around her eyes to frighten small children and her face is unnaturally pale. Her real name is Debbie. I've just learned Morticia is 28, which seems a little old to be decked out in this sort of Goth get-up, or whatever they call it, especially when we're about to cross the border from Canada into the U.S. and I can't imagine the American border patrols will take kindly to her freakish attire.

Morticia is with me because she read the notice I placed on the University of Guelph ride board:

CALIFORNIA OR BUST. LEAVING NEXT WEEK. CALL IF YOU WANT TO COME ALONG AND SHARE DRIVING AND GAS.

Debbie was the first reasonable person to call, or so she sounded on the phone. Before that, I'd had a variety of calls, all sounding like potential nutcases, although the seventeen year old named Jason who wanted to move to the desert and start his own band could have been inspiring. The middle-aged Polish woman who was escaping her husband would have been trouble and the student who said he'd never consider sleeping anywhere but in a hotel was a definite no. Hadn't he ever slept in his car even once? Thrown his sleeping bag on the ground in a field under the stars one night? What was wrong with twenty-two year olds these days?

I liked Debbie right away. She sounded fun. Debbie said she was a grad student and she wanted a ride to St. Louis,

Missouri, where her boyfriend lived. St. Louis is only twelve hours from Guelph, not even a third of the way to California, but she sounded so high-spirited and level-headed on the phone, I said yes. We spoke over the phone again a few times to make arrangements but we didn't meet in person until today when I picked her up at her place in one of the student housing areas of town, a neighbourhood of tall trees, large old houses in varying stages of disrepair, and dented cars parked on the road with bumper stickers saying things like *Think Globally, Act Locally* and *Mean People Suck* and *Think Whirled Peas!* The woman who answered the door seemed to be dressed for Hallowe'en even though this is June.

'Is Debbie here? We're driving to St. Louis.'

'That's me. I'm almost done packing. Hold on. Oh, nice to meet you.'

I waited on her front porch under the scorching sun while she disappeared into the darkness of the house. I heard laughter inside but couldn't see any faces through the screen door. From somewhere in the back of the house a male voice said, 'Are you really taking that thing, Deb? Hot damn!' When she reappeared on the porch carrying a knapsack, a black leather case and a rolled-up army sleeping bag I couldn't help noticing she was beautiful. She thrust her hand out to shake mine, the normalcy of the gesture taking me by surprise. Under the layers of black fabric she seemed to carry herself with the grace of someone with long slender limbs and a slow gait. Her eyes, beneath the metallic layers of eye shadow, were large and green and of an uncommon clarity, almost childlike, as if they were focused at a wider angle than most, allowing more of the world inside. Although her straight hair was dyed black from her ears down, its roots were shades of mahogany and red like tones of polished wood. Her skin looked as if it had never been touched by the sun, the colour of cream, and although some sun would have given it a cherry glow, she hadn't a single line or wrinkle.

As we walked toward my car she struggled with the zipper of her leather case which wouldn't close because it was bulging full of clothes. When I helped her hold the case while she pulled the zipper, I noticed that on top of some folded black jeans, a long strip of leather was coiled around itself like a black snake. 'Looks like a belt, doesn't it?' she said.

'I guess. Is it?'

'It's a whip!' she said as she yanked the zipper across the top. She tossed the case and sleeping bag into the back of my car, hopped in the front seat, waved out the window and shouted goodbye at the house. As we drove off, she chuckled to herself, as if she knew something I didn't. Terrific, I thought. I'll tell the American border guards she's a hitchhiker and I'm dropping her off at the Beat Me in St. Louis S&M convention. I should have gone for the Polish woman with the mean husband.

Morticia and I have been trying to have a conversation but I think her outfit is getting in the way. It's as if we're from different countries and we don't know the right questions to ask. Already I can tell we're both the sort who prefer asking questions rather than answering them. This conversation is like a game we're playing, tossing a hot potato back and forth as fast as we can so we don't have to think things through, so it doesn't burn us.

'So how long are you going to St. Louis for?' I lean toward the open window to let the wind cool my face.

'Don't know yet. I have to wait and see how I like it. Why are you going to California?' Her feet on the dash. She's wearing army boots. The heat, I keep thinking. I'm in sandals and even they seem too hot today.

'I love California. I've been there lots of times. Hot day for a drive. Too bad I don't have air conditioning. So you're visiting your boyfriend in St. Louis?'

'Yep. Can't wait. What's so great about California?' she asks.

I turn to look at her eyes again, and this time I don't notice their clarity, but how they're expertly rimmed with smooth black eyeliner that grows gradually thicker from the inside until it reaches the iris and then tapers dramatically to a feathery tail just beyond the corner of her eye. I'm wearing cut-off shorts, a cotton sleeveless top and no make-up. Suddenly I feel very unfashionable. 'Lots of things. The coast for one thing. Most of the California coast is rugged and undeveloped. People don't realise that. They associate California with L.A. But so much of the state is wilderness. It's full of scenic beauty. So what are you studying?'

'Physics. And some other stuff. What are the people like there?'

'Physics?' I look over to see she hasn't rolled down her window at all.

'I'll probably do a post-doc in physics. The Californians – what are they like?'

'I guess you find all types there,' I tell her. 'The place is full of variety. People actually from the state and all kinds of people who've left winter and pollution and their old lives somewhere else. California's very progressive, lots of environmentalists, social activists. No smoking allowed in public in the whole state, not in bars, restaurants. They don't even allow it in outdoor cafés out there. But it doesn't seem to matter much because hardly anyone seems to smoke there any more. They talk about it as if it's kind of a quaint and embarrassing idea from the past.' I pass a slow-moving RV. 'Where are you from?'

'Toronto originally.' She picks up her knapsack and begins rifling through it. 'You?'

'Guelph. I was born in the States but grew up in Guelph mostly.' She's looking intently for something. Cigarettes perhaps.

'I have way too much stuff in this thing. So how long are you going to California for?' She's emptying the knapsack's contents onto her lap. One by one the items tumble out – a giant hairbrush, a clear plastic make-up bag, two tattered paperbacks, comic books that appear to feature leather-clad women in black masks holding whips, an electric toothbrush…

'For the summer,' I tell her, although it could be much longer. I might actually be moving there for good. I might actually be leaving my entire life behind. Everything. I might be leaving my nice boyfriend and a hundred other friends, work, maple trees, streets where people know my name, a hometown where every block contains a memory. 'Hey, comics. I used to love Archie comics,' I say. '*Betty and Veronica* was my favourite.'

'No way. Me too.' For a second her eyes flash wide. 'They're worth a lot, if you have the right ones and they're in good shape.'

'There must be five hundred Archies in my parents' basement,' I tell her. Maple forests stretch back from both sides of the highway, occasionally interrupted by a dairy or cattle farm. I look at the collection of odds and ends piled on the black clingy nylon of Morticia's lap. She must be boiling in those clothes but she's not even sweating. She actually seems cool. I keep thinking she'll explain something about herself, like her appearance, but after over an hour's drive it doesn't seem she will. Couldn't she have ditched the costume just for today? We're about to cross an international border.

'Is that rain?' she asks. Big drops are starting to spatter the windshield. The sky has become suddenly leaden.

'Yeah, rain will be nice. Cool things down. I love summer rains.'

'Me too,' she says. 'I love how rain smells.' She takes a deep breath and closes her eyes. We're discussing the weather. She's dressed as a witch for Christ's sake. Is her appearance supposed to pass without comment? 'Smells like dust rising,' she adds.

Dust rising? I'd expect someone so urban-looking, dressed as if she prefers the night and all its dark offerings, midnight taxi rides and full moon coven get-togethers for instance, wouldn't care or even know about the smell of summer rain showers. Yet she does. She tells me how as a kid she'd run into the street during thunderstorms, how her mother hated it, how she loved to feel drenched. Our conversation turns to Lewis Carroll, whom she loves. The rain is pounding harder, instantly cooling the air like a gift. Cars have switched on their headlights and I can hardly see the highway. Morticia and I discuss European medieval history and poetry. She likes T. S. Eliot and Emily Dickinson. Me too. This is wonderful. Morticia is thoughtful and self-possessed, a bright mind with a youthful confidence, happy even. I wonder why she's showing the world this dark image of herself. Is it a reflection of a personal tragedy she's projecting? Perhaps it's more subtle, something fragile and vulnerable deep within her that's not apparent by anything other than the way she presents herself, this physical fact of her black outfit. Maybe it's fashion, something she and her friends can wear to be distinguished in a crowd, to pretend they're different, more interesting than the rest of us, possessors of a secret knowledge. I can't fathom what it could be but perhaps that's what separates the young from the rest of us. The young, anyone under thirty, are still open to the world, still believe it can be new, offer fresh ideas. Those of us over thirty, even by a few years like myself, have started shutting the door on anything new. We've grown suspicious, weary. We've already allowed enough of the world in to last us a lifetime. Anything new would be confusing.

'So are you excited about seeing your boyfriend?'

'God yes.' She peers in her knapsack again and looks up, puzzled, as if she can't remember if she brought something.

'So how long have you known him?' The rain is splashing the side of my face and feels so good I leave the window open.

'Over a year now.'

'How did you meet him?'

'On the Net. There it is! It was in the pocket!' She holds out a Kit Kat chocolate bar in front of her with both hands.

'I didn't know they still made Kit Kats. No kidding, the Net? In a chat room or something?' I glance over to see she's still holding the chocolate bar up to the windshield like a trophy. Somehow this lightens my heart. 'Remember Bar Six? You can't get Bar Sixes any more. Or Pixie Stix either. So, a chat line?'

'We like the same music, Alex and I, that's his name. Kind of a music chat line.'

'Really? What's he like?'

'He's funny. Super intelligent, a little out there. Lives in his head, one of those types. Pretty cute too, sounds like.' She offers me two sticks of the Kit Kat, half of it.

'Thanks. Sounds like? Sounds like what?' I bite into the melted chocolate.

She takes a bite and chews slowly, contemplating; then, scrunching up the red wrapper she says suddenly, 'Like he's cute, not that he's actually said that about himself, but I can tell a lot about him by the way he writes. I know more about him than I do about my own brother. It's amazing what you can learn about a person you've never seen.'

'You've never seen him?' I keep my eyes on the road but say it cheerily, so she'll go on.

'No. That's why I'm going to St. Louis, to see him.'

'Oh… right.' I swallow the last of my Kit Kat. The rain has stopped as suddenly as it arrived and already the sky is brightening. Ahead is a sign saying, 'Bridge to the United States.' We pay a toll fee and cross the half-mile expanse over the St. Clair River where it flows out of Lake Huron. The view from the bridge is a glorious surprise. The sun has escaped from the rapidly moving clouds and its reflection on the water is blinding. A rainbow enlivens the sky and far below sailboats emerge looking like toys. At the end of the bridge we drive straight up to the immigration booth without having to wait in a line. I say hello and smile at the white-haired man behind the glass. He slides open his little window.

'Nationality?'

'Canadians.'

'Purpose of visit?'

'Vacation.'

'Where are you going?'

'I'm going to California and she's going to St. Louis.'

The man leans out the window to get a closer look. Morticia twists her wrist up to give him a wave. He takes a deep uncompassionate breath. 'Yeah, right, and I was born yesterday.'

'Excuse me?'

'Would you mind telling me where you're really going?'

I repeat what I just told him.

'Look ladies. I don't have time for this. Where are you going today?'

'Why wouldn't we be going to California and St. Louis?' Don't people go to those places? We have to go somewhere. I look over at Morticia. She shrugs. Maybe he thinks someone who looks like Morticia wouldn't be caught dead in the Bible-belted flatness of the Midwest. I turn back to the border guard. 'Would it make a difference if I said Chicago? Nevada? … South Dakota?'

Ignoring me, he writes something on a little piece of paper. 'Pull your vehicle over there and step inside the main building.' The man hands me the piece of paper and with no warmth in his voice whatsoever says, 'Think about telling the truth once you're inside.'

We pull into the mostly empty parking lot and stop the car. Morticia says to me quickly, almost under her breath, 'Let's just say we're both going to California.'

'But why?' I ask, incredulous.

'Because it sounds weird to say we're going to two different places.'

'Why? We have nothing to hide. We just tell them the truth. If we lie they'll trip us up. There's no point. Let's just tell them the exact truth. We're not doing anything illegal.'

'But they don't trust the Internet. Don't tell them I met Alex on the Internet.'

'OK. I doubt they'll ask that anyway. This should be over in five minutes.' As I open the car door I glance into the back seat at my pile of things. It's true. I have nothing to hide. When they search the car they'll see my tent, my camping gear, my books, my maps of the Rockies, maps of California, my hiking guides, Morticia's whip. What's the big deal? I begin to feel my pumping heart as we walk to the inspection station.

The spacious, air-conditioned U.S. immigration building, impeccably clean with freshly painted white walls, is a far cry from the bleak and grey immigration offices I've seen in developing countries. Those offices usually have peeling paint, cheap fluorescent lights, too few windows and men standing around holding unreasonably large guns. Sometimes, giant warning signs declare, 'Anyone Caught With Drugs Will Be Hung.' Things never seem on the up and up in those offices.

Another white-haired man is waiting for us, although this one's hair shoots up in mean military spikes like a bristle brush, perfectly flat on top. Pallid blue eyes narrow to slits as he watches us take the long walk up to his counter. He taps his fingers. Four or five people behind him sit at computer screens in a brightly-lit office. When we arrive at the counter he doesn't say anything at first but continues tapping his fingers, eyeing us, and then, 'Your story?'

'For some reason the guy out there didn't believe us.' I hand him the piece of paper that seems to be written in scrawl, perhaps in code. 'I'm going to California and I'm dropping her off in St. Louis.'

'Aha,' he says, 'and why should he believe you?' He's still tapping his fingers.

'Because it's the truth. Don't people go to California any more? Do you want to see my maps of California? Addresses of friends I have there? What can I show you?'

'Some I.D. for starters.' His tongue is perched on the side of his mouth as if that's its usual resting place. He has a crowded bulldog face.

I fish through my bag and produce a driver's license, a library card, and some other photo I.D. Canadians and Americans aren't usually required to show a passport when crossing each other's borders so I never take mine with me when entering the States.

'What do you do for a living?'

'I'm a teacher.' I don't tell him I'm also a writer. That sounds suspicious to people like this.

'Teacher?' He turns around to the people behind him at the computer screens and shouts, 'She's trying to tell me she's a teacher!' A few of them look up from their screens, not particularly interested.

'Why wouldn't I be a teacher?'

'You don't look like a teacher to me.' Again, that narrowing of his eyes set back in his hardened face.

'Why not?' Does he think all teachers wear hair spray, navy suits and sensible shoes?

'So if you're a teacher you're really smart. You should know all the capital cities.'

'I know capital cities. Try me.'

His eyes are barely visible now, mere cracks of watery blue. For some reason he doesn't want to play this geography game after all.

'What do you teach?' He turns around. 'Listen to this, guys.' The office people don't seem to be listening.

'Lots of different things. High school English, E.S.L., adult education. I used to teach...'

'Prove you're a teacher.'

In my wallet I find my teacher identification card, something I acquired ages ago, after teacher's college, to give me discounts at museums and on trains overseas. It never worked very well for discounts, although once it was enough to get me a teaching job in Fiji. He takes the card, holds it at arm's length for a better view of my photo, as if he's farsighted.

'That you? Your hair's different here.' I lean over and we both look at the picture together, trying to discern how different my hair was. Morticia looks also.

'Not really,' I say. 'Hardly at all. My hair was a little longer then maybe.' Morticia agrees.

'Well, this could be forged.' He tosses the card onto the counter. I notice the skin around his jowls hangs in unpleasant folds.

'Forged? Why would I forge this?'

'Why would I forge this?' he mocks, in an unnecessarily prissy version of my voice. My face is starting to get hot. I hate this man. There's definitely something wrong with him. 'How much money are you taking into my country?' He emphasises the 'my' by drawing it out with an exaggerated southern accent. 'Hey, guys! This should be good!' He says this loudly enough for his co-workers to hear but this time doesn't bother turning around so it's as if he's shouting this at us.

'Well, I have lots of money in my bank account and I'll be using this ATM card and my credit card. I could also show you...'

'Did you guys catch that?' he barks, still facing us.

'I could also show you my bank book. It's in the car.' I pass him two bank cards.

He looks at each of the cards, turns them over, holds them at arm's length. Then, with an alarmingly vicious twist of his mouth, he says, 'Oh, excuse me, I think these are plastic. Do these pieces of plastic look like money to you?' He pauses, waiting for an answer, and proceeds to do something bordering on the unforgivable. He tosses my two plastic cards up above the counter so they do little flips in the air, bounce down, and land on the floor.

'Of course they're plastic.' I'd like this man to suffer a massive cardiac arrest, right here and now, I think as I bend down to retrieve my cards. 'Haven't you seen credit cards before? What do you want? Traveller's cheques? People don't need to use those any more, not with bank machines everywhere, with ATMs. Do you want me to carry American cash across the border? What's the point of that when I can get it in five minutes at the nearest ATM around here? That's what everybody does.'

'That's what everybody does,' he repeats. He's smiling. 'Did you guys hear that?' One of his co-workers seems to be taking a passing interest in this exchange. I look to this other man, exasperated, in hopes he'll add some sanity to the situation. He smiles slightly, shakes his head, and looks back to his computer screen. What's going on here? Why is this man not believing a word I say? Do I look like a criminal? And why is he picking on me alone while Morticia over here looks as if she's on her way to a satanic cult meeting? This guy's a complete bastard, an American Border Bastard. Mr Border Bastard sighs deeply and says sternly, 'I don't want you going into my country and running out of money. I don't want you on the street, young lady.'

'On the street? What do I look like? A bum? A bag lady?' I take a step back, hold out my arms, look down at my shorts, purple top and sandals. I don't think I look like a bum, not at all. In fact I look like Mary Tyler Moore dressed for a summer day. 'Do I? Do I look like a bum?' Both Mr Border Bastard and Morticia look me over and seem to consider this. Despite Morticia's obvious sense of good fashion, she shakes her head. No, she doesn't think I look like a bum either. Is this man deranged? I want to ask him if he gets paid to be a jackass, if it's part of the job description. He's just waiting for me to blow up at him. I can feel it. He wants that. I decide to change tactics. I step back to the counter. 'Would it make a difference if I told you I'm American?'

My words drop like lead. Mr Border Bastard's face empties of expression. 'Excuse me?' He cocks his head as if he didn't hear me right.

'I was born in the United States, in Madison, Wisconsin. I have dual citizenship.' I cringe when I say 'dual citizenship' because from past experience at American borders I've learned they don't take kindly to that term.

The contours of his face begin to change. 'Oh is that so? Is that so? Prove it.' He folds his arms and stands up straight but this time doesn't shout anything back to the others.

I look through my wallet and hand him my birth certificate. He takes it without removing his eyes from mine. At first he just fingers it before taking a look, as if he knows the feel of counterfeit, then he turns it over, holds it at arm's length to read every word with his beady rat eyes. He frowns. He's unnerved, disarmed, furious.

'Why did you lie?'

'When?'

'You said you were Canadian. Did you not say you were Canadian?'

'I am Canadian, but I'm also American. Dual citizenship.'

'What's that? We don't recognise dual citizenship here.'

'OK, fine. I'm American.'

'Well, this will have to be checked. It could be forged like that teacher one.' He puts the birth certificate down on the counter and doesn't seem to know what his next move should be.

'So can we go now?'

His face is actually flushed, as if he's lost his composure. 'I can't stop you, young lady, from entering the United States at this point. I can't turn you back.' He clears his throat.

I've really pissed him off. This is great. Since I'm free to go, I wonder if this is a good time to ask him if he was a member of Hitler Youth. He's a little young to have been an actual Nazi. Or perhaps his father was a Nazi and he grew up under a fascist influence right here in Michigan. Both the US and Canada let in all kinds of Nazis after the war. They thought Nazis could help in the fight against Communism. I'm wondering how to phrase the question when he says to me, 'You can go, but who's your Friday the thirteenth friend over here?'

For the first time his attention is turned towards Morticia. Great. We've already been here 45 minutes. A light returns to his eyes as he looks over his new prey. He leans over the counter, feigning weariness. 'And where are you going again? Chicago?'

'No, St. Louis.' Morticia is actually beaming, perhaps anticipating meeting her Internet boyfriend at the mention of St. Louis. I'm amazed she can appear so calm in the face of such evil.

'Why on earth would you want to go there?'

'To visit a friend.' She says this almost dreamily. She's serene. This is impressive.

'What kind of friend?'

'Just a friend. I have his address here.' Morticia reaches into her knapsack to find her address book but he stops her before she shows it to him. Clearly he doesn't like the orderliness of this, her unruffled composure in the simple act of presenting an address which he fears will be there, neatly written on the white pages of a little book.

'Hold on there, Missy. First of all, how did you and this one over here meet?' He tilts his head in my direction but doesn't look at me. 'What's the story with you two?'

We tell him about the ride board at the university.

'Well that's the biggest cock and bull story if I ever heard one.'

This man is a cretin. I wait for him to shout something over his shoulder to the others but he must realise they aren't listening. He begins to grill Morticia about her financial situation and isn't satisfied that she has enough money to go to St. Louis. He asks her how long she's going to stay there to visit her so-called friend.

'Two weeks.' She says this with the faintest expulsion of disheartened breath, as if two weeks can't possibly be long enough for what she'll encounter there.

'Aha. And how are you getting back to Canada? Is Miss California over here gonna come sweeping back from Hollywood to pick you up?'

'No, I'll take a train probably, or maybe my friend will drive me back. He wants to visit me in Canada.'

'Get your story straight! You don't know how you're getting back?' He scrunches up his face into a knot of wretchedness. 'What kind of a friend is this? Look here, young lady, if you want into the United States you're going to have to show me a train or a bus ticket exiting the United States, a ticket that leaves in nine days or less. You'll also have to show me an updated account of your financial situation. That's the only way I'm letting you in.' He pauses, and for the first time we see his eyes widen to surprising proportions. 'The ONLY way.'

As one by one the words slither from his mouth and coil inside me I realise that Mr Border Bastard must be the keeper of some rare wickedness stored in a bitter heart. He's not a normal person. How can he do this to us? Now we have to go back across the bridge to Canada and drive all over the city of Sarnia to find a train or bus station and a branch of Morticia's bank. That could take hours. This is ludicrous. I look at Morticia and expect to see her as exasperated as I am. But, standing tall in her pagan outfit with her flowing shoe-polish black hair, Morticia is smiling at this pitiful man, smiling as if she doesn't hate him, smiling from the depths of her pure, free heart and shiny green eyes. I think this must be love that's doing this to Morticia. I think this must be life's blessing, that we can stare down the face of hatred any day of the week if we can write a letter to someone who will write us a letter back. Life's prayer for us is easy and everywhere in the world you find people who either listen or don't and everywhere in the world you find people who are hateful.

We leave Mr Border Bastard officiously filling out some form, shaking his head in disgust as if he knows there's something we're hiding from him, some truth we haven't told. We cross back over the bridge to Canada and spend an hour going from train to bus station then back to the train station so Morticia can buy a return ticket from St. Louis. It's much more expensive doing it this way and she really was hoping to drive back with Alex instead of taking a train. When we get to a branch of her bank to request an updated statement of her entire bank account, Morticia is surprised to learn she has over $15,000 deposited in her account. For some reason her mother had deposited some investment certificates into her account without Morticia's knowledge. It seems Morticia is from a wealthy family. Fifteen thousand dollars should make Mr Border Bastard happy, if happiness were possible for him.

Fortunately, we never find out what Mr Border Bastard would have thought of Morticia's motherload of cash because we don't see him again. The second time we attempt to cross the border, along with Morticia's return train ticket, updated bank statement and our heated determination, another man is sitting at the immigration booth at the end of the bridge and this one looks different from the others. He doesn't have a military haircut and he's younger, seemingly more relaxed. 'Of course he's probably just as mean as the others,' I say to Morticia as we drive up to the white line. 'Probably worse!'

'So where would you two be headed today?' He smiles, displaying a set of unnaturally white teeth. His uniform is starched. Ranger Smith comes to mind.

'St. Louis and California.'

I hold my breath. Morticia thrusts out her documents, holds them steady in front of my face. I stare at the windshield, clenching the steering wheel.

'Have a good one.'

I turn to him. 'Excuse me?'

'A good one.' He's smiling as if he's advertising America. What does he mean? Have a good what?

'Step on it! Go!' says Morticia.

'Go?'

'Go!'

I squeal the tires, not actually meaning to, but it feels right for the occasion. We're free. A peculiar lightness takes over my body and everything around us – the highway and the sudden and numerous interstate signs, the duty free store, the green grass on the boulevards, the ATM machines, the convenience stores, the blinding sun setting low on the horizon – feels like the hatching of a strange and marvellous dream. I'm allowed to be here. I'm American.

'Cool!' says Morticia. 'Now I can put on some real make-up. I feel so naked like this.'

Chapter 2

An hour of Michigan green farmland has gone by and I'm working up the courage to ask Morticia about her fondness for black and the puzzling hold the colour seems to have over her life, what its intrinsic purpose in her world could be. For some reason I don't know how to broach the subject. She seems lost in her own world, just as I am. My mind drifts to another woman I encountered once, a woman who remains as mysterious today as she did that night all those years ago. In a far corner of the universe must be a place where all the world's mysteries travel.

Naxos Nights

No single incident in my life has been so strange, so hard to grasp, so totally lacking in feasible explanation. I came to Naxos by mistake, but maybe there are no mistakes. Maybe sometimes we're meant to be led here and there, to certain places at certain times for reasons beyond our understanding, beyond our will or the spell of the moon or the arrangement of the stars in the sky. Maybe all the dark and eternal nameless things lurking around us have their own purpose and vision for us. Who knows?

KISS THE SUNSET PIG

When I was 23, I was travelling alone through Europe. Travelling alone seemed to come naturally to me, and that solitary trip was just the beginning of what would become a habit in the years to come. I'd been in the rain for two months in Britain and discovered I didn't like being wet. I wanted to dry out. And perhaps I wanted more than that – an inner light, a deeper understanding of life's complexities, a friend. With all those rainy days travelling alone, a fire had been extinguished within me and I needed rekindling. One morning I woke up soggy. I was on a beach in Scotland at the time so sogginess was to be expected, but I was also shivering and miserable. I decided to escape to Greece as fast as possible.

Three days later I was on a midnight flight to Athens. At six in the morning, dragging my sleepless, jetlagged body around the port of Piraeus, I came to a clapboard sign of a ferry schedule for various Greek islands. I was still dripping wet – although that was probably psychological – and dead tired, but I wanted things: a beach, the sun, a warm dry place to sleep, a Greek salad. I bought a ticket for the island of Paros because the ferry was leaving in ten minutes. Arbitrary, yes, but I was young and still arranged my life that way.

Six hours later we pulled into the Paros harbour. From the wooden bench on the boat where I'd been napping, I looked up to see a large crowd of passengers jamming the exit doors. Since I was groggy and exhausted, I decided to stay on the bench a few more minutes and let the crowd disappear. When I looked up again, I was appalled to see the boat pulling away from the harbour, the passengers all gone, and me left alone on the boat. For the next two hours I worried we were sailing back to Athens and I was too embarrassed to ask the men who worked on the ferry about it.

Fortunately, in two hours we arrived at another island. I got off the boat on what turned out to be Naxos and walked with my backpack along the dock, where I was immediately swarmed by a sea of short, round, middle-aged women in black polyester dresses and black socks who wanted me to stay at their guesthouses and sleep on their roofs. Assuming the roles of eccentric aunts, they took my arms and patted my hands, trying to pull me into their lives, their doughy bodies.

I didn't go to the houses of any of those women. In the recesses of my drowsy mind I remembered I needed a simple combination of a beach and sleep. Leaving the busy little port town, also called Naxos, behind, I headed south along the beach, walking for a long time through scatterings of bodies lying on the white sand, topless French women playing Frisbee, nut-brown boys throwing balls, incoming waves, and tavernas off to the side. A pure Aegean light fell on my head like a bleached curtain draping from the sky. It was a lean and haunting landscape, savagely dry, yet the light was uncannily clear with a blue sky big enough to crack open the world. The crowds thinned as I walked farther along the beach, and music from the tavernas faded in the distance. Finally, I spotted something under the shade of an olive grove – a small bamboo wind shelter that someone must have constructed and recently abandoned. Perfect. I'd found the place to drop down and sleep. And, although I didn't know it at the time, I'd found the place that would become my home for a month.

I slept the rest of that day in the bamboo wind shelter under the olive grove, and when I woke up it was dark and all the people were gone. A night wind danced across my face and shooting stars crashed across the sky. I ran along the beach, delirious, exalted, and finally dry.

My days on the beach took on their own rhythm. In the morning, rose coloured rays of sunrise from behind a dark mountain would wake me, and if they didn't, the island's omnipresent roosters would. The sea would be calm at dawn and I'd go for a swim before the day's beach crowd arrived. Walking back to my bamboo shelter I'd say hello and chat with the smiling waiter, Nikos, at the nearby taverna as he set out his chairs for the day's customers. Nikos was handsome in the way many Greek men are handsome, which has more to do with the way they look at you than how they themselves look. Nikos was good at looking rather than good-looking, which was almost the same thing in the end. When the sun got too high I'd escape its burning rays and read books in the shade of my olive grove. I'm a redhead – an absolute curse in a desert climate like Greece's.

The waves would gather momentum as the day passed and at some point every afternoon they would be at their fullest. That's when the old men would appear. From seemingly out of nowhere, a gathering of weathered, mahogany Greek men with sunken chests and black bathing shorts would converge to stand on the shore and survey the sea. The Aegean in dark blue spasms would reach its zenith there in the afternoon light and, from my olive grove, I'd watch it also. The old men would enter the sea together, simultaneously turn to face the shore, and hunch over with their knees slightly bent, skinny arms outstretched, waiting. They'd look over their shoulders at the ocean beyond, ready to jump up and join it at precisely the right moment. They always knew when that was. I would join them and always laughed when riding the waves, but I never saw those men crack a smile. I decided that when I was eighty I would take the waves that seriously also. After that many years of life on earth, what could be more important than playing in the waves?

Sometimes I'd walk into town to explore, buy fruit and bottled water, and watch old men argue politics over Turkish coffee served in tiny cups. The coffee was sweet and strong and one third full of gooey sediment.

At sunset the men would turn their chairs to face the sun as it melted the day into the sea. They'd sigh and drink their ouzo or citron or kitro – a specialty of Naxos lemon liqueur – and stop talking until the sky drained of colour. Parish priests with stovepipe hats, long robes and beards would stroll the narrow alleys with their hands behind their backs looking exactly like movie extras. Old women in black would watch me as I passed and occasionally ask me about snow. I'd wander through the maze of white-washed houses, the stark lines of white and blue, and stumble back home over the rocky land of dry absolutes in a heady daze.

Nothing is murky on a Greek island like Naxos, nor hazy, nor humid, nor dewy. Lush doesn't live there. This part of Greece is a rock garden of shrubs and laurel, juniper and cypress, thyme and oregano. Wild flowers spin colours that surge out of a pure clarity and in this clarity the forms of things are finer. In the hardy heat of this arid place, donkeys sound off at all hours, as if agitated. They'd wake me even in the dead of night.

One evening at sunset a man on a moped zipped by as I was walking along the beach. He came to a stop in the sand ahead and turned to ask my name. I'd seen him before at the taverna, throwing his head back to laugh when Nikos the waiter told jokes. The man on the moped offered me a ride down the beach and I took it. Naxos has one entire uninterrupted beach and in twenty minutes or so we came to his village, a cluster of houses and an outdoor restaurant overlooking the sea. The man let me off, smiled without speaking and disappeared. I went to the restaurant for dinner and chatted with some tourists. We didn't say anything significant. Mostly we watched the sky, which by then was blood-red cracked apart with whisky shots of amber. Shortly after, I found a bus that took me back to the town of Naxos.

By the time I finally arrived at the olive grove it was dark except for the light of the moon heaving itself full over the mountain. I came to my bamboo wind shelter and found it creaking in the wind, desolate, as it was the day I arrived, abandoned by its inhabitant. My backpack and the little home I'd made with my sleeping bag and pillows were gone, taken.

For approximately three seconds I felt a panic spread through me. This didn't seem healthy so I looked at the moon. Seeing that dependable milky rock hovering up there like the planet's eccentric uncle made me smile, and I remembered that in the great scheme of the universe, this kind of thing didn't matter. I had my money, traveller's cheques, and passport with me and could buy the few things I needed. My backpack had been too heavy anyway and travelling light would be a relief, a new challenge, something to write home about in postcards. Sitting on the sand I thought of the stolen things I would miss: my journal, my camera, some foreign change, a pair of Levis, my toothbrush, my shoes. My shoes!

I fell asleep surprisingly quickly under the full moon that night. Luckily the thieves hadn't stolen the floor of the wind shelter – the bamboo mats – and I was comfortable and warm, but an hour or so later a group of hysterical German women came and woke me. They'd been staying at a campground down the beach and they, too, had been victims of an annoying petty crime. Standing with them was a quiet, tall Dutch man with a blond beard and thick glasses. His belongings had been stolen also, even an expensive camera, but I noticed that, unlike the women, he wasn't the least perturbed by it. In fact he was calm, even amused, and I felt an instant affinity for this unusual man. In the midst of the German panic, three Scottish backpackers came along and asked if this was a safe place to camp. I laughed, which seemed to irritate the German women, while Martin, the Dutch man, said it was safe except for the occasional theft in the area, but really quite peaceful during the day. The German women went off to search for clues down the beach. Martin and I lay back on the sand and watched the stars whirl over the wine-dark sea as we discussed the faults and betrayals of the modern world.

We should have been helping in the search, but what was the point? Our possessions gone, we felt free in a funny way. We didn't care. We were two whimsical souls colliding in the land of Homer. Half an hour later, the German women came running back, exhilarated and out of breath. 'We found everything! Our things! Come!' It was true. Over a sand dune not far away, most of our belongings, including my backpack, were piled together like a happy heap of children hiding in the dark. My backpack had been slashed with a knife and anything of value, like my camera, was gone, but my journal was there and so were most of my clothes, even my toothbrush. It felt like Christmas. I found my sleeping bag and tent in another sand dune and since I hadn't used the tent since Britain anyway, I gave it to Martin because his had been taken. Somehow losing everything and so unexpectedly finding it again had given us a new perspective on what we valued. One of the German women gave me a book. A festive night! The best part of the thievery was that in the semi-crisis of getting our stuff ripped off, I'd met the strange, fair-haired Dutch man and he made me laugh.

Martin and I spent the next two days together talking continuously. Just being with him filled me with an excitement and a calm, deep knowledge. There are people with whom you feel mute and around them you forget you have a head and a heart full of ideas and wonder, poetry and longing, and there are those who can reach straight into your chest and pull songs and stars out of your heart. Martin wasn't quite like that – I didn't sing around him

– but he was close, and he was the best friend I'd made in months of travelling. Travelling is so temporary. Sometimes you forget you need friends. When you find one, you remember the miracle of another person and you remember yourself. Talking to Martin made me feel I was availing myself of whatever was extraordinary in the world. He had a special interest in the spirit world, also in plants and modern history. He was a storyteller, with stories of his long journey through India and Tibet, stories of love, betrayal, auto accidents. I told stories also, most of mine involving medical mishaps in foreign countries.

On the third day Martin left to catch a plane. I walked him to the ferry. He limped because he'd stepped on a sea urchin. He was sunburned. I waved goodbye from the dock to the Dutch man with gawky glasses and violet eyes and I wondered if I'd ever see him again.

As the days passed, I found it increasingly difficult to leave my wind shelter. I had the moon, sun, stars, my books, the old men in the waves. Why would I leave? I'd seen enough of the world and I liked where I was. Perhaps the more you stay in a place, the more it grows on you, the way some people do. I'd wake at dawn thinking today should be the day to go to another island, go back to the mainland or to another country. But then I'd go for a swim and read a little, take a walk, jump through the waves. The sun would sneak across the sky making its way towards its great dip into the sea and I'd still be there like a lotus eater – lazy some would say, if they didn't know better. One day I decided to take an excursion away from my beach. I wasn't prepared to leave Naxos yet; I'd just see more of it. I took a bus to the other side of the island and was gone for four days. It felt like forever.

The bus driver could have gotten us killed several times as he rampaged around hair pin curves into the mountains.

From the window, I watched the dramatic patchwork of Naxos, its gardens, vineyards, citrus orchards, villages and Venetian watchtowers. Farmers ploughed with donkeys in the fields. Children played barefoot along the roads. The people of the island may have had only a scruffy flock of goats or a small grape orchard, a rowboat to search the night waters for fish or a taverna with three tables, but they weren't poor. Life brought them regular random encounters with friends and relatives each day, not just occasional carefully selected lunches with them. Their lives were rich, plentiful and cheerful.

I stayed at a fishing village called Apollon on the roof of a house of one of the women in black. In Greece, a woman puts on a black dress when her husband dies, and often wears a black dress the rest of her life. That's devotion. That also cuts down on clothing expenses. Some women also rent out rooms to tourists and, if the rooms are full, they rent the flat roof. That's a good head for business. By this time I was so accustomed to sleeping outside, I chose the roof over an inside room. The woman in black gave me a fine example of a 'tsk tsk', and she said something in Greek, which was truly Greek to me, and gave me an extra blanket. For hours I watched the stars and thought of our dark ancestral past far away, the stars where we originated in some distant, long forgotten explosion. Under the weight of the stars I could hardly bear the full force of the universe, the randomness, the chaos, the chance of it all. What is one to do with a life when eternity surrounds us?

One could return to a wind shelter under an olive grove. That was one option.

So I returned. And that's when the strange thing happened, the one for which there is no logical explanation.

On the first night back from my excursion I had fallen into a deep sleep in my shelter when I had the distinct and uncomfortable feeling that something was moving towards me along the beach and I should wake up to chase it away. I tried with all my might to wake up, but my eyes felt glued shut and I couldn't open them. The thing was approaching fast, faster every second it seemed, and it was determined, perhaps running, and I knew it was looking for me. Although I couldn't fathom what it was, it felt horribly dangerous and I knew it was imperative I wake up to protect myself.

Yet waking was impossible. My body and eyes were paralysed. Like a great black shadow the thing was coming across the sand, and still my body was catatonic. Then I could feel it close by, and I knew suddenly this dark and unknown thing was with me in the olive grove. My heart seemed to bang out of my chest, loud enough to hear. I forced myself to climb up through layers and layers of a deep sleep, the sleep of centuries, it felt like, and at last I broke out of it and woke up, or so I thought. Pulling myself up on my elbows, I saw what the thing was: a tiny woman in black, no more than four feet tall, and very old. She lay down beside me, curled her body against mine, and shivered.

Whatever she was, she was very cold and wanted inside. I knew she didn't mean inside my sleeping bag – she wanted inside me.

No, I said, you can't come in. I live here.

She pulled herself closer, and her long, damp, silver hair fell like mourning, like misery, like an ancient sad longing. She needed a home, a warm body to live in, a place with a fire. Her face was that of a crone and I could feel her wrinkled icy skin on my cheek. Even her breath was the frigid night air of winter. Her eyes seemed bottomless at first, empty, like black holes, but buried deep inside were two brilliant stars for eyes, blazing stars light-years away. Again and again I told her no, which seemed to make her unbearably sad. Please let me in, she pleaded. No, you can't. This is my body, this is me! For a moment an uncanny intimacy hung there between us as we stared at each other across the distance of two worlds. Her eyes shone so brightly they burned my own, burned straight through to my inner core. No, I told her again firmly. No. With that, she raised herself up and drifted off down the beach, still shivering and still wanting a home. She left as she had come, with the night breeze.

The incident itself I could easily have dismissed as a bizarre dream, and did in fact do so the next morning when I woke to the call of the roosters, shaking my head at the previous night's dark madness. Although the dream had been unusually vivid, tangible and oddly lucid, it had to be a dream nonetheless. A four-foot-tall woman in black trying to pry her way into my body? What happened later that day, however, made me wonder how far dreams travel into the waking world.

That afternoon, the taverna near my wind shelter where I always ate lunch was closed, the tables, chairs, and the owner, Nikos, nowhere in sight. Strange, I thought, since I had never seen it closed in all the weeks I'd been there. Perhaps Nikos was taking a holiday. I decided to walk down the beach to the campground restaurant instead. By chance, my table happened to be next to some backpackers who were discussing where they would travel after Greece. As I ate my fruit salad, I listened to their conversation, which fortunately was in English since they were of several nationalities. The conversation took a twist when a German woman began to tell the others about a strange dream she'd had the night before.

'It was horrible, a nightmare. I dreamt a little woman came floating along the beach. She was kind of like the women here in Greece, the ones who wear the black, but she was tiny. She was cold. It was terrible, terrible. Such a clear dream.'

My spoon fell from my hand and I felt a sudden constriction around my heart. Had I heard her right? Was this too a dream? 'Excuse me,' I said to the German woman, 'I couldn't help overhearing you. What did the woman want?' The German woman looked over at me, startled, almost familiar. Her face was pale.

'To get inside me.'

In a land where myth and reality swirl around each other in a luminous haze, lessons clear and absolute can be found after all. I said nothing is murky in Greece but I was wrong. A woman came to me on the mist. She crossed over from the other side and sent me a gift. In all my life I have never known such a moment as when those haunting eyes from eternity stared into mine. Although she may not have intended to, she gave me a message: a human life is an extraordinary treasure. She wanted to feel life, maybe feel it again as she once had, and she wanted it desperately. I was alive, breathing, warm, strong, with a fire and light inside me she ached for. When I pushed her away, proclaiming my life as my own, never had I felt the life inside me so intensely.

I left on the ferry the next day. I didn't need to stay in Naxos any more. I needed to see the rest of the world. To stay in my wind shelter and live amidst the lure and myth of Greece would be to believe in magic and fate, superstition and dark mysteries. I had this world to explore first, the one with cities and rivers, foreign faces and Woody Allen movies. From the boat I watched the island shrink on the horizon, getting smaller and smaller like a puddle evaporating in the sun. Yet I knew then as I still know now, that from the shore where the sand dunes begin, the olive grove grows old, and from the bed where we sleep, the shadows of secret things lurk, forbidden, timeless, and forever calling our name.

Chapter 3

Morticia and I are driving through Indiana in the dark and I can't get that little woman from the beach in Greece out of my head. Looking back on it, I think it must have been a dream, and what the German girl said was just a bizarre coincidence. But whether it was a dream or not doesn't really matter. What matters is that I felt someone or something was trying to take me over, burrow into the centre of my very being, as if there was a hollow place needing to be filled. That was the feeling that sometimes crept over me after too many months travelling, that my life had no direction, no purpose. I was an aimless wanderer without an axis.

Sometimes I think I'm still looking for an axis.

'Have you ever been to a pagan witch gathering?' asks Morticia out of the blue.

'I don't think so.'

'I go to one every year. It's amazing. It's called Vermont Witch Camp. We could drive there together in August when you get back from California. You might find it interesting.'

Instead of jumping at the idea, as I probably would have ten years ago, I have the urge to make a joke. I imagine the most politically incorrect outfit someone could show up in for a witch get-together. Recently, a friend told me she often goes to the Michigan Women's Festival, a week-long gathering exclusive to women where, my friend said, those who aren't card-carrying lesbians and don't walk around topless the entire week are made to feel boring and unenlightened. I told her it would be fun to go to the Michigan Women's Festival in really girly tops that say 'BOYS!' or 'CUTIE', wear lots of make-up and high heels, and ask everyone where the guys are.

'So for the witch gathering, could I come dressed as the witch from *The Wizard of Oz*? I could wear a black pointy hat, fake wart on my nose and pretend to cast spells.'

'Umm… huh? Oh, ha ha,' says Morticia.

'Just an idea,' I say. I wonder when I became this jaded. As we drive through the night I think about how I seem to have lost my enthusiasm for things. At twenty I was full of enthusiasm. I wonder if this happened as a result of an event that disappointed me in some fundamental way – perhaps teaching on the native reserve or something in my world travels – or perhaps was simply a culmination of everything I've seen and done since I was in my early twenties, every small disappointment and shattering of illusion from when I was that spirited idealist who believed that although the world was rotten, it could be changed, revived back to a golden age. Now, I don't believe in golden ages. As we get older, we grow these shells around our hearts and minds, shells which young people don't have yet. If only we could keep that openness all our lives, that belief that the world is shot through with blazing stars. I wonder how I can get my whimsy back, my positive attitude towards life.

I'm sorry to be bypassing Chicago on my way west this time, but since we're going to St. Louis it doesn't make sense to go through Chicago also. I love Chicago, its architecture and friendly streets. One gets a sense of history there that you don't find in Canadian cities outside of Quebec. On my first trip to Chicago, when I was 21, I was driving out west from Ontario to California with three friends from South Africa. Two of these South Africans – a couple in their late twenties, Shana and Connor – had never in their lives been outside of South Africa where they were born, or Zimbabwe, their adopted home. They were white, extremely anti-apartheid, and decided not to set foot in their homeland of South Africa again until apartheid was abolished and Nelson Mandela was released. This was 1985. Shana and Connor were in Canada that fall visiting Shana's sister, Luanne, who was my roommate at university. Luanne and I had spent the previous two summers studying French in Quebec, going to music festivals and working at a Guelph health food store. When Luanne's older sister and husband came to visit, we left our jobs, and the notion of returning to university, and the four of us drove to California in Luanne's tiny Chevette. I'd already been to California once, just that spring, and was anxious to go back.

American society and landscape astounded the South Africans. Connor commented on how watching the American Midwestern countryside out the window was like watching scenes from old westerns, but in the cities and towns they were appalled at the blinding ugliness of the neon strip malls that went on for miles with the same chain stores in every town. What, they kept asking, distinguishes this town from the next? Every American city seems familiar as you approach it with the same Burger King and the same KFC. Rapid City's Wal-Mart isn't any different from Tampa's, or Tempe's. American malls are filled with the same kids wearing the same fashions, watching the same lousy movies and eating the same junk food. The South Africans were also shocked at the sheer size of Americans. Only once, on a TV documentary they'd watched about Disney World, had they seen such ample-fleshed people, and they recalled how all their African neighbours gathered around their TV to gawk in horror at how some of the Disney tourists were so large they even had trouble walking. This trip out west was the first time in their lives Shana and Connor had seen real live obese people, and the first time they'd seen what is meant by The American Cult of Food, where one can't drive down a main street or turn on a TV without images of food attacking. For me it was fascinating to watch this land of my birth through fresh eyes, this land where I'd already travelled so much and which is in some ways – although Canadians hate to admit it – so similar to Canada. Canada is just less a nation of extremes – less commercial, less exciting, less obese-ridden, less fitness-crazed, less outgoing and fun, and less – actually, a lot less – violent. Canada is also a lot less religious and right-wing. Canadians constantly press their noses to the glass, looking through with fascination, outrage and admiration at the antics of the great republic to the south, while most Americans remain serenely oblivious to everyone but themselves. In Canada we sit on the fringes of the Great Circus of America, living within the media fallout of American pop culture, continually amazed at our neighbours and infuriated by American ignorance of Canada and the rest of the world. Yet the Canadian and world view of America is also coloured by stereotypes and folk wisdom. Many foreigners, including Canadians, imagine that Americans are Bible-thumping, gun-worshipping yahoos. Yet when Canadians and other foreigners actually travel or live there, they see what a small proportion of Americans really are yahoos. Which isn't to say that wild, big, brash, we'll-do-as-we-damn-well-please America is a myth. In the U.S., you can buy a handgun at a local department store. And, if you break your ankle and aren't covered by private health insurance or Medicare, you actually have to pay the hospital or doctor bill yourself.

These two facts are astounding not only to Canadians, but to most of the world.

Morticia is sleeping and I'm playing a Joni Mitchell tape that I keep rewinding to hear the song called *California* that I used to sing when I was travelling through Europe. In the song is a line I can't decipher. Joni Mitchell is travelling by herself around Europe, just as I was, and she's lonely, tired of Europe and the cold, and is yearning to go back to her adopted home of California (she grew up Saskatchewan). I remember hitchhiking on rainy roadsides in Wales and singing that song to myself over and over. I didn't live in California, but I'd visited, and even then, dreamt of moving there some day. I sang that song in some forlorn woods in France, in Greece, and on several lonely nights in Spain. But I've always been confused by the lyrics. She sings about how she wants to go back to California to see the 'folks I dig' where she'll even 'kiss a sunset pig'. Surely she means she'll kiss a sunset pink. What's a sunset pig and why would you kiss one? Nobody I ask ever seems to know. Nonetheless, hearing the song again makes me think of all the travelling I've done over the years, what I've been looking for and how I always seem to be searching for a home. It also makes me think of California and my cave. I have to find that cave this time. Every time I visit California I look for it and haven't been able to find it, as if it never existed at all. But I have pictures to prove it. One is a sunset picture where you can see part of the cave wall. I saw six sunsets from my cave because I stayed there six nights, and although I'm not sure any of the sunsets were purely pink – more mauve and burnt orange as I recall – I know none of them resembled a pig.

It was on that same trip with the South Africans that I found my cave. After two months together we parted ways because the South Africans wanted to go north to British

Columbia, and I wanted to stay longer in California. The last evening we spent together was Hallowe'en and we just happened to be in the city that treats that festival as it should be treated, San Francisco, where Hallowe'en is the biggest holiday of the year. We walked up and down Castro Street watching the famous Hallowe'en parade and none of us had ever seen such outlandish costumes in our lives. Most memorable was the man dressed as Dorothy from *The Wizard of Oz*. He wore ruby slippers, a gingham dress, and carried a real dog that looked exactly like Toto. That night, the four of us decided to camp in Golden Gate Park, a large wooded park right in the city. Shana and Connor tried to sleep in the car while Luanne and I laid out our sleeping bags on a groundsheet and slept on the grass. At two in the morning I was awakened by a large dog accompanied by the annoying beams of flashlights shining in my face. Four policemen had surrounded us. Apparently, sleeping in Golden Gate Park just isn't done. In my most innocent 21-year-old voice, I said, 'Oh, we thought you could camp in parks. We're from Canada.' They seemed taken aback that we weren't at least noticeably crazy, and politely suggested we find another place to sleep. The next morning, other parades were taking place all around town, which for San Francisco, is nothing unusual. Some North Koreans were protesting their government and causing major traffic jams, while just a few blocks away, members of the Cacophony Society, the original organisers of the Burning Man festival, were gathered, as a joke, outside a movie theatre which was showing *Fantasia* to protest Mickey's unnecessary waste of water. All that throwing and carefree splashing of water in the animated film offended them somehow. The year before we were there, televangelist Jerry Falwell came to San Francisco to denounce the city as the 'Wild Kingdom'. His presence drew a group of transvestite nuns on roller skates, the Sisters of Perpetual Indulgence, who organised an exorcism of Falwell. On the edge of the fault line and edge of the continent, dangling precariously over the ocean, the eccentric city of the far west has always been quirky, fascinating travellers since the forty-niners rode over gold-laden hills. Jack Kerouac wrote of 'Ole Frisco' as 'the last great city in America... where poets and bums could come and drink wine in the streets'. I thought if I were ever to live in a big city, San Francisco might be my first choice, but at that time in my life, even if poets and bums were celebrated, a big city wasn't what I was looking for.

After Hallowe'en, I waved goodbye to my South African friends until their little car became lost in San Francisco traffic. I was alone now and although it felt strange to be without my travelling companions, I was elated about the possibility of finding a quiet place by the ocean to camp, contemplate and to figure out what to do with the rest of my life. The fall days were still warm, the nights cool, and most tourists would be long gone. In a secondhand shop I bought a cooking pot, a jackknife, a transistor radio, a few other supplies, and in a used bookstore, a load of books that weighed down my backpack to the point of absurdity.

I was planning on hitchhiking as much as possible but took a bus as far north out of the city as I could get on public transit. In Sausalito, I got a ride to the John Muir Forest where I spent a rainy night camped in a fallen hollow tree; the perfect cover from the weather, although a little damp. That's the sort of thing I did then when the world was at my feet. I remember not caring what strangers thought. I slept on park benches if I felt like it, spoke my mind and never worried about fashion. When I entered a new place I didn't mind being a little ragged and dirty because I was anonymous, and being anonymous, I discovered, made me free. Travelling alone as a stranger sharpened something in me, called upon inner resources I didn't know I possessed.

Sometimes I wonder whatever happened to that girl, where she came from and why she left.

The next day I walked and hitchhiked on small back roads and recall finding a farmer's field where I stole some green onions which tasted sweet but later made me queasy. Eventually, a man and a woman picked me up and told me they were headed for Point Reyes National Seashore. I was happy to go with the couple, even if they were on their first date.

At Point Reyes, we drove a long way on a lonely winding road through emerald rolling hills dotted with cows and, occasionally, with elk, until we reached a far-off parking lot full of wind. The place was deserted. We walked for five minutes or so down a steep path until we came to a beach cove with red sandstone cliffs and a little stream running towards the ocean. We strolled up and down the shoreline collecting shells and rocks and splashing in the waves. Just as the sun was setting I turned to see if the rays were casting light on the sandstone cliffs behind us. That's when I spotted the cave. The cave was carved into a cliff, up high where you'd have to scramble up a cliff-side path to get inside, and it looked big enough for me and my backpack. I knew right away the cave was where I'd spend the night. I told the couple my plan and instead of looking at me as if I'd just told them I was about to swim to Japan, they said they thought it was a good idea. This was California, after all, where people tend to do things that would be considered abnormal anywhere else.

After the couple left I climbed the cliff to investigate the cave. My new home was about six feet deep and three feet high, larger than the hollowed-out redwood tree I'd spent three days in earlier that year in northern California. I rolled out my sleeping bag, ate some dried mangoes and started writing in my notebook, a notebook that strangely has the last half of its pages torn out.

Before leaving on this trip with Morticia, I found that tattered notebook again to see if I'd written any clues as to the location of the cave because it seems crucial that I find it again. I'm taking the notebook with me to read along the way. I've already read the first few entries:

Cave Journal

I'm so excited! The whole spread of the Pacific Ocean is on fire in the sunlight. The Quaker couple who brought me here (on their first date! They were so awkward with each other that I think they enjoyed my company as a diversion) has left and I'm all alone here on an isolated, heavenly pink beach. Those onions have given me violent stomach cramps but it's forgotten in light of what I see in front of me: the sun dropping into the sea, a sorrowful red disc so softened by the ocean mist that I can see straight into its inferno heart. Farewell Sun!

Why do we always assume the sun will reappear tomorrow?

Next Day

The sun did return today, hotter than it has been in weeks, and I've been warming my skin in it all morning after a night of shivering in the cave. My day has been so filled already and it's not even noon. I've investigated the beach from one end to the other, have started collecting firewood, have found a big black rock in the waves full of mussels that I might be able to eat, have started reading Zen and the Art of Motorcycle Maintenance, have found a stream for drinking water, have washed some clothes and laid them out on a big rock to dry, and have named some of the landmarks on the beach: Rocky Point, Mystery Cove and Jagged Little Shells That Hurt Your Feet Beach, or Jagged Beach for short.

Next Day

Hawks and gulls are a constant here. I watch the hawks circling overhead, drifting and rising on thermals, swooping down for kills. The gulls here are different from city gulls. On this remote beach they're wary of me where all they know are cliff, wind, sand, sun and a clear view of the sea.

It's another perfect day after a near-freezing night. I'm basking in the warmth of the day's sunlight. I'm filled with the blue of the sky, storing the light and heat inside me for when the sun falls away always too soon.

Later

I've forgotten that I love solitude. I'm trying to recall if I get this kind of exhilaration and peace of mind when I'm with other people. I go for long walks along the beach which is full of tiny animals, shells and insects, all of them worth observing.

I've made a friend with one of the gulls. When my back was turned, it walked right up to where I lay on the beach and tore half a page from my book. He's watching me but pretending not to. I wish I had a copy of Jonathan Livingston Seagull.

I've been trying to make a fire but all the firewood is damp. I have only two matchbooks with me and wasted almost an entire one today and still no luck with a fire. How frustrating. If only I had dry kindling. I want to boil water to cook the mussels. I'm sure I'll tire of my supply of dried mangoes and granola soon.

The evening mist is beginning to gather as the light fades. Soon the night will creep over me. I'll grow cold and be filled with starlight while the roar of the waves rides through my dreams. Without the roar of the waves it would be hauntingly silent here.

It's almost 3 a.m. Morticia took over the wheel a couple of hours ago and I've been trying to sleep. Even though I'm groggy I realise we must be in St. Louis because we've slowed down and are driving through well-lit suburban streets with names like Ptarmigan Crescent and Hickory Circle. Suburbia is where they tear out the trees, kill the wildlife, and then name streets after them. At this hour, mine is the only car in these suburbs. In the occasional house, I can see the eerie blue glow of TV and the shadow of someone transfixed to its brain-sucking power. The cordless moon is crawling up the sky, looking down over a damaged planet. Morticia stops the car in what looks like a parking lot for townhouses set back in the woods. 'This must be it. Oh God. I can't believe we're here,' she says. We sit for a minute, still dazed from the droning rush of the interstate. Crickets are chirping and house cats are prowling. Ten minutes ago we were hurtling through the country, bypassing one small town after the next, and now we've entered an American summer night. Morticia has invited me to crash on her Internet boyfriend's couch, which seems a little creepy, but these ritzy townhouses look kind of appealing at 3 a.m. after a day inside a car.

It takes almost half an hour of wandering around the townhouse complex to find Alex's place. If I were a little less tired this would be completely bizarre. Still, the oak trees seem to be dark with suspicion, the navy sky wary and hapless above this eerily typical neighbourhood. Morticia is cool as a white sheet, or so she seems. Finally we see a note taped to a door.

'Debbie, got tired of waiting up, have gone to bed, come find me, xxoo Alex.'

We walk in. I'm not sure what I was expecting – satanic dolls nailed to the ceiling, black leather dinnerware, discordant music – but Alex's apartment looks like an accountant's. On the wall are Ikea-framed posters of people with muscled, tanned legs hiking in the rainforest; there's a tank full of tiny goldfish and you can tell Alex has just vacuumed. The computer set-up in the corner looks expensive and must be where he writes Morticia all those e-mails. The view out his window beside the computer must look out to his neighbours, so when Alex writes his Canadian girlfriend whom he has never seen, a row of identical clean white townhouses stares back at him. The kitchen is small and tidy with an open recipe book on the counter. I think of how weird this must be for Morticia. She's going to meet her boyfriend for the first time in his bedroom. Does this kind of thing happen often? Surely there must be more unusual things in the world. Women in many Islamic countries don't see their husbands until their actual marriage ceremony. At least Morticia has been writing this guy and she could leave tomorrow if she feels like it, if she realises he doesn't brush his teeth or is irritable or eats kids' cereal for dinner. Maybe he watches those daytime talk shows where people yell and throw things, maybe he eats Cheesies while he's watching and throws them at the TV because he's angry about his childhood. Maybe he commits road rage, is obsessed with golf, or maybe he's bald and does the comb-over thinking he's fooling people. Maybe he's 83. There are lots of things you wouldn't pick up about a person by writing letters. Morticia and I look around the apartment. We seem to be hesitating, perhaps waiting for something. We seem to be in a moment that resembles a teenage horror made-for-TV movie just before the commercial break.

Then, from the bedroom, we hear Alex clear his throat and suddenly we know without saying anything that Alex is a nice guy. It's not the hiking posters or goldfish or the recipe book that tells us he's OK, but the way he clears his throat. It's a funny thing and not at all logical, but sometimes all you need to know about another person is contained in one small human act, like the way someone yawns, or nods off when he thinks nobody is watching. That sort of vulnerability must be a human being's greatest appeal.

I head straight for the couch after the throat clearing and Morticia heads into the bathroom. Within a few minutes the living room is dark, Morticia has gone into Alex's bedroom and the apartment is quiet except for the pump of the goldfish tank. I'm lying on a plush leather couch and staring at the fish, praying to the god of an innocent world, if such a god exists, that I don't hear the crack of a whip coming from the bedroom.

I'm in St. Louis, Missouri, about to embark on a westward pilgrimage to a land I might some day call home, and I haven't been this fully and happily wide awake in months.

Chapter 4

I wake up on the accountant's couch and decide to leave immediately. Scrawling a thank you note for the hospitality and wishing Morticia a happy visit, I rush out the door. Morticia will be fine, I think when I step into the scorching sun, off to have her own adventure different from mine, her own black-dress-up, Midwestern-boyfriend adventure.

When I reach the parking lot I realise I have no clue where in St. Louis I am and ask directions from a man cutting a hedge. In the nineteenth century, Charles Dickens came to see the famous American West and got no farther than St. Louis, nine hundred miles short even of the Rockies. He went home convinced he had seen the West, and declared it to be a fraud. St. Louis seems friendly and has lots of big trees which, when you come down to it, are the two most important things you want in a city. Driving through the suburban neighbourhoods I find it interesting to think that T. S. Eliot came from St. Louis, and only 85 years before his birth, this city was a beginning point of westward expansion on the St. Louis Trail. Lewis and Clark started from St. Louis in the spring of 1804 with a sixteen-year-old Indian girl, Sacajawea, as their guide. Thomas Jefferson's orders to Lewis and Clark were to open up a river route for a continental fur trade, study the Indian tribes, their languages and customs, and most importantly, be nice to the Indians on all occasions, while being sure to convey the message that they now belonged to the Great White Father back in Washington. Sacajawea lived into her nineties and must have been pissed off in her old age. The great expedition had doomed the hope that her people would keep their native land. All her life she must have thought, damn, if only I hadn't run into those two bozos that night in St. Louis.

T. S. Eliot left St. Louis as soon as he was old enough to appreciate the larger world and eventually moved to England, and all those pioneers left as soon as spring arrived and the trail was free of mud. If it were cooler I might spend more time here, but I'll have to save St. Louis for another trip. It's now my turn to leave St. Louis, as soon as I find the interstate.

I seem to be suffering a complete breakdown, or rather Marcia my car is. I'm barely out of St. Louis and it sounds as if a sick animal is screeching underneath me and the car is rapidly losing speed. I pull off at a gas station to have a mild panic attack and spend five minutes cooling down in an air conditioned convenience store. Maybe my car is like me, just overheating. I'll check under the hood, look at the rad fluid, and hope some garage guy will come look with me.

When I open the hood I'm immediately blasted with a surge of heat and billow of blue smoke that stings my eyes. If I stand over this hood long enough, looking exactly like a woman who knows next to nothing about cars, which is exactly what I am, surely someone will come over to help. It appalls me that I've never taken a simple mechanics course and must rely on the knowledge of strangers. I look up from the hood to see a man in blue overalls sauntering my way.

'Got some problems, looks like,' he says. He has a chiselled face, the kind of face you see more often on TV than on real people, which seem incongruous at this sweaty roadside garage. He takes over my position by the hood while he drinks a bottle of lemonade. 'Don't look good.' I stand next to him, heavy with determination, nodding in agreement, lusting after his lemonade. I ask about the overheating possibility because it's 104 degrees this morning. Just standing under this vindictive sun is almost killing me. He takes out a rag and starts unscrewing things. I can feel him becoming aware of me leaning over with him. 'Could be the heat,' he says. 'Could be a lot worse. I'll give her some water and see how she does.' He saunters back inside and returns with a styrofoam cup of water for me to drink, and a jug of water for the engine. As I watch this oddly attractive guy's tanned hand slowly pour water into the radiator, I suddenly see Marcia as a fellow travelling companion from a cold climate – perhaps she's never experienced temperatures like this before – and we're quenching our thirsts together for our long voyage into the western sun. I'm also suddenly wishing I'd left on this journey two months earlier, when it would have been cooler. However, that would have meant leaving my teaching job before school ended. Besides, it never occurred to me there would be a heatwave this intense in June. I guess I should watch the Weather Channel more often.

I'm back on the highway and no longer hear the squealing pig under the car, although something is still wrong with the engine. The garage guy wasn't convinced it was just an overheating problem, but I'm hoping he's wrong, or else the problem will fix itself, as if that ever works. The wind is blasting into my car like a hot air furnace. The sun is beating down on me like a weapon. I'm noticing that the cars around me all have their windows closed and the air-conditioned people inside are chatting or singing to their music, oblivious to the murderous waves of heat just outside their windows. One driver is wearing a sweater. I hate him. I've come up with a defence for the heat and sun; a soaking wet towel over my head. It takes about twenty minutes for the towel to become bone dry so I keep re-soaking it with water from a bottle. I've soaked another towel to wrap around my face covering everything but my eyes. People in passing cars steal quick, nervous glances my way and speed ahead.

Something I love about the United States is bumper stickers. No other country's citizens display their opinions on how they feel about the world so openly. You don't see many bumper stickers in Canada. Canada is too boringly polite. The car ahead of me has a bumper sticker that cracks me up. 'Jesus Loves You. Everyone Else Thinks You're an Asshole.' A speeding car that passed both me and the car ahead had a bumper sticker that said, strangely, 'Fish Can't Walk: Darwin Was Wrong', which goes to show that the first guy's bumper sticker made a good point.

Gallivanting is what my mother calls this, taking these long trips by myself, but I can't help it. I crave the thrill of travel and, in the back of my mind, I'm always searching for the perfect place to live. I hate to think I've been living out a life in the wrong place. The thought terrifies me. That's one reason I'm going to California. I have to find out if it really is better there. California offers so much of what I crave: a year-round summery climate and growing season where I could eat out of my garden 365 days a year, year-round blossoms, a thunderous roar of the ocean beneath green cliffs, redwoods, opportunities for the kind of work I like – something combining writing with travelling and teaching perhaps – and people who've come from all over the planet bringing with them new ideas and a worldly outlook on life. In moving to California, however, I may also be doing something called fleeing, which includes leaving my boyfriend Andre because I also to hate to think of living out a life with the wrong person. But I'll think about that later.

For now I like to think I'm off in search of an idyllic land, because, after all, this life we've all fallen into is a blessing, fleeting and miraculous. I don't want to look back when I'm 90 and realise I didn't try hard enough to be the happiest and most fulfilled I possibly could be with all the world has to offer. The world contains perhaps hundreds of heavenly places to spend the rest of your life, places with just the right combination of what's important. I'm searching for a place where you can walk out your door at night and the sky is scattered thick with stars and you can think wide open thoughts and not get eaten by mosquitoes or get frostbite, a sunny place of rare and wild splendour alive with trees and blooms and deer, a place close to clever conversation and good-hearted, community-minded people; close to art, foreign films and good used-book stores, a place where even small towns have an international magazine stand, a juice bar, a natural foods grocery, an outdoor market, outdoor patios and community events. I know California is overflowing with places like this because I've seen them. The problem isn't whether they exist or not; the problem is being overwhelmed with how many of these utopias there actually are and trying to choose among them.

It's not as if my hometown of Guelph, which is an hour west of Toronto, is so terrible, but it could use a little work. Guelph is a university town that's green and hot in the summer, grey and cold in the winter, unpleasantly sprawling into a cancer of suburbs on what was once farmland, on a mildly rolling-hilled pocket of southern Ontario. There are two pleasant but unswimmable and dirty rivers, thirteen nuclear reactors not far enough away, and air pollution warnings on muggy days. Yet if you're downtown you're surrounded by history and friendly faces, and century-old buildings and homes with perennial gardens and sunflowers, by students strolling – drunk at night, politically active by day – and people on porches in the shade of leafy trees. There's an impressively large pocket of people who have a strong social and political conscience, an undying community spirit, and desire to make their town better – they've been fighting against building a Wal-Mart for years. Guelph has a farmers' market every Saturday morning which takes forever to walk through because you keep running into people you know, and a big eclectic music festival every summer by a lake just outside of town. People know their neighbours in Guelph and they stop to chat on the street. It really isn't that bad, but it's miles from the perfect place. Mainly, it's not majestic, and the winter is long, damp and dreary. I want to wake up every day and inhale the vapour of a coastal forest or the salt spray of the seashore, hear the rush of a mighty river, the echo of loons calling over a clear still lake, or be able to gaze up at a range of snow-capped mountain peaks. I need a powerful place of inspiring beauty and a reasonable climate. I need the coast of California. Or, perhaps, some place I might find on the way.

I sometimes wonder if this is my life quest – finding the perfect place, where I belong. Whenever I come across a stretch of rolling green hills and a grove of trees, a river or a cliff by the ocean, or a remote island, or a funky college town, I think *I could live here*. This has happened to me all over the world: on the island of Taveuni, Fiji, where I once stayed a long time and almost stayed for good; in Madeira; New Zealand; the Yorkshire Dales; Wales; small towns in Vermont; college towns all over the world; the Gulf Islands of British Columbia; Boulder, Colorado; Eugene, Oregon; Taos, New Mexico; and it especially happens to me in California, where one afternoon you could be driving through a grove of redwoods and the same day pass beneath a canopy of eucalyptus trees and their cool menthol scent permeates the air along the winding road for miles. When you exit the canopy you may find yourself facing the intimate shock of the ocean, aquamarine, eternal and crashing, and you think you've arrived at the edge of your senses because here, after all the magnificent sites of the West, is finally the place where nature's combination of land, sky, water, weather, vegetation and space is perfect. Egrets, pelicans, monarchs, coyotes and bobcats grace the land and sky while far off somewhere is always the sound of a lone seabird. In California, you always feel as if you're meandering through a canyon deep in secrets of another life that could be yours.

In the critical recesses of my mind, I wonder if I will always yearn for some place else. It's not as if I've been a malcontent who always needs to go somewhere new. For the most part, day to day, I've been happy. But more and more lately, I've been feeling this pull towards California, this inexorable draw to the rocky cliffs of my own salvation.

I suppose I've always been split between the desire to stay in a familiar place, the desire for home, old friends and connections, and the equal passion to shut the door and go, to see the world. I feel very at home in Guelph but I don't think it's the place I should spend the rest of my life. Right now, my desire for California in all its promised land glory is overwhelming my desire to stay in Guelph, which isn't quite enough for me, not when I know so much more of what I love exists in California.

I can hardly wait to get there but I have to remember to see this country, the United States, through new eyes. I was born in the U.S. – in Madison, where my father was doing graduate work in geography at the University of Wisconsin – but have heard the U.S. ridiculed much of my life. When I was four my parents, who are Canadian, moved us back to Canada. Since many Canadians are staunchly anti-American, I was teased as a kid for being a Yank, and my sister, who was older, got teased much more. Many Canadians consider Americans to be too loud, crass and, strangely, not as well educated as Canadians, which even as a kid I knew was suspect. The uninformed and unfair anti-Americanism gave me a strange affection for the U.S., sticking up for its citizens. Were Canadians secretly jealous of its success and warmer climate? Canadians seemed to feel overshadowed, which is understandable since the American population is ten times that of Canada's, but some Canadians also seemed to feel inferior, which often made them act superior, painting all of their American neighbours with a general brush of ignorance. Perhaps the Canadian view of the U.S. is reasonable given the sheer ethnocentricity of America the superpower – and I admit I understand many of the complaints about 'the ignorant American' who couldn't locate Ontario, or Spain, on a map – but why pick on *all* U.S. citizens? I never understood. Even at university when I spent much of my time protesting the American government and its support of the Contras in Nicaragua, I still defended the American people. Any place that swings that far to the right of the political spectrum must also have its pendulum swing equally over to the other side. Although not evident if you're only exposed to mainstream American media, you find far more progressive movements going on in pockets of the U.S. than in placid Canada, but most Canadians don't know that.

I'm so hot I start to watch for places on the highway with air conditioning. I see a sign for a Dairy Queen ahead, an establishment I don't frequent in regular life, and suddenly have an uncontrollable craving for the icy sweetness of a root beer float. I was once in a Muslim town in northern Malaysia on a broiling hot afternoon when I spotted, right beside a mosque, an air-conditioned Dairy Queen. I ducked inside for a root beer float. The local girls who worked behind the counter were completely covered except for their eyes, their uniforms and veils the exact Dairy Queen bubblegum-pink striped colours with the A&W logo on their head scarves. They smiled and spoke the few words of English they knew: 'You like Billy Buster Parfait, yes?'

I pull off the interstate somewhere in western Missouri, and at the Dairy Queen, strike up a conversation with a woman mopping the floor. Her long hair hangs in grey strands and her teeth look as if she has drunk too many root beer floats. She complains to me about Bill Clinton and Monica Lewinsky, which I find fascinating because this is the first American I've talked to who actually thinks Clinton should be kicked out of office because of a few blow-jobs. All the other Americans I've met don't think Clinton's sex life is any of the nation's business, but that odd American Puritanism seems to have slithered down through the centuries and ended up in people like this woman. 'I didn't vote for him,' she says, 'that hippie drug addict, pot-smoking Commie who doesn't go to church.' Staring at her open jawed I realise I'm in the heart of the Bible Belt. We don't have any such belt in Canada. I can only think of a handful of people I've ever met in Canada who go to church, while 41 per cent of Americans say they read the Bible regularly, and 43 per cent attend church regularly. If a Canadian politician were to mention God in a speech, Canadians would definitely find that weird, yet in the U.S., politicians seem compelled to mention God at least once every time they open their mouths in public.

I smile weakly at the woman as she goes back to mopping the floor and think there must be thousands of small towns like this one all over this country, each as peculiar and full of gossip, church picnics and suspicions of the larger world. Still, I'm a sucker for small towns and find them infinitely intriguing. I know I'll live in one some day, although it'll have to be an enlightened small town with big trees, bike paths and a thriving downtown, not the redneck variety full of big box stores and religious fanatics. It'll also have to have its share of small town eccentrics, mildly brain-damaged people everyone in the town calls by name – perhaps Kenny or Lenny – and Kenny or Lenny will have to be in his fifties, live with his parents and stand at the end of the driveway waving to every passing car. When I was a kid and walked to school with my friends, we'd always stop to watch 'the spinning lady' who spun around and around in front of her elderly parents' living room window. We'd heard the spinning lady had once been a math genius at the university and we thought her spinning must have been a way to divine the cosmic powers of the universe. All the kids knew about the spinning lady, but I doubt that she would have been noticed in a big city.

When I order my root beer float, I ask the teenage girls behind the counter what there is to do for fun in this small Missouri town. It soon becomes apparent that the teenage girls are ignorant of every aspect of their hometown, except to say that it's boring and I should get out fast.

After my sickly sweet root beer float, the last of my life I swear, I drive into a wall of Kansas heat and think of tornadoes and Dorothy and how a nice tornado would cool things off right about now. This is my first time ever in Kansas and I'm secretly thrilled, not only because arriving in Kansas means I've now been to all 50 American states, but because I'm going to visit a *Wizard of Oz* tourist site in southwestern Kansas. In the 1970s, the financially struggling town of Liberal decided to set up a museum in an ageing farmhouse which they claimed was Dorothy's House, and since the movie wasn't set in a real township, nobody could challenge them. The farmhouse supposedly looks exactly like Dorothy's farmhouse in the movie. Dorothy's House, on a list of the most bizarre tourist destinations in America, has a collection of young Dorothys who dress in Dorothy clothes, carry around a Toto dog, and lead you through the house stocked with vintage appliances. I really have to see this for myself, teenage girls having a summer job I would have died for at 15.

But Kansas brings to mind more than tornadoes, amber waves of corn, munchkins and the memory of a young and tormented Judy Garland. Kansas is also very historic, once part of the Wild West where cowboys roamed, although now the state is full of wheat fields and abandoned missile silos. During the Cold War, nuclear missiles were stored underground in places like Kansas, ready to take off at the press of a button. Today these storage silos are largely obsolete, with some being used as people's homes, although not normal people, but people who prefer to live underground.

So far, Kansas looks the same as Missouri. Somewhere near Boonville, my car begins to lurch, speeding up out of control, then slowing down again just as quickly. I pull off into the small town to find a mechanic. After a few minutes underneath the hood, the elderly mechanic informs me the problem is my fuel filter. I need a new one, which he'll have to order from a nearby town, but he can have it installed by sundown. I thank him and wander off to wait in the shade on a nearby curb. Torrents of Kansas heat roll down from above and fill my lungs with hot air and my head with a dazed longing. Cicadas screech, the road melts and dogs are probably dying around the corner. Somewhere in the world, the wind is rippling gently through trees and gliding across a flower carpeted meadow. Somewhere, the air is fresh, brisk, even a little chilly by this time of day, and people are putting on jackets. But I don't remember what cool air feels like.

Chapter 5

Yukon Summer Sky

A big golden light is plastered all over the Yukon summer sky 24 hours a day. When the sun catches itself falling just below the horizon, perhaps a little tired, it bounces up again towards the next day, never for a second allowing darkness to enter the picture. In those moments the sky, in vague and moody shades of orange, sage and violet, considers blackness and the stars. It recalls a celestial silence that only comes with pure dark winter nights. Essentially, and quite understandably, the sky longs for the piercing clarity of the moon.

We wrote the word YUKON in black marker on a piece of cardboard and held it up to the oncoming traffic on a June morning in my hometown of Guelph, Ontario. The man in the truck who picked up my friend Kevin and me said to us, 'What's the yuck-un?'

'The Yukon, out west, way up north. The Yukon.'

'Never heard of it.'

'Beside Alaska.'

'Way up there?'

It's true we were 3,000 miles from the Yukon that morning, but I found it alarming he'd never heard of the place. It is part of Canada, after all. A woman with caged rats in her backseat picked us up next so she could tell us her life story. Then came the hairdresser, the mute truck driver, and the woman on her way to Wawa. Wawa is the northern Ontario town with the big concrete goose on the side of the highway and it's a known fact amongst all hitchhikers who have been to Wawa that they don't take kindly to the concept of hitchhiking there. The drivers in that area seem genuinely nervous, visibly uncomfortable as they pass us by in their securely locked cars. Even though the highway stretches endlessly along rocky, pine-covered hills for hundreds of miles, the drivers, on seeing a hitchhiker, divert their eyes and turn the other way as if they've suddenly noticed something of remarkable interest on the other side of the road. Look at that tree, Helen! Look at how different it is from the two million others! Did a gruesome murder involving a hitchhiker take place there years ago? I must know.

Luckily for us, Tiny, the Vietnamese mechanic, didn't know about Wawa and its aversion to hitchhikers. He was just passing through it, as we were, on his way to somewhere else. Tiny picked us up because he wanted someone to drive while he slept.

When Tiny's fifteen-year-old orange Pontiac broke down in the black of night an hour outside of Thunder Bay, he opened the hood, jumped up, and squatted on the front of the car to peer inside with his flashlight. Whatever the problem was, he fixed it by employing his burning cigarette to solder two wires together. I'm always impressed with this sort of ingenuity and I could tell Tiny was impressed with himself also. When he jumped back in the car he was wildly eager to tell us how he had lived off grubs and roots while hiding in the jungle for three years to dodge the Viet

Cong. He had travelled daily for miles on his stomach through thickets of tropical undergrowth to carry food to families living underground. Being tiny, he was good at hiding. That's what I love about hitchhiking; it's always a surprise study of human beings.

A few days of hitchhiking later, Kevin and I were on a back road in northern Alberta when a farmer gave us a ride and invited us home for an overnight stay. After dinner, he and his wife took us out to their strawberry patch where the four of us picked enormous berries as the late evening sun set crimson over the rolling hay fields. A strange intimacy, that mysterious connection strangers feel as they behold the majesty of nature, occupied the strawberry patch as we all turned to watch the sky.

It was the late eighties and I was 24, back from my trip to Europe where I'd stayed under the Greek olive grove a year earlier, and still on my way to everywhere. By that time, I was beginning to realise I possessed a gypsy soul and needed to travel as I needed to breathe. I'd learned already that travel could mean hours, even days of despair, rain, heatwaves, snow, mosquitoes, late trains, no trains, followed by a single moment of dazzling elation. It was those single moments one tended to recall.

I'd met my travelling companion Kevin a few years earlier when I was 19 and on a rafting trip on the Ottawa River. Kevin was at the end of a two-year hitchhiking trip around the world, and when his ride had let him off where we were camping, he bought the last rafting ticket. My girlfriend and I were drawn to Kevin immediately and it wasn't because he was probably the best-looking guy we'd ever had the nerve to talk to – he was tall with broad shoulders and clear sky-blue eyes – but he possessed a rare combination of qualities one doesn't often find in ordinary humans, especially in men. His favourite TV show as a kid had been *Little House on the Prairie* because he'd wanted to live a simple rural life.

He'd grown up on a farm and had loved the cows so much that he stopped eating meat for life when he was ten. He wasn't afraid of anything, especially not hitchhiking. He said hitchhiking was how he'd met the most fascinating and compassionate people in every continent. He was more excited about the world than anyone I'd ever met, and full of unbridled and youthful enthusiasm for travelling. His eyes shone when he told his travel stories, stories which inspired me to try travelling his way myself. After talking with him for hours around the campfire on the banks of the Ottawa River, it was obvious I'd found a kindred spirit, someone I could learn from, someone with a pure heart, unclouded and open like a child's, ready to take in all the universe had to offer. The next day, after paddling down the rapids, a houseboat came along to take us back to the campsite. On a table they set out big plates of fruit, cheese and bagels for the rafters, and I noticed Kevin stuffing his pockets with as much food as they would hold. I really did have a lot to learn from this guy, I thought. After the rafting trip, we gave him a ride home, to his family farm a couple of hours north of Guelph, and a few months later, I saw him walking down a hall at the University of Guelph where he'd enrolled in an agriculture course. The thing is, even though most of my girlfriends were infatuated with Kevin, I never thought of him as anything but a friend, which seemed a little baffling at the time, but years later would make perfect sense.

Kevin and I took six days to hitch across Canada to northern British Columbia where we would begin the three-day dusty drive up the Alaska Highway from Dawson Creek to the Yukon. After the Japanese attack on Pearl Harbor, the U.S. government felt an inland route to Alaska was vital. Ten thousand soldiers, four thousand of whom were blacks from the Deep South, built the 1,522-mile-long road by working twenty-hour days for eight months through a winter with temperatures as low as minus 60 degrees. The road winds through old-growth forests, hot springs, ice fields, tundra, lakes and some of the highest mountains in North America. Few towns or gas stations exist on the Alaska Highway so drivers must carry gasoline. The road wasn't paved when we were there so for three days we experienced a tyre-eating dust-fest of ruts and potholes approximating the size of large hot tubs. The road is paved now but this doesn't mean you travel any faster. With such a short summer to repair all the damage inflicted on the highway from the north's bad tempered winters, construction crews are as common a sight as the retired couples snapping pictures beside their RVs.

The Alaska Highway seems to be some sort of rite of passage for RVs, but no wonder. The scenery is spectacular and an hour can't pass without some sort of wildlife encounter. One morning, a moose galloped along beside the pickup truck we were riding in, like a racehorse from Uglyville.

We saw a lot of German bicyclists charging determinedly along the road's shoulder. At least we figured they were German. What other country's citizens would bicycle up a dusty, pot-holed highway through swarms of mosquitoes and black flies day after day for two months? Germans are a different breed, I thought, and normally should be approached with caution, although every so often you meet an extremely friendly one.

The Alaska Highway even has its own roadside attraction, a sanctuary for signs, any sign at all that people have lugged along in their vehicles and hung up on a giant wall for all those who stop to see. These people must know about the sign shrine in advance because no other explanation exists for signs stating the population of Wichita, or the 'Tampa: 60 miles' and 'Repent Now!' signs. What really impressed me was the massive green interstate sign: 'You Are Entering Atlantic City.' Somebody went to a lot of trouble to haul that one up there. It's amazing when you think of it: retired couples dismantling and tearing down those signs in the middle of the night, stealing forty pound pieces of metal so they can carry them thousands of miles in their RVs and desert them in a no man's land in the wilderness. It must give them a demented sense of importance. Kevin and I were getting a ride with a couple who had a sign that said: 'George Peterson Quality Meats. Just Up Ahead!' They nailed it up there with the hundreds of other signs and stood proudly underneath it while I took their picture. That was a big day for them, and for George Peterson too, I imagine.

When we arrived in the Yukon, our ride let us off at Haines Junction where we went in search of a good meal. We were surprised to find everything closed down for dinner until we learned it was midnight. This was our first night in the Land of the Midnight Sun. We set up our tent on the grass outside the information ranger station and were immediately ordered to take it down because the ranger told us it looked bad. In the parking lot sat eight giant gas-guzzling RVs running noisy generators, self-contained movable houses that took up three parking spaces where people were sleeping or watching *Dynasty* or playing video games or eating microwave popcorn. The RVs looked good, slick, air conditioned. Our little nylon dome tent, although brand new, looked bad. We moved it into the nearby woods where it wouldn't be criticised, and slept soundly.

The next morning we hitched to the entrance of Kluane National Park, 8,500 square miles of glaciers, marshes, mountains and sand dunes, all unsettled and all virtually untouched. Kluane contains Canada's highest mountain, Mt. Logan, and several massive glaciers including the largest non-polar ice field in the world. Once in the park, we began our hike into the utterly remote Alsek River Valley, straight into the heart of the largest breeding ground for grizzly bears in North America. We didn't know about the grizzly bears until six days later, when the woman who picked us up in the rain had to pull her truck over to the side of the road after we told her where we'd been camping. 'You were where? Good God! Hear any strange noises at night?' she asked. Actually, we had heard strange noises, especially one night in particular. As we lay awake in our tent we kept very still and listened as some monstrous clumsy visitor clamoured around our campsite. All we could do was huddle in our sleeping bags hoping the thing would go away. We weren't entirely stupid. We didn't keep food near our tent. We even jingled tin cans and sang as we hiked. I think the bears were happy to let us alone in our naiveté. At that age, I still hung on to the belief that if you don't invite fear into your heart, nothing out there can spoil your dinner party. It's based on the theory of attraction: you can't attract what's not inside you. That was the way I liked to regard the world back then and I love my younger free-spirited self for that reason. Only later would this conviction cave in on me to varying degrees, but certainly that summer in the Yukon, no grizzly bears trampled through my sweet theory of life.

We didn't see grizzlies in the Alsek River Valley. What we saw was this: snow-capped mountains, towering fir trees, a wide and calm river of jade that was too old and smart to rush hurriedly down to somewhere else, and masses of purple flowers. We called this place the Valley of the Green Sand and Purple Flowers. Fireweed stretched along the green clay valley for miles in every direction. We saw no people, no indication of humans anywhere. With each day we spoke less and less, settling into our own private silences. One day we climbed a mountain to be able to peer down and gain a new perspective on our ancient valley. Although many millions of years old, the mountains were likely to remain for eons after the last people had been wiped out by a stray meteor, or a change in the weather, or any of a thousand human disasters likely to wreak havoc on the world. I sat on a rock and watched the mountains for a long time and it occurred to me that life doesn't have to be a struggle. Life can be as simple as this.

We stayed for a few days with a friend of mine at his cabin outside of the Yukon's capital city, Whitehorse, on a road in the woods called Squatter's Row. The population of the entire Yukon is just 31,000 in an area the size of France, and two-thirds of that population live in Whitehorse, one of the few towns left in the world that still has a frontier feel to it.

One morning we woke up and decided to canoe down the Yukon River. It was that simple. All we had to do was rent a canoe in Whitehorse, which we'd drop off at our destination in Carmacks about ten days later, and buy a big garbage bag of food and some cooking pots from a second hand shop. In one of the stores in Whitehorse we met a group of Swiss men who were embarking on the same canoe journey. They told us they'd been preparing for the trip for over a year and had spent thousands of dollars on it already. Their gear consisted of fishing rods and tackle, shotguns, and all the high-tech European camping gear they could stuff into their canoes. Kevin and I weren't that prepared, but at least if our boat tipped we'd only be wet, not broke.

Our canoe trip down the Yukon River began in the cold rain of a foggy afternoon in July. We got as far that first day as the southern tip of Lake Lebarge, the lake immortalised by Scottish poet and adventurer Robert Service in his poem, 'The Cremation of Sam McGee', about the character who froze to death and was cremated 'on the marge of Lake Lebarge'. The rain was pounding down too hard to push further, so we decided to take shelter and camp at a cabin we noticed along the river. As we were pulling ashore, we spotted two male figures in an extraordinarily fast-moving canoe appear out of the thundering rain and heavy mist. Their canoe and its crew we came to call the German-Japanese Team, for it consisted of one of each of those nationalities, both determined to paddle faster than anyone else on the river. Neither the German nor the Japanese guy spoke a word of the other's language and we often wondered how they fared on their trip. Due to the pace they set, we only saw them that first day, although we heard stories about them from other canoeists as we travelled further down the river. The German–Japanese Team paddled ashore and the four of us went to investigate the apparently abandoned cabin. Rain was beating us to a frozen pulp. We peered inside the building's windows to see an empty room and a wood stove. The Japanese guy took his machete and swung it above his head with a pained expression on his gleaming wet face, ready to thrash down the door. Kevin stopped him and tried the door handle first. It was open.

For entertainment that night, Kevin and I watched the German-Japanese Team eat alarming amounts of barely cooked meat they'd heated over their camp stoves. Afterwards they cleaned their shotguns, then rolled out their sleeping bags to snore all night long. We studied the map, then listened to the rain pelt a rhythm on the cabin's tin roof, helping to dull the snoring so we could dream of river adventures in the light of the night.

For the next two days we attacked Lake Lebarge. A fierce wind pushed us along the thirty-mile narrow lake which made for a thrilling ride in the waves, although difficult to steer through at times. At the end of the lake where it became the river again, we reached an abandoned miner's camp and stayed for the night in an old trapper's cabin with hard beds, five hundred mice and the voices of dead gold seekers in the walls telling us to go back home.

Few places in the world exist where there were once many people and now there are none. All along the Yukon

River are the rotting and rusting relics of a population long since disappeared. In the gold rush to the Klondike thousands used the river like a highway leading into the far reaches of northwest Canada and Alaska. Hand-made boats of every conceivable construction set sail or paddle for the Klondike gold fields in 1898. Twenty thousand dreamers floated north. Few returned rich with gold, and some, in their dangerous pursuit, didn't return at all. Hundreds of shacks, cabins and tents dotted the hillsides all along the river. No one is alive today who remembers the Klondike boom days and all that remains are some faded photos, a few surviving journals and tattered letters home. The Yukon is a museum the length of a river, a land of artefacts – rusting tin cans, crumbling cabins, old roads barely visible, rotting carcasses of dredges and steamboats, gravestones, crosses, abandoned villages, ruined roadhouses. Paraphernalia of the past are strewn along the river like an antique collector's dream. The land seems untouched, looking as it must have hundreds of years ago with the forest rolling endlessly back from the riverbank. But once you step into the forest, rusty cooking pots crumble beneath your feet, releasing untold tales of a gold seeker's life.

Where the river resumes at the north end of Lake Lebarge, purple shadowed cliffs begin to close in on you, the water having cut down through the centuries into the land as if quenching a deep thirst. I'd never seen anything like it, that many sheer unspoiled miles of pure untamed wilderness, almost frightful in its isolation. Kevin said it reminded him of the Yangtze River valley in China. Mountain goats and moose drank from the river, ignoring us entirely. Above us, bald and golden eagles soared. The water was crystal clean green and the mountains that rose straight up beside us were reflected in the river at our paddle. We had been thrust magically back in time. All around us was magnificence and we were paddling into it.

'I can't help thinking,' said Kevin one day, 'that at the end of our lives, when we look back, we'll remember this river, not where we camped on it or its colour, but how it sounds. It's completely quiet, except for this faint rippling.' He went on to tell me about a time he was once on another river, a much noisier one, the River Ganges in Varanasi, India. He spent the first night in the crowded city in a flea-infested hotel. The next day, he took his belongings on a boat with a driver down the river in search of better accommodation. When the boat stopped in the part of the city he wanted, he got out with his backpack, paid the driver, and was immediately swarmed by a flock of people trying to talk to him. In the confusion of the crowd, Kevin didn't have a chance to get his knapsack from the boat, and almost immediately the boat became lost in the hundreds of other boats along the bustling river. A moment before while riding along the water, he'd been enjoying the women's brightly coloured saris in passing boats, the many languages spoken all around him, the lazy morning breeze, and now suddenly he was without his essentials: his passport, his money, his traveller's cheques, his journal, his plane ticket home. He went to American Express and they refused to replace his traveller's cheques without his identification. He went to the Canadian Embassy and was scolded by a woman for being so careless, and told they couldn't help him without his Canadian passport. With only a few rupees in his pocket, he realised all he could do was find the boat driver, which seemed like an impossible task in a city of thousands of boat drivers, but he had no choice. He went back to the place where he'd first boarded the boat and started talking to people, telling them his story. He spent the entire day talking to people, making sure to say the incident had been an accident and not a theft, and if the driver returned his knapsack to his hotel, he'd give him a hundred dollars. That evening he went to the police station and found a policeman who was very friendly, so friendly he wanted to chat and find out the names of all Kevin's relatives, what Kevin did in Canada, what he thought of India, what Indian food he liked. Finally, the policeman got him to write down every detail of what had happened that morning, and then he made him write it all over again on another piece of paper. The policeman took the two copies of Kevin's statement, stamped them, gave one to Kevin, and put the other in a dusty file box. With a big smile, he said, 'There, all done. Thank you my friend.' Kevin returned to his hotel wondering how he'd survive India penniless, when, standing outside his hotel room, was the boat driver with his knapsack.

'So the driver heard from someone you'd talked to where you were staying?'

'Yes, and he was so apologetic and kind. I was so relieved. Seeing him standing there was like a gift from the gods or something.'

'Didn't you want to break down and cry?' I asked.

'No, I somehow knew it would all work out, even if I didn't find my knapsack. That's what I love about travelling. You're surrounded by adventure. You have no idea what's in store for you, but if you let yourself go along with the flow of the unknown and accept whatever happens, things seem to work out.'

Kevin's words were mysterious and mesmerising to me. I thought perhaps he ought to have been a hermit or a monk, so intimate he was with the infinite wisdom of the world. I remember looking back at him as he paddled and being deeply grateful I'd found him on this earth, a lifelong friend who radiated such calm and assuring energy.

As we continued to paddle along the Yukon River each day, what slowly dawned on us was that the river was moving at such a steady clip by itself that paddling wasn't necessary. The river cruised along at about five miles an hour so we could average almost fifty miles a day by barely paddling at all. Once we got over our psychological need to keep ourselves pointed downstream we enjoyed a lazy 360 degree panorama as the canoe gently rotated to her own rhythm. One of us could lie back in the boat and watch the sky and mountains, read a book, or doze off while the other would keep watch. Things to look out for were the gravel bars and innumerable trees swept down the river during the spring floods. The Yukon is one of the few great rivers of North America untamed by dams. This means the river goes berserk with melt water every spring, with ten times the volume it has later in the year. The river rips out new channels, chews out acres of riverbank on the curves and wipes out islands while spawning new ones. This is how all big rivers once were: uncontrolled, wild and ravenous.

We weren't the only canoeists on the river. About a dozen people were paddling along the same route at the same time. We all had our own pace and stopped at different times, but two or three times a day, we'd come across the same people, especially at campsites which were usually abandoned miners' camps or old Indian sites. We got to know our fellow river people, even fairly well sometimes, all of us part of a friendly assemblage of people of different ages, different countries and lifestyles but all encountering the same scenery, the same rain, sunshine and wildlife, and all with the same whimsical compulsion to paddle the Yukon River.

Even though we were in Canada, we were among the few Canadians on the river. Most of the other canoeists were German, Swiss or American. Every day we'd pass the same spiky-haired Germans, two guys with leather jackets, tattoos and lots of little metal rings protruding from their flesh. They were usually fishing, which seemed incongruous. Another pair of Germans we saw just once because they were hell-bent on making it to Dawson City as fast as possible. Since it was 24-hour daylight, they refused to waste light and were paddling around the clock. The six women from Florida we came across at least three times a day. They were in their early fifties, on a college reunion, and this was their first canoe trip. Every time we met them they were laughing at a minor catastrophe they were either entering or escaping, and always the one named Marge was the butt of their jokes since she insisted on applying make-up and styling her hair. 'Mr Right could be out here, honey, any time, around the corner,' she told me. 'You just don't know!'

The Albertan Brothers was the name we gave to a pair of bald, not terribly bright twins from Alberta, each with his own canoe equipped with a small outboard motor. Often the Albertan Brothers would come ashore at a campsite for the 'night' and cook dinner just as Kevin and I would be eating breakfast and preparing to set off for the 'day'. The 24 hour daylight was confusing. We'd wake not knowing if it was 7 a.m. or 7 p.m. As time passed, I kept waiting for it to get dark. I felt as if I was missing something essential as each day continued on into the next without the familiar dream time to replenish what the day took away. The Albertan Brothers would never fail to ask us what time it was whenever we saw them. We never did know the time and I never understood why it was so important to them. 'Does it really matter?' I finally said to them one morning, which was one evening, for them. They had no reply but looked at me as if I'd told them I was holding secret meetings with the Pope deep inside the earth.

One morning as we paddled down the river we heard a voice shouting wildly. We looked up to the top of a metal look-out tower beside the river, and there we found the voice's owner in the form of a giant man yelling at us. Dressed in army fatigues, he was nearly hysterical, waving his arms frantically. Incoherent and panic-stricken, he seemed desperately to want to tell us something. When we asked him if he wanted us to pull in, he shouted down, 'Well, if y'all can, I'd mighty appreciate it.'

We pulled in for him. He wasn't half-way down the tower when he started telling his tale, how he and his partner, hunters from Georgia, had capsized their canoe the day before in some monstrous rapids not far ahead, how he'd swum to shore and walked hours back along the riverbank to the tower he remembered passing, while his partner, who he thought was now probably dead, had stayed floating in the river to chase after the canoe, and save the ham. The lost case of beer was OK. His wife was always nagging him to cut down anyway, but that mother of a honey-baked ham brought all the way from Georgia, they'd really been hankering after that. All that food, all that beer on the bottom of the river. It was a crying shame.

He told us his name was Ernie and plunked himself down in the middle of our canoe, causing it to sink so deeply into the water I feared a river disaster myself. Almost breathless, Ernie commenced a one-hour monologue. 'Those rapids are a-comin' soon and I ain't gonna fall out again. I'm gonna hang on. My wife. I gotta call my wife. I almost died yesterday and do ya think she cares? Probably not. I'm callin' her as soon as we get to a phone. We lost our ham, we lost our beer, shouldn't have been sittin' up on that beer case. Too shaky. Better to sit down low like this here. What part of the States you two from? (The Canadian part, Kevin told him.) Hell, I gotta find my partner. I doubt he's alive.'

Shortly afterwards we reached *the rapids* where the southern duo had met their fate. Nothing more than a few barely discernable ripples in the water, these rapids made us wonder how they'd managed to paddle through Lake Lebarge. 'It ain't what it looks like. She's a trickster this river. Hang on.' We paddled along as always, waiting for something terrible to happen. 'OK, maybe this is a better canoe. Those rapids were powerful yesterday. Nearly killed us. Jimmy, my partner, he's probably dead. Yep, won't be shootin' ducks with Jimbo no more.'

Not far after the rapids we came across Jimbo, but Jimbo wasn't dead. He was relaxing with his face aimed into the sun beside a little campfire. Next to him sat a sleeping pad propped on its side with the word HELP written across it in large letters. 'Howdy all,' Jimmy said, with a casual wave of his hand as if this were a picnic. 'Thought you'd be showin' up soon, Ern.' Jimmy, in contrast to paunchy Ernie, was long and lean, slow-talking, with a scraggly red beard and felt hat on his head.

We pulled ashore. Ernie hauled his massive body out of the canoe, walked up to Jimmy, grabbed hold of him, and pulled rigid Jimmy into the wide spread of his sweaty chest, displaying a degree of tenderness I found surprising from this man who'd lamented his beer and his honey-baked Georgia ham. Jimmy, looking vaguely bewildered, didn't hug Ernie back but Ernie didn't seem to notice. 'We ain't dead, Jimmy, we ain't dead. I love you, man. I love you… Where the hell's our canoe?'

'Gone.'

'Ham?'

'Gone'

'Where's everything else?'

'Gone.'

'How'd you get this fire lit? How'd you get this here sleepin' pad?'

'Some friendly folk come by. They helped a bit. They left.'

That's when it struck me for the first time. Kevin and I may have to take Ernie and Jimmy with us for the rest of our canoe trip. I looked over at Kevin and could see the same dreadful thought was occurring to him. A silent shudder passed between us.

But then, miraculously, from around the bend the Albertan Brothers were approaching, each with his own canoe, even outboard motors which would help lug the extra weight of Ernie. 'Come ashore,' we called to them. 'Have some lunch.'

At first the Albertan Brothers were happy to take along Ernie and Jimmy. Apparently the twins had been fighting, sick of each other's company, and were thankful for the distraction. But later that day, when they finally came across the Americans' upside-down canoe caught in a mass of dead trees near the shore, the Albertan Brothers were no longer on speaking terms with Ernie. We spotted Ernie and Jimmy ahead of us on the riverbank with their canoe: Ernie jumping up and down and waving at us, Jimmy lying on the ground, the pair of them stranded once again, at the mercy of whoever came down the river. Their canoe badly needed patching and the Albertan Brothers had unceremoniously dumped them there with it and left. 'Stupid rednecks,' said Ernie. 'Trying to tell us everything we done wrong yesterday. As if they're any smarter.' Since we didn't have room for the two of them, or any patches for their canoe, we were of no use to them and free to leave.

That evening, at a campsite called Big Salmon, we learned that Ernie and Jimmy had been rescued by the six women from Florida. Marge was beaming at the campfire, her rouged cheeks flaming, her coiffed hair all astray. Jimmy, pulling on his beard and stealing quick shy glances her way, was a changed man, a man whose last name apparently was Right. Marge and Jimmy had fallen in love.

And so it went, the Yukon River, inspiring love and languor and a never-ending light. In the day we floated and at night we recalled, trying to rehearse the scenes of the river in our minds: the eagles and the leggy moose, the impossible green of the river and the mountains rising up so close like sudden thoughts. The nights never failed to bring with them, on schedule and at an alarming decibel level, the not-too-distant voice of Ernie telling his story of the river disaster which almost took his life, the story of how he'd been so close to death he'd spoken to God and asked forgiveness – forgiveness for what we never asked – how he'd swum miles alone along the river, searching for his partner, a tale of heroic proportions we didn't even recognise, a tale that Kevin and I, by its fifth telling, had been cut out of entirely. 'I don't understand,' said a Swiss man to us one night around a campfire. 'Every night we hear this same story and every night the story grows more dangerous.' The Swiss man told us he also had canoed by the hysterical Ernie in the tower, but hadn't stopped for him. He simply waved and kept paddling, thinking Ernie in his army fatigues must be an escaped lunatic from the military. 'This sometimes happens in Switzerland. The army drives them mad and they head for the wilderness. I didn't want to go near him.'

On the tenth day we looked up from the river to see a bridge approaching. The bridge seemed intrusive and alien and meant civilisation was ahead. A few minutes later we passed some shacks along the water and a clearing of the forest. Sadly, we'd arrived at Carmacks and the end of our canoe trip. Carmacks was a forgettable little town with three restaurants all owned by the same man, which explained our ten dollar salad consisting solely of iceberg lettuce.

That night, camping in our tent beside a river that felt like home, I thought of the drifters, homesteaders, and renegades who had tramped across an unimaginable expanse of country and sailed down a river to find gold, or their spirits, or a new life. I thought of the ones who had died on the way, their bones left at the river's bottom, polished, and fragile. You could almost hear their voices, a murmur around your sleep, as if the dead souls were babbling at the edge of the river. And I thought of Ernie, whose bones the river didn't want, and whose babbling at the edge of the river was enough to waken the dead.

We spent another two weeks in the Yukon, hitching from Carmacks up the Klondike Highway to Dawson City, the site of the 1898 Gold Rush, and found the lively little town to be full of commotion, wanderers, dilapidation, fiddle music and the last century. In Dawson City we found an abandoned miner's cabin to stay in and we volunteered at a music festival that was just starting that weekend. After the weekend, we couldn't imagine turning south. South meant going home. At the end of the summer, I would go to teachers' college and after that, planned on teaching in the Arctic, all of which made me nervous just thinking about. We decided to keep heading north and hitchhike up the Dempster Highway, a 456 mile mountainous road, to Inuvik, the town at the end of the highway and the end of just about everything else. The Dempster Highway is the most northerly public road in Canada and nowhere else in the country is it as easy to penetrate the harsh and mysterious lands of the Arctic as along the Dempster. I've never seen a road like it. The highway passes through rugged volcanic mountains, rolling plains, tundra, and at that time, in early August, stretching for hundreds of miles in all directions along both sides of the road is a flaming carpet of fireweed, a roller-coaster ride shrieking with bright pink flowers. The scene is almost too much to believe, both dramatic and serene, like a forgotten dream of some infinitely protracted moment out of childhood. It would be inspiring to live along that highway, but few people do. On the Arctic Circle you can't exactly drive down the road to pick up some bagels or go out to see a movie without spending at least a week in your car.

On the first day up the Dempster, some forest rangers dropped us off at a campground in the Tombstone

Mountains. We set up our tent, cooked dinner and met the five other people at the campground. A lone camper in his sixties from Seattle noticed I was reading a Hermann Hesse book. He came over to where I was lying on a picnic table to tell me he remembered going through his own 'Hermann Hesse stage' and informed me I'd soon grow out of it. I thought it was an arrogant comment at the time, and now, looking back on it years later, I still think that. Amazingly, the four other campers were women from Guelph, my hometown. They'd been travelling together all summer and apparently all hated each other. The bossy one asked Kevin and me our opinion on a debate they'd been having over whether or not it was right to pull apart two copulating dogs if the dogs were copulating in front of children. Evidently the bossy one had done this, to the horror of the children I imagine, although she admitted pulling the dogs apart wasn't easy and it made the dogs scream in agony. The other three women had varying opinions on the subject, although tended to think generally the act was cruel, stupid and unnatural. The argument was quite heated and involved yelling. In the midst of all this, a German couple on bicycles came flying into the campground. They set up their super-practical tent and started preparing dinner as they told us they'd bicycled up the Alaska Highway and now were heading up the Dempster for Inuvik. I imagined that their journey thus far must have been akin to trudging through the torture region of hell as the Dempster Highway is unpaved and its gravel consists of irregular sized rocks, the smallest approximating the size of a baseball. They were visibly exhausted but with true Teutonic efficiency they unpacked, cooked dinner, washed their dishes, set up their tent and were inside it within half an hour. The next morning they were nowhere to be seen and we could only assume they had been rattling down the highway dodging semis for hours before the rest of us opened our eyes.

Four Swiss travellers picked us up that day. We ate lunch with them on the Arctic Circle and that night camped out on a desolate tundra that looked like the surface of the moon. At midnight, we went for a moonwalk and stepped over some gigantic grizzly prints, freshly planted. We were in a very different land from any place I'd ever been, far beyond the trees, and I got a sunburn at midnight. The tundra exerted a strange hold on me. It felt primitive, barren and fiercely private, a place not meant for humans ever to find.

People told us not to expect much in Inuvik but we didn't listen, thinking that a city amidst so much icy wilderness and close to the Arctic Ocean in one of the most remote regions in the world must have something of interest to offer. It doesn't. I've never felt such an anticlimax, except for my first kiss at age sixteen when Peter Chaloner jammed his tongue down my throat in his parents' dark basement. I hadn't realised tongues were part of the set-up. Even though Inuvik was ugly – most of the buildings are of the pre-fab-pastel-paint design and all pipes are above ground because of the permafrost – we managed to enjoy ourselves because we spent our time searching for Northwest Territories license plates shaped like polar bears. We eventually found a mechanic willing to rummage through a junk pile and sell us three plates for five dollars, which was cheaper than the bananas selling in Inuvik for five dollars each.

On our trip back down the Dempster, at a rest stop called Eagle Plain, we waited ten hours for a ride, but since it was hailing, howling and raining, we abandoned our game of guessing which cars might stop for us, and decided to wait inside Eagle Plain's hotel and restaurant lobby in front of a TV instead. The TV was airing seventies re-runs and during commercial breaks, Kevin would go out to the parking lot to ask if anyone was headed south. That's another form of hitchhiking, one that doesn't involve thumbs, and it can be a refreshing change from standing beside highways. After two horrendous episodes of *One Day At A Time*, Kevin found a lovely retired couple who said they'd take us in their colossal and luxurious stream-lined RV that resembled a jet plane. They said they'd meet us in the parking lot after they'd eaten lunch. We were elated, but soon became so absorbed in the final episode of *Magnum P.I.* that we didn't notice when the lovely retired couple left without us. Next came *Get Smart*, a favourite of mine as a kid, followed by *Maude* and *Miami Vice*, a truly crappy show. Just as we were starting to think we'd have to spend the next week at Eagle Plain in a mindless, glazed-eyed state staring at the TV and every so often looking out to the rainy parking lot where no cars were headed south, a truck driver, whose truck Kevin had helped load when *Miami Vice* became intolerable, told us he'd take us to Whitehorse. We were saved from having to watch the next show, *Emergency*, and to this day I believe I am a better adjusted person because of that.

Our sixty-something driver wasn't the most charming of men. He didn't speak for the entire first hour, until finally he uttered this: 'I always regret picking up god-damned hitchhikers.' After that, the silence was broken only sporadically when he'd mumble, 'God-damn the whole thing to hell,' whenever we encountered another vehicle.

'Are you married?' I asked him. He didn't answer that with words but made some snorting, guttural noises which I assumed meant that no, he wasn't married but had been once to a miserable and crabby woman, as all women obviously are, and never again would he even consider the idea of marriage, or women in general for that matter, in this lifetime. I was so happy to be on the road again, to be bumping along and back among all those pink flowers that rambled into eternity, that I actually started singing Willie Nelson's 'On the Road Again', refusing to let this man's unpleasant disposition ruin my day. Kevin sang also but we only knew the words to the chorus so kept repeating it. 'God-damn it, don't you know the verses? What's wrong with ya? It goes like this...' Our driver not only knew all the verses of 'On the Road Again' but his voice possessed a haunting lilting quality and, occasionally, sounded operatic. We must have sung for two hours with the man. I think he had fun. By the time we reached Whitehorse the next day, he actually asked for our addresses and said he might drop by for a visit if he was ever in Ontario.

We decided to take the ship from Skagway, Alaska down to the coast of British Columbia, a three-day sail, rather than hitchhike the Alaska Highway again. Over the preceding weeks we'd met numerous German travellers who'd told us they'd taken this same boat ride and had only paid eight dollars for their passage. How could three days on a ship only cost eight dollars? we'd asked. They'd told us that all you needed to do was buy a ticket in Skagway for the first stop, Juneau, Alaska, four hours away, and then simply stay on the ship until you reach British Columbia. You can go all the way to Vancouver if you like and only pay eight dollars. They never check walk-on passengers' tickets, said the Germans confidently. They don't care. They make their money from the RV passengers who have to pay a fortune to ship their vehicles. It sounded suspicious, not to mention dangerous and illegal, but so many Germans assured us of this, that we thought we'd try our luck at being stowaways also.

We bought our eight dollar tickets, boarded the ship in Skagway, and lay down our sleeping bags under the sky on the ship's top deck where some other travellers, mostly Europeans and Americans, were already camped. I wondered how many of us had bought these 'special' tickets, as the Germans referred to them, but didn't know how to broach the subject. Four hours later, when the ship pulled into the Juneau harbour, all of the travellers got up to look over the deck and listen as a voice on the loudspeaker called out, 'All passengers debarking in Juneau, this is your final call.' We watched nervously as people below walked off the ship while we stood frozen at the railing, now official stowaways, guilty of international crime, impulsive folly, and believers in the word of Germans. Germans had tried twice in the twentieth century alone to take over the world. Perhaps they knew something we didn't in how to be devious.

By the afternoon of the second day, we began to worry about our special tickets because the ominous voice over the loudspeaker had changed its message. 'All passengers debarking here, this is your final call. Have your tickets ready for inspection.'

We leapt to the railing to look down and see if they really were checking tickets but it was difficult to say in the rain, fog and commotion of crowds coming and going under their umbrellas. Kevin went downstairs to investigate while I stayed up on the deck imagining scenarios of getting hauled off to a concrete federal prison somewhere in the Nevada desert, spending ten years in jail fighting off murderous inmates, missing out on my prime years and eating spam sandwiches. It was all too much and I considered going straight to the captain to confess my crime.

But then something unexpected happened and suddenly I didn't care about prison any more. It had become dark. I hadn't seen real darkness in two months and I'd forgotten what that meant. The night had approached from somewhere across the sea and had come crawling up to where I stood on the deck. Up above was now a great net of stars looming so close I could almost reach for them, almost swipe them with my hand. How strange was this blackness that had grown around me, silent and dense, hanging like a shroud, devouring my arms and legs. I was erased, swallowed by a velvet night, and I found consolation in that, in whatever was secret and eternal in a dark night. My fears of getting caught as a stowaway, of my future as a teacher, melted into the night sky. I knew the sun would rise and the sun would set and the world would keep steady its gentle swirl. Here and there the world would blow up, people would shout, and fluorescents would glare, but tonight it was dark, so dark I could wrap myself in its cosmic origins, jump up and down, dance the tango, and, if compelled, blow a kiss up to the stars.

Maybe, I'd even watch for the moon.

Chapter 6

I'm back on the road in eastern Kansas long after darkness has fallen. My car has a brand new fuel filter and the brand new oil filter isn't making the slightest difference. In fact, I think Marcia is even worse than before. Thinking back to that summer in the Yukon it seems as if my life was blissfully simple then. I had no major life decisions to make, no pressure, and I never had car troubles because I didn't own a car. So much life was ahead of me, and although I didn't know how it would all turn out, I was convinced I'd continue along as always: lighthearted, optimistic, full of dreams, letting each day bring whatever it felt like. We never did get sent to prison for being stowaways. I distinctly recall my heart pounding violently, however, as we walked down the gangway, watching an official ahead of us nod goodbye to each passenger, wondering if he'd single us out and ask to see our tickets, eye us sternly as we pretended to search for them until finally he'd holler into his loudspeaker that he'd captured criminals and call for everyone to hit the deck. He didn't do any of this. He smiled and nodded goodbye. We smiled back. The Germans were right. We walked off the gangplank onto the next adventure.

Somehow I've allowed my life to become more complicated, or at least more weighted down, than back in those rambling hitchhiking days, and I wonder if this is a byproduct of age, the pressure of society, or something else. I used to wake up every morning and practically jump out of bed. I don't do that any more. Is this gradual deflating of life's balloon ride to be expected for everyone as each year passes into the next? Perhaps so, since for millions of years the average life expectancy was 34, my age now. In this alarmingly short time span of human history since we've suddenly begun living into our eighties, we're expected year after year to keep up our zeal, our romantic notions, our dreams, our get-up-and-go. Perhaps our genes simply haven't evolved to sustain the enthusiasm for all the years beyond 30. Or perhaps I'm just feeling what many women who've recently arrived in their thirties feel, a pressure to start a family, own a house, invest in the future, be more responsible, all of this when we're not even sure we're doing what we want to do, or living where we want to live. Or perhaps I just have a harder time letting go of my youthful vision than other people. In fact, I refuse to believe we have to, and would like to say I follow in the footsteps of those who never gave up their passion for life. It always breaks my heart to think of Thoreau who wanted to 'live deep and suck out all the marrow of life', and how on his deathbed he asked to be lifted up to the window so he could catch one last glimpse of spring. However, now that I think of it, he was only 44 at the time.

This is something I love about a North American road trip, especially out here in the Midwest. I discover that nowhere is actually where everything is. The expanses are so vast that hours can pass dwelling on all manner of things. Every mile I drive along this dark interstate I seem to be unravelling thoughts that have been swirling inside me for ages but haven't had the chance to surface until now. I'm also recalling my old self, bringing her back. It's like driving to find my whole past. Memories of my youth pass by in other cars, sneak up in the transport truck beside me, or lumber along in the trailer I saw a mile back. Every summer when I was a kid, my parents would pack up our Starcraft pop-up trailer and our family car, a rusty 1965 Ford Falcon station wagon and we'd set off on an epic camping trip. My dad was a geographer with a love of maps and any road leading to someplace new. We'd go to the Maritimes, the Canadian Prairies, Pennsylvania or New England, the Great Lakes, Wisconsin, the Canadian Rockies, sometimes Quebec, or the Appalachians. Every summer was different. My sister hated those camping trips, but I didn't. Those camping trips cultivated my love of the open road.

Memories of places spring up from a childhood well, and memories of people and old friends appear on the roadside. Recalling the Yukon trip makes me think of Kevin, and how having him as a travelling companion was like wearing a good-luck charm. He never seemed to let much bother him and he could turn every lousy, rainy, hard-ground situation into something funny. Or so it seemed at the time. Later, he told me that during our summer in the Yukon, he'd been plagued the entire trip with the thought that he might be gay. For the first time in his life he'd allowed the dreaded thought – dreaded since he came from a tiny rural community where he doubted his parents even knew what homosexuality was – to take form in his mind, and he said I'd helped him with this radical notion in a conversation we'd had on one of those eternally-light days meandering along the river. Apparently he'd asked me what I thought of people discovering they were gay, and I'd said I thought that could be great, certainly no big deal, and it would probably be a huge relief to discover something fundamental and biologically inherent about oneself, like discovering one's true destiny after years of searching. Apparently that comment had a profound impact on Kevin. A year after our Yukon trip, when he was 28, he invited everyone in his entire life – his large extended family, all his friends, his teachers, everyone who'd meant anything to him over the years – to a small country church near Georgian Bay, Ontario. There, he got up to give a sermon, in which he explained, gradually and not without suspense, what it was which made him different, how he'd wished like hell he'd been born left-handed instead. As it began to become clear what exactly he was referring to, several people walked out of the church and didn't speak to him for years. I had to miss this stirring event because I was teaching school 600 miles north of there, but just before I left, I got to hear him read me this secret speech. My parents were invited to the church service – my mother had always adored Kevin and hoped I'd marry him some day – and they said it was one of the most moving addresses they'd ever heard. I'm sure, however, that my mother must have been disappointed Kevin would never be her future son-in-law, and that I, her daughter, would continue to date men who were never quite ideal, never quite Kevin. When I heard about the occasion, I was once again inspired by my friend, in awe of his brute strength, and glad for him that he'd found at least part of his destiny. Finding one's true destiny, who we really are beneath all the layers of what we've piled on ourselves over the years, is, I suppose, why we're here on earth, so we can enter and know that inner bright core.

I can't help wondering if my destiny is waiting for me at the golden end of this long highway.

Damn! Marcia is making clunking noises again, which jolts me out of my reveries. This is depressing. This is chaos creeping closer. What a thoroughly helpless feeling to be at the mercy of a beaten-up car in the Midwest at midnight. I've lived this carefree life and look where it has gotten me. Living like this, all these years of traipsing around places like the Yukon and too many other places, has led me here, tonight. I should have been working all this time at a well-paying and fulfilling job so I could afford a decent, reliable car. I should have a membership with the AAA.

After several hours of chugging through the night I can hardly keep my eyes open so pull off in a small town to look for a place to sleep. If there were a Wal-Mart around I might actually sleep in its parking lot. Wal-Mart allows free camping so people will eat at the Wal-Mart cafeterias and shop for lawn chairs, coolers and whatever else might be needed for a good time in a Wal-Mart parking lot. I think a motorcycle gang or fifty bus loads of hippies should take Wal-Mart up on its offer and stay in a parking lot for six months. I'd pay to see the look on those managerial faces.

At this hour, the black summer trees are rustling down sweet air in this little town, and I do find a parking lot, but not Wal-Mart's. It's a parking lot under a grove of elderly oaks at what looks like an old folks' home. Finding a place to sleep in your car is easy if you know what to look for. Small quiet towns and shady parking lots are always a good bet. And although I never do this, ideally, it's best to stop before dark to dispel the fear that you've accidentally parked on a traffic meridian, a runway airstrip, or beside a gas station pump, like I once did years ago. Unlike sleeping in a hotel room where the surroundings are always pretty much the same, sleeping in your car in a different place each night is a thrill: crawling under your sleeping bag in the dark and lying there perfectly still listening to whatever strange sounds might be out there – a train whistle or the wind or far-off human voices – then in the morning getting to look out your car windows to see where you've spent the night, knowing you've saved a bundle of money on a room, and feeling that sense of invigoration from living outside. As long as the car windows were open, that is.

But aren't I a little too old to still be sleeping in my car? Would Mary Tyler Moore have done this? I don't think so. She would have driven her little convertible to an old-fashioned homey motel, quiet and neat with thick plaid blankets on the beds, and the good-looking manager would have asked her on a date. Her hipper seventies sitcom counterpart Rhoda would have slept in her car. I've become Rhoda. I guess that's something. I liked Rhoda's creativity and her ability to laugh at herself. Still, I always thought I'd be Mary, one of my role models as a child – along with Nadia Comaneci, Laura Ingalls and Laurie Partridge, which I just realised is completely frightening since I only knew those people from TV.

Still, like Mary, shouldn't I have 'made it after all' by now? I climb into Marcia's backseat, lie down under my sleeping bag, and listen to crickets and the distant but distinct sound of teenage girls, who somewhere tonight in this little town, are laughing.

At approximately 7 a.m., there seem to be people surrounding my car in the parking lot. Someone is tapping at my window, which I find a little rude. 'I think it's a girl sleeping,' says a woman's voice. 'Maybe it's Irene's niece.' I keep my head hidden under a T-shirt. 'She's from Ontario. Long way from home,' says another. Not being an early-riser, I don't feel like getting up yet, but since it probably isn't good manners to sleep in an old age home parking lot, I grudgingly force myself awake. Besides, it's better to drive in the cooler parts of the day and I can already feel today will be another scorcher.

When I climb out of the car, feeling dishevelled and rather disorientated, five old women and a caretaker holding vine clippers are staring at me. I explain to them about using their parking lot as my motel and they seem to find the idea amusing, if a little unusual. Two more elderly women approach, the younger one supporting the older one, whose ankles spill over the tops of her black orthopaedic shoes. Her pure white hair is knotted in two perfect buns on each side of her head and she has that lovely soft peachy skin that only old women seem to have. Even though she needs help walking, she's squarely built with a surprisingly sturdy voice: 'What do we have here? You just waking up? Who ya comin' to see?'

'Actually, nobody. I was so tired driving last night I pulled in here to take a nap. I hope that's OK.'

'Well it's hardly a nap if it's a full night.'

I consider this. 'Well if it's just for a few hours it's more like a nap.'

'A few hours? You're burning the candle at both ends. You sleep here at night, in my book, that's no catnap. How old do you think I am?'

I think she looks at least 95, but I say 82.

She says proudly, 'Eighty-five.'

The caretaker makes a whistling sound to show he's impressed. 'Wow!' I say. 'Good for you! Are you from Kansas originally?'

She yells into her companion's ear, 'What'd she say?'

'She's wondering where you're from, Ellie.'

'Oh.' She looks vaguely downcast and doesn't answer. Then, she pipes up, 'We don't get many like you around here. Need more action around this dump. Food's no good here either. Why don't you stay a while?'

My heart goes out to her. 'I wish I could, but I have to be going. The sun's getting too hot already. I'm going to California.'

'Take me with you! We'll live in a teepee!'

Looking into her face, I feel as if I'm seeing my future self, or else, my old self – I used to dream about living in a teepee. Will I want to again at her age? Why don't I now? For a second I wonder what taking her along would be like. 'But it's such an unpleasant drive in this heat. I don't have air conditioning and there's something wrong with my car. And besides, I sleep in my car.'

She knits her brow for a moment, looks my car over, and then shouts, 'Well, maybe I'll just meet ya out there.'

'OK,' I say, 'OK. And you know it really is lovely here, all these big trees and the garden.'

She shrugs as if she has heard it all before. 'Take lots of naps!' she yells as I get in my car and start the engine. 'Lots of naps!' I'm not sure if this is advice for me or whether she's telling me how she gets through the day. The others wave, and as I drive off, the group of them shouts out goodbye. I wave back until they're out of view, and turning the corner, I get that energising light traveller's feeling of having just made new friends I'll never see again.

Still, I wonder, why *don't* I want to live in a teepee any more?

After finding a Taco Bell – the preferred haven for car-sleeping vagabonds like me who need to wash their hair and brush their teeth in a clean, anonymous restroom where nobody asks questions, and the only place on the interstate to get a bean burrito with guacamole for less than a dollar – I approach the town of Hays, Kansas. The movie, *Dances with Wolves* was set in Fort Hays so now the old fort, where 600 troops were once stationed to defend railroad and white settlements, has become a tourist site. Wild Bill Hickok, Buffalo Bill Cody and General Custer were all here at one time, as were black troopers known as Buffalo Soldiers. As I wonder whether I'll visit the fort in this irrational heat, my car begins to smoke. I pull over at an exit and decide to escape into the chilled air of the giant shopping mall while my car cools down.

After over an hour of wandering through the mall I momentarily forget where I am, lose all sense of place. What's in here, in this cold sterile complex, has nothing to do with what's outside. I'm no longer in Kansas: I'm in the American Mall. I could be at any mall on the continent, I think, as I stare at a row of familiar lacklustre chain stores which inhabit every shopping centre in the country. I watch teenagers walking in groups, gossiping and talking into their cell phones. They seem to be playing out their own impossibly complicated soap operas with plots too convoluted to understand: so many teen dramas all over the country, so many teen heartbreaks, complexion problems and wondering how to get noticed. What a lot of work.

Gazing at the faces of the fashion-conscious teens and the heavy-set parents pushing ice-cream-eating kids in strollers I long to see the face of a true eccentric, someone who doesn't belong. But in this culture of sameness I can't find anyone like that. That's something I love about outdoor markets, especially those in the developing world or in big cosmopolitan cities: eccentrics are everywhere. The North American mall is one of the West's less enlightened ideas for only occasionally does the enclosed mall exude a noisy excitement of a meeting place. Mainly, instead of being colourful, outlandish, and pulsing with life, malls are sterile; they smell like air freshener rather than ripe fruit, spices and sweat; the music is canned instead of live; and the people inside the malls seem bored, more concerned with buying the latest trend marketed at them than engaging in lively conversation.

Still, I have a craving to sit in this mall's cool dark movie cinema sipping an iced mocha, forgetting completely that I'm in Kansas with a crappy car during a heatwave. Perhaps I should have flown to California instead. But then, how could I do that when I might be moving my whole life out there? There's a lot of stuff in my car, and besides, people don't move their whole life somewhere else in a plane if they can drive there. At least, I don't.

I escape the mall and find a hotel room in Hays. I can't stand the thought of driving straight into the sizzling heart of the sun any longer today and besides, I've taken Marcia to see another mechanic. After I explained the lurching problem, the mechanic's words were courteous but clearly expressed his readiness to view me as several different kinds of airhead at once. He, like the last guy, thinks he knows what the problem is, however, and I can pick Marcia up in the morning. I go for a swim in the little hotel pool, then sit for hours on the hotel bed in the air conditioning watching a mini series on the saga of the young Kennedys. This is heaven, evading the 103 degree temperature and the afternoon drive through the monotony of cornfields. Or, in Hays, Kansas, this is about as good a time as I'm likely to find.

Shutting the door on the cold hotel room air this morning is almost unbearable because it means shutting the door on escapism and facing the unmerciful tedium of driving through the horizontal brown patch of America known as the Midwest in a baking, unreliable steel capsule which may fall to pieces at any moment beside a cornfield. I really should stay in the hotel room until winter.

When I walk along a strip of highway to pick up Marcia from the mechanic, I see two morose youths wearing angry black ripped clothing and so many rings punched in their bodies they could be dangled from strings like marionettes designed to terrorise children. They seem out of place in Kansas, I think as they approach, but then they say hi to me like regular kids, all boyish and scruffy and sweetly awkward, and my heart is lightened.

The mechanic seems a little wary of me for some reason, as if Marcia's problem is something foreign and infectious, carrying a disease no car in Hays, Kansas would ever carry. He says he tightened some things in the engine, then took it for a test drive and nothing seemed wrong. I drive 30 minutes out of town before Marcia starts lurching again, but I don't have the heart to turn around and go back to the mechanic in Hays. He'd take it for another test drive and Marcia would sail along pretending everything was fine. The notion of ditching this car and hitchhiking seems perfectly sensible right now. Through the searing heat and flat, parched pasture, I spot a truck stop where I immediately pull over to keep my mind from unravelling into a wheat field. I need three things: a phone, air conditioning and a mango juice. Mostly, I need a phone. Just like Marcia, I might be breaking down a little. I'm going to phone Andre, my nice boyfriend, the one I'm fleeing. My nice boyfriend not only is nice, which I tend to think is overrated; he also knows about cars. Also, I think I miss him. As soon as I hear his voice, which will be melted in reassuring kindness, I'll confess I may not be coming back at the end of the summer after all. I've told him I'm just going on a summer trip to California, and he's perfectly happy to oblige me my wanderlust while he stays in Guelph with his five-year-old son and does his carpentry work. Perhaps I *will* return after the summer. This trip has started so badly with the heat and the car and the border crossing. And I really do miss him, even if nice isn't everything. Or maybe it is. Right now, someone being nice to me seems like the most important thing in the entire world, and moving to California seems like a far-off and ill-conceived fantasy.

I had thought I'd figured it all out. For years I've wanted to live in California and this seemed like the perfect time: when I was stuck in a relationship with a person without obvious flaws, with someone I would, if I were slightly less restless, slightly less interested in travelling or having worldly conversations, or perhaps, slightly less interested in laughing out loud on a daily basis, consider actually marrying and having kids with while living in a log house we built by a river. Maybe I was too rash in coming out here.

Even in the parking lot of the truck stop, country music is blasting, greeting its swarming devotees like a sermon from heartbreak hotel. In a twang impossible to imagine coming from a real person, the singer laments how his wife ran off with his best friend, how her teeth were stained but her heart was pure, and how he's got the hungries for her love. 'I miss ya baby,' twangs another singer inside. I think I miss Andre. I look for the phones.

The truck stop is a massive air-conditioned, noisy emporium designed to entertain and feed truckers with large appetites and large sweat circles under their arms, their uniforms consisting of the mandatory cowboy boots and the tight jeans squeezed up under their gargantuan beer bellies. As I enter, one of these men eyes me as he leaves. His beard is halfway down his chest and his red road-weary eyes peer out through masses of facial hair. A century ago he could have been in the circus for his impressive size, a giant among men, tall and hugely fat. He's wearing a black Harley T-shirt and is about to light up a smoke. The phones are all in use so I head for the refreshment stand and discover they don't sell real juice. How can I be in the same country as California with its fresh organic mango-a-go-go juices, its peach passion berry immunity boosters, its daily squeezed orange and its vitamin packed wheatgrass shakes available in every corner store in the state?

Since they don't sell any real juice, I buy overpriced bottled water instead, along with a key chain that says 'If I Only Had a Brain' with a picture of the *Wizard of Oz* scarecrow on it, and decide I won't settle for anything less than what I know California offers, at least not until I try living there. When I finally find a free phone, I get voice mail, and although it almost crushes me not to speak to Andre in person, I know it's probably for the best. I don't want to talk to him in a place like this anyway. I have to keep going.

I rush back to the car and the corn realising that the truck stop was my visual stimulus for the day. Sadly, I also realise that I'll have to skip going south to Dorothy's

House because of Marcia and the heatwave, and just like all those forty-niner gold-seekers and all the thousands of sun-seekers after them, find what's over the rainbow on my own in California.

I'll even kiss the sunset pig… California I'm coming home…

To remind me how much I need to see California again, to keep my resolve in going ahead with this trip, I decide to dig out my California cave notebook, find some shade to read under, and look at more entries.

Cave Journal

When I live like this, eat this simply and explore the beach all day, my mind goes wild at night with exhilaration and I can't sleep, am awake for hours watching the voyage of the stars. I have to remember that I always want to live with the natural beauty of the world. I have everything I want here: the sea, sun, sky, and the golden hills behind me. I have a brook with delicious clear water and the possibility of more food – those mussels on the rocks, as soon as I can get a fire going. (I never knew starting a fire was so difficult!) I have my cave, which already feels like a little home, a nest, a fort I would have tried to build as a kid. What is it about kids building forts? I used to build forts with my friends in the woods and we'd spend whole days designing those forts, living in them, guarding them, fixing them up, always keeping them highly secretive from everyone else for some reason. I'd also build forts and caves out of maple leaf piles, blankets and tables, and snow. The desire to live in a cave must be instinctual. Humans must have a basic need to make cosy, private spaces where we are free to be ourselves, to hide from the world. So here I have my fort, my cave, but most importantly, I have myself in it, hours upon hours of myself living at a beach cove. I'm really getting to know myself being all alone like this and I like it.

When you're with other people all the time and constantly distracted, you forget to get to know the person whose body you're occupying.

In living like this it seems clear that deep happiness lies buried beneath layers of convenience and comfort and schedules. Stripping down one's needs brings us closer to our fundamental source of joy. Here in this beach cove my life is simple yet nothing in the man-made world can be as complex as the small spiral seashell I found on the beach this morning.

My life here has a rhythm like the sea, following its own timeless order. With every passing day, life grows less complicated with less of the world to think about. But maybe I should be thinking of the real world, what I'll do in it. I'm so heady with elation it hardly seems to matter here. But what about university? Should I really have just quit after only two years? Did I make the right decision? I quit because I thought I could learn more on my own, in places like this, from people I meet around the world, from reading my own books, educating myself. I hate the idea of paying for a piece of paper. I wanted to live for the moment instead of the future. But living for the moment is difficult. It means hitchhiking without a destination, not knowing which side of the road to stand on to get a ride.

The sea seems lonely and restless today. I sit by its ragged feet trying to hear its message, a song sent over the water from afar.

The sun is falling down my side of the world, pulled into a pink bath. The waves, stirred by an ageless clock, pull the continent back to sea, grain by grain. Behind me, the cliffs and my cave burn crimson and will soon grow dark.

Later

All across the shimmering night sky the history and future of the universe are unfurling into bright bands of mystery and possibility. Here from my view in the cave I could almost fly up to join the arrangement. I'm not that far away.

Whatever happened to that girl in the cave? I can almost remember her, like someone or something half-forgotten, glowing at the far edge of my mind.

In reading this cave journal I'm reminded of a particular dilemma I occupied myself with back then: whether to live each moment fully as a footloose explorer, not worrying what the next day or even next hour would bring, or to live for the future by working towards something meaningful, leading a more traditional life. To live for the moment or for the future: I used to think about that a lot. I tried living for the moment several times, and although sometimes it was truly enlightening, other times it was the hardest thing I'd ever done. Actually, it was terrifying. In the spring that I turned 21, I left university after two years, disillusioned with academics. I went off on a westward quest by myself, perhaps to get a more first-hand knowledge of the world. In seven months, I would find my California cave, but that April I started out in Alberta where I worked as the only chambermaid in a lonely old mountain lodge. One day I went skiing in Banff and at the day's end, when I realised I missed the bus that would have taken me up the Banff–Jasper Highway and to my lodge, my only choice was to hitchhike. The truck driver who gave me a ride dropped me off directly in front of the lodge, and as I was getting down from his truck, he mentioned casually that he passed my road regularly and onward to Vancouver if I ever wanted another lift. I was shocked at how easy it all seemed. The possibilities astounded me. A couple weeks later, after quitting my job, I walked to the end of the little road and stuck out my thumb. Two days later, I was in Vancouver, and a few days after that, was hitchhiking down the West Coast through Washington and Oregon.

My parents would have been horrified had they known, so I didn't call to tell them I'd quit my job in Alberta. My life became a constant adventure travelling that way. I was a waitress a couple of times, once in Seaside, Oregon, a town known for being the end of the Lewis and Clark trail. But mostly, I hitchhiked, meeting all kinds of intriguing people – mainly men since women seemed resolved never to pick up hitchhikers, not even female hitchhikers, not even someone who looked like me: 21 years old with a backpack, smiling and wholesome, usually holding a map, obviously harmless. For most of that time, I felt very intrepid, although a little lonely, but one frigid night I slept on a picnic table in the mountains of Oregon and almost froze to death. Towards dawn, a warm feeling started to spread throughout my body even though I was chilled to the bone. I bolted upright, realising I may be in the early stages of hypothermia. I decided right then that this was no way to live, and I really needed to go someplace. I just didn't know where. Back to university? To my sister's in Colorado? Further south to California? I'd never been to California and had always wanted to go. That morning in the rain, on some remote back road with hardly any traffic, I had no destination, not a clue as to where I should go, and it frightened the hell out of me. I was truly alone, thousands of miles away from anyone I knew, completely out of my safe environment full of friends and school and a plan. Never had I felt such an utter aimlessness, an empty-gut feeling of not knowing what to do next. What good was living for the moment if this was what the moments were like? Shouldn't the moments be filled with something, like a solid idea of the future, a dream? Perhaps we create all this stuff around us – social lives, problems, material things, schedules, the busyness of the day-to-day, just so we never have to experience moments filled with absolute nothingness, moments when we have only ourselves all alone with nothing to do and nowhere to go. Luckily, a businessman in a rented car came along, out for a day trip from Portland, and he cleared all this up for me.

I don't remember his name – I might never have known it – but the businessman in the rented car was ecstatic to pick up a hitchhiker, not because of anything unseemly, but because he was bored to death with his job, his business meetings, his retirement savings plans, his suburban life. Years earlier, he'd hitchhiked a lot, and I reminded him of that. In fact, he was driving around that morning just for the sake of going someplace new, to see what he'd find around the bend in the road. He had found me out there, standing in the rain, and it had made him slam his brakes. He said he'd drive me wherever I wanted to go, and when I explained about not knowing where that was, we just drove and talked. In fact, we drove and talked all the way to southern Oregon, since we decided that if I really wanted to see California for the first time, I should. He was a godsend for me, a kindness lodged in a difficult world. According to him, my life wasn't pointless at all. I was just doing what people my age, and maybe any age, should be doing: travelling around to see what the world was like. It made me feel a lot better about things. As for him, our talk made him decide to quit his job and start living again. A few days after that, I found a hollowed-out redwood tree in northern California where I stayed for three days to keep out of the rain, and because I loved it in there. I was back to living for the moment.

That businessman also put a curious idea in my head. Through the course of our conversation he learned not only that I was Canadian and liked the idea of travelling, but that I liked to write. He suggested I write a book some day about the U.S. from a Canadian perspective – a Canadian looking down from the north at the mad carnival below the forty-ninth parallel. I wonder what became of that man in the rental car, if he quit his job after all, if in any way our encounter changed the course of his life.

That's what I always found so fantastically mind boggling about hitchhiking. Which car stopped for you not only affected whom you met and where you were dropped off, but who would pick you up after that, and who after that; and where you went next and where after that – a chain of serendipitous encounters all collaborating to form a journey. If someone else had picked me up that morning on that lonely Oregon road, I may never have gone to California that first time or any time after that, even now, and may never have decided to write about my travels.

I have to remember on this trip with Marcia that I'm indebted to all the people who picked me up hitchhiking throughout my twenties, the people who unknowingly shaped my life's journey. It would be bad karma not to pick up someone out there on the road, at least the ones who don't look like they're homicidal maniacs.

Here I am headed for California again, just as I was with that businessman, and just as I have been so many times in my life, only now I'm crossing the blistering hot plains to get there. These are the same plains the pioneers crossed in covered wagons journeying fifteen miles a day, braving hostile weather and Indians, an unforgiving terrain, little food, dirty water, disease, starvation and death. The majority were stoic families from the East – some farmers, some city folk – who journeyed west to find decent soil to farm. Here in Kansas, a family might have ended up with a thousand acres of soil that was as hard as cement and barren of all water and shade. Many families came to settle in Kansas with hopes of self-sufficiency and found their acreage too arid or tough to work, and the weather – droughts, hailstorms, winters – had a savagery beyond anything they'd ever known. The disenchanted had a bitter rhyme: 'In God we trusted, in Kansas we busted.' Those who pushed further west to look for land found the situation even worse. Sooner or later, lousy weather and mishap befell every party, and the scorching summer heat made tempers flare, fights break out daily. A mistaken road, a broken axle, a disabled draft animal, a lost child, a lay-over to recover from illness, a serious accident, some seasonal perversity of the earth – a rainstorm or flood or tornado – anything might happen on the open road. Once mountain passes were closed by snow, once food was gone, once the animals were exhausted, a party might have to leave everything behind and pack their belongings onto mules in a desperate effort to reach the journey's end. The most disturbing thought wasn't just dying, but dying and being buried where wolves could dig you up. This was a real fear of settlers as they headed west.

As I think about all those poor weather-beaten families struggling across this forsaken landscape, the sun burns my skin through the glass and the hot wind belts me like a boxer in my gasping, clonking car, and I think, THIS IS NO FUN EITHER!

I thought I once travelled through the world with a light step of joy. I could find something good in almost any situation, and even have fun hitching on rainy cold deserted highways, just as Kevin and I did in the Yukon. Perhaps the seed for my gradual disenchantment with things began to grow during my first teaching job. Perhaps my first teaching job has something to do with why I don't want to live in a teepee any more.

Chapter 7

Among the Cree

My first teaching job, when I was 25, was a lesson in humility. I taught a third grade class of Cree natives in a village called Kashechewan in Canada's sub-Arctic. It proved to be a cultural learning experience, and a complete unravelling of almost everything I believed in until then. Until then, I romanticised things, like the Third World and native cultures, which probably wasn't fair because I was putting those people on a pedestal, somehow expecting them to be wiser than people from my own culture, more connected to the land, perhaps even possessing an ancient knowledge that our culture had lost eons ago.

That first morning, I prepared everything just the way they'd taught us at teachers' college. I was going to have the kids make name tags out of coloured paper in the shapes of various local animals: moose, goose, fish. On their desks, I arranged crayons, glue, paper and scissors.

'Be firm but kind,' I kept telling myself, as if I was the teacher on *Little House on the Prairie* and an obedient group of timid children were about to enter the room. As I waited for 9 a.m., I looked over their list of names again: Elkanah, Zachariah, Malachai, Shem, and Sue-Helen, Betty-Ann and Verna. How strange, I thought, this mix of biblical boys' names and all-American 1950s girls' names on an isolated fly-in James Bay reserve, as far away from Israel and apple pie as one could get.

The bell rang and my heart thudded as I rushed out to greet my new students who were to be waiting in line outside. Immediately I noticed they weren't shy in the least, but looked me squarely in the eye. I asked the kindergarten teacher why some of my students were so big and she told me some were eleven years old and had never been to school before. The kids began bombarding me with questions: 'What your name?' 'Why you wear that?' Then: 'Me hate school.' 'Me go inside now.' Before I could stop them, a storm of kids charged inside without me, shrieking, running, shoving and punching each other's heads.

Let me relate some highlights of that first morning: dead animals were thrown around the classroom – mice, sparrows, small rats. At one point, something I thought might have been the tail of a mink torpedoed across the room. When the rusty coloured object landed on my desk I looked down in horror at the braid of my hair. I reached up to feel my newly cropped hairstyle. Somehow, during the chaos, one of the kids had put his or her scissors to use. The curtains were torn down and used as a giant swinging hammock. Books were cut up, scribbled upon and chewed. The sand-table region was turned into a war zone as mud balls flew across the room with paint stands used as barricades. Recalling what occurred at the water table that day can never be erased from my subconscious. Nothing I did to try to prevent any of this had any effect. I was a non-entity. Already I'd aged five years, lost my voice, and my hands were curiously shaking. It was 10 a.m. I'd get 'used to it', the other teachers told me.

The other teachers were wrong, not to mention antisocial and a little strange. I never got used to it. It never got better. But at least I had the advantage of knowing that if I really wanted to I could escape that sad little ice village and join my own culture again. These children and their parents were caught in a no man's land, lost between cultures.

As time went by I realised that very little native culture remains today in sub-Arctic Canada. Once, small bands of nomadic Cree roamed the territory, hunting, fishing and gathering. Today, most live in a village year-round in prefab houses, are unemployed, get their money from welfare, and shop for highly processed food at the Hudson's Bay store – the vast quantities of sugar consumed daily by the kids is evident in their rotting teeth. Here and there, some of the old ways still exist: twice a year, school is shut down for a week-long goose hunt. The children were excellent goose callers. They demonstrated this daily in class.

I was astounded by the discipline problems in the school until I considered the reason for them. These children's lives weren't structured the way most children's lives in the south are. Bedtime is a foreign concept in this land where rules don't seem to exist. Children are rarely told what to do or not to do. They may sleep at a different house every night. Meals are rarely eaten together as a family. I used to ask the kids what they had for lunch. Mars bars, Coke and potato chips were the usual replies. TV, it seemed to me, was the main culprit in destroying what little the people had left of their culture. Within a year of the first TV arriving in the village in the late eighties, the nurses told me, children began to fight regularly and swear at the teachers when this was rare before. No longer were they content with their homemade toys; they wanted plastic guns instead. Kids in my class would often fall asleep on their desks. They'd been up all night watching videos.

In the times when the Cree led their traditional lifestyle, their ancestors' method of parenting would have worked. Children being allowed to roam freely without rules and to discover and learn on their own probably developed useful survival skills. Now, since the people no longer hunt and gather to survive, but spend much of their time watching TV, this child-rearing method no longer works. Children have little direction and often become depressed and hostile in their early teens. The anger lasts into adulthood, where it's often accompanied by hatred towards all outsiders. Teachers would sometimes be pelted with rocks and snowballs as we walked down the road. Across the river, where my friend Charlie was teaching, someone had hung the woman principal's dog by a noose, hung it so it dangled dead on her front porch when she stepped out to work one morning.

Most parents were not the least interested in encouraging education or reading in their children. I had to remind myself that up until the 1960s, generations of parents had been taken away to residential schools at early ages. No wonder many of these parents had no parenting skills – they'd never had the chance to learn these skills from their own parents. All responsibility was taken from them for two centuries: education, religion, means of living. No wonder they often acted in ways we would call irresponsible. It often seemed to me that the people craved the least desirable aspects of my own culture – *Friday the 13th* movies, TV wrestling and deep-fried chicken – while they seemed to reject so much of what had been valuable in their own culture, like a connection with the land.

It was on the reserve, however, that I learned the value of quietness. In the classroom, the noise was often unbearable, but any of those kids, when I was alone with one out of class, was as quiet as a fawn and, like the adults, never felt the constant need to make conversation the way we do. Time spent together among friends can be just as valuable in silence. The kids amazed me in many ways. One kid could shoot a spitball from a straw across the room at another kid. The kid who got hit, not seeing who shot the little wad of wet paper, would pick it up, sniff it, then turn around and yell at the kid who shot it. They recognised each other's individual scents, a skill our own ancestors must have lost in the Stone Age.

Despite their highly developed sense of smell and other intriguing cultural traits – such as their ability to shriek in high pitched voices which got dogs howling – I dreaded going to class every day. The principal of the school seemed to have permanently shut himself up in his office even though most of the classes, mine especially, were completely out of control. I'd been given a 'problem' class among a problem school of kids to begin with, and 20 out of 29 of them were boys. Every day in class, these boys performed wrestling moves on each other, which usually ended with a pile-up of all 20 of them. The fattest boy, who weighed more than I did, waited to jump on at the end as he roared out an attack call. My trying to break up the pile of boys not only would have been pointless, but might have killed me. Not a day passed when I didn't see blood.

The day after Hallowe'en, all the kids brought bags of candy to school, and one chubby girl ate so much candy that she shit her pants, and was so enraged when the boys teased her about it that she reached into her underwear to remove the offending rank mass, and began throwing it around the room. I distinctly recall the considerably large contents of her bowels splattering on the blackboard *way* too close to where I was standing. All I could do was yell, 'Hit the deck!' to warn the others, and hide under a desk myself. I figure that a kid who hurls her own shit at other kids inside a classroom might be participating in an activity that even the worst behavioural problem kids in inner city schools would consider unseemly.

One day I tried some native drumming in my class. Some of the kids brought in drums and we also made a few. Days later, a group of native elders came to tell me to stop the drumming because they didn't want 'evil Indian ways against Jesus'. All I could do was stare back at them in disbelief, wanting to ask them if they thought Jesus liked *any* percussive instruments.

After three months, I began waking up with headaches and dark circles under my eyes. One day in class, perhaps the day when the kids had stolen my house keys – they regularly stole things, but I really needed those keys – I felt so defeated and exhausted that something in me simply gave up. I sat at my desk and watched bleary-eyed as they whirled around the room like dervishes, destroyed every remaining book, and sprayed glue into each other's faces, events they'd pretty much been carrying out in all along but which, that day, I couldn't fight against any more. In one last-ditch effort, I tried inviting the parents into my class to help me, but none of them showed up.

When I left the job at Christmas, I left as a different person. A few days after I returned to Guelph, a woman I knew who saw me on the street looked at me aghast and asked what had happened, as if I was suffering from some incurable wasting disease. Other than my physical appearance, which frankly, wasn't as bad as that woman made out, something else in me had changed. No longer was I a bright-eyed idealist yearning to live in a teepee and voice the virtues of native culture. I'd lost something essential on the reserve, perhaps a faith in humankind, or, perhaps, part of the old me.

I went to Kashechewan naively looking for a culture that no longer exists, and therefore was continually dismayed by the abuse I saw every day – to the children, the women, the animals and the land. On the reserve, open sewage was emptied into the streams; garbage was thrown all over the place; and every year, on Dead Dog Day, stray dogs were shot and thrown into the river, turning the water an alarming, brilliant red.

Chapter 8

I wonder if it's inevitable that as we get older, we all, in some way, become disillusioned with the world. Gradually, and in varying degrees, a disenchantment seems to grow within us, and not until years later does an awareness come that a vital sense of mystery and innocence in the way we saw the world has deserted us without our consent.

Two years after teaching on the reserve, after living in a cabin in the woods of northern Ontario, I travelled to the South Pacific and South-east Asia, again expecting those cultures to be somehow 'better' than my own. At first I was enchanted with everything I saw. Most people, when they travel, are attuned to the deficiencies of their own culture and the marvels of others, which is one reason we travel. As time passed on that trip, however, I began to realise that all of human nature the world over is the same. In all cultures you find greed, dishonesty and exploitation of other people and the land, and you find people who are prejudiced, superior and mean. Yet in those same cultures you find people who are unbelievably kind, honest, caring, and so generous it can break your heart. No one place has 'better' people than another. Everywhere you find idiots and everywhere you find jewels.

Jewel – my mother once referred to Andre as a 'jewel' after I'd broken up with him the second time. 'He's such a jewel! There aren't many in the world like him,' she'd said, and I went back to him the next day because of that one remark alone. But perhaps I'm still romanticising things, like California. Perhaps I should try calling Andre again.

Or, am I just romanticising him too? Damn!

Since it's late, I find an old dirt road and pull on to an even smaller road in a farmer's field where I stop the car. A thunderstorm is setting the western sky on fire and it's better than watching a movie at a drive-in. Sheets of lightning are opening up the secret night and taking it by surprise, like a parent with a flashlight at a slumber party. I close my eyes and see the frostbitten faces of those kids on the reserve, faces forever etched in my mind. Usually when I recall those kids, I think of how they wore me down, but oddly, what I recall right now is their laughter. They laughed all the time. I sleep to the roar of a furious wind with nothing to inhibit it for hundreds of miles, and all night long am rocked by the promise of a storm which never comes. Still, I have a wonderful invigorating sleep induced by the distant storm and powerful winds, and I know that soon I'll leave this heatwave behind, and soon, I'll arrive in California.

In the very early morning as I lumber down a farm road in my semi-obsessive state of driving a smoking car across the continent, I watch the huge expanse of dawn sky that I normally never see turning ever so slowly from black to violet to lavender to soft rose. The day slinks in so quietly that it's hard to believe this is how all days start, not with a loudspeaker announcement or the clanging of bells, but like this, a pale pink rising.

I get stuck behind an old couple going 20 miles an hour. Their car is even older than mine, although seemingly in pristine condition. The man's shoulders are hunched and he's wearing a fedora hat like my father wore in the seventies. I wonder if he's driving this slowly because he finds it enjoyable, or if he's half-blind and afraid to drive faster, or perhaps he's trying to make a statement, namely that the world used to be a gentler place and people travelled through it at a slower pace, so go to hell!

I think back to a story I heard. Somewhere in America one summer, not long ago, an elderly couple were driving down an interstate, pulling a camper trailer behind them. What they failed to realise as they drove merrily along was that their whole camper was burning up in flames. The passing drivers honked and waved and pointed to get their attention but the couple continued on oblivious, wondering what all the fuss was about. The man was probably shaking his fist at the other drivers who honked at him, 'We're going as fast as we want to!' The couple continued to drive until they came to a rest stop where they found all that was left of their trailer was a hollowed-out blackened chunk of carbon. It reminds me of that joke: When I die, I would like to go peacefully, in my sleep, like my grandfather did. Not screaming and yelling, like the passenger in his car.

The radio stations in this part of the world are mind-boggling. I keep getting Kansas farm reports – advice on fixing tractors or paying taxes – or else Christian rock stations that blare lyrics like, 'Pray, pray, pray, three times a day!' Occasionally, when I'm near a college town or medium-size city, I hit upon a National Public Radio station and for half an hour or so, while I'm within range, I get to hear intelligent commentary, educated and witty people discussing literature or music or the latest political theories on what's happening in Ireland, Zimbabwe or the Middle East, and then the station starts to crackle and fade until it's back to 'Yeah, Jesus is my boyfriend!' sung by a bratty teenage girl. Christian rock, and for that matter, all

Christian fundamentalism, is an American phenomenon which makes people in other countries suspect Americans can't be that smart. Fundamentalism is found in other parts of the world, whether in the Jewish occupation of the West Bank, or in certain fanatical Islamic sects, but it always seems surprising to find it in a place as modern as the U.S. It's possible that many Americans are so religious because their country is simply too big, complicated and violent and the only way to combat this alienation is to join a church to feel part of a small, safe community, or to feel in touch with some divine force greater and wiser than the suburban or inner city estrangement surrounding them. However, most religious people in the U.S. aren't in the big cities but are here in the countryside. I just passed through a small town and saw this clapboard sign at a gas station:

LUBE JOB
OIL CHANGE
CHRIST SAVES
CIGARETTES $3.49

This fervent American Christianity coupled with the loud American tourist in Europe who can't seem to help but blare his ignorance to anyone within a thirty-foot radius only adds to the unfortunate stereotype that the average American isn't too swift. Of course, the average citizen of Spain or Canada or Poland or Chile might also be uninformed about the world but they don't travel as much and there aren't as many of them as there are Americans. And, since those countries are smaller, its people tend to learn more about the rest of the world and perhaps have a wider world view. Mainly though, it's a question of volume. People in other countries simply aren't as loud as Americans. The average non-American may be ignorant, but he doesn't advertise his ignorance at fifty decibels in the Louvre, for example. When I was thirteen my family went to Europe for the summer. We rented a caravan camper in London, travelled around Britain, and then went to the continent. At the Louvre in Paris, we were standing in the lobby buying our tickets to get inside when a middle-aged American couple beside us started attracting attention. The husband was practically in hysterics, animatedly pointing to a plastic back-lit image of the *Mona Lisa* used to advertise *Mona Lisa* posters. He called across the lobby to his wife. 'Here it is, Helen, here it is! I'll be damned! Right here in the lobby!' He waved his wife over as he started fiddling with his camera. 'No, no, Harold, that's not it! That's not the real *Mona Lisa*.' He refused to listen and, as I recall, told her to fix her hair. She stood next to the plastic *Mona Lisa*, patted her curls in place, pulled down her stretchy nylon shirt and smiled for the flashing bulb. The couple moved happily on to the exit door having seen what they came for.

Stories like this are always terribly unfair – Americans are among the most highly educated people in the world with a body and history of superb literature, music, art, unrivalled scientific invention, past and present great thinkers in every major academic field – but every traveller seems to have one of these stories. We think, if Americans are so rich and so privileged, why don't they educate themselves to learn about the rest of the world? It's easy for the rest of us to become annoyed with American ignorance and arrogance, especially when their foreign policies affect the entire world. Most of the Americans I meet don't fit this image – rather, they're worldly, intelligent and interested – but we choose who we want to befriend and even talk to in a group of strangers. Lately, however, I've noticed in my travels that it isn't the loud American tourist that travellers are making fun of so much as the rude German. Again, this is probably also unfair, as I believe there are a lot of very polite Germans who actually do have a sense of humour.

I'm still on the highway and, unbelievably, still driving in Kansas, a state the same size as the former West Germany. In trying to define America in a sentence, Gertrude Stein once said, 'Conceive a space filled with motion.' She was right for the most part, except for out here where nothing is in motion, where even the cows, so trampled by the heat and their dismal existence, are at a dead standstill. I can't believe how remote it feels in the endless fields of yellow grass where I'm dwarfed by the colossal dome of the blue sky. I can see everything from a long way off, my past behind me as it gets smaller and smaller in the rear-view mirror – a young woman living with an endless variety of housemates in a pleasant, historical university town where single, educated women outnumber single men by five to one, a city of century-old limestone homes, a growing number of factories, subdivisions, and a famous mental institution: a young woman working at various teaching jobs, leading an active although sometimes bewildering social life, and dating a series of Mr Right Nows instead of Mr Rights (in fact, previous boyfriends have covered the full range of personalities, except for that time she dated three guys in a row named Michael, and all three Michaels happened to live in cabins in the woods, had long brown hair and beards, and all were a little too solitary. Sometimes the boyfriends have even been embarrassments, not quite worthy, messy, sometimes even a little crazy, or not good at conversation in a crowd. One drank too much, and one had never seen a moonrise, not even once) – and my future ahead, somewhere off in a green valley by the sea in California where winter doesn't exist, the men might be more like me, the air is clean, and people seem more free, think bigger, live larger, than in my home town. I wish I had more time for everything between, for my life caught somewhere out here in the middle. But I seem to be passing it by in this clanging car, the land sliding by in a blue and yellow blur, the earth an endless, windblown painting drawn against the sky. Perhaps I'm not meant to be fleeing so fast. I try to imagine how these Great Plains looked years ago when they were an intricate fretwork of plants: peppergrass, salt grass, gamma grass, porcupine grass, buffalo grass, prairie June grass, cat's foot, knotweed, mustard and chokecherry. Now, most of what they called the Great Plains have been ploughed under and replanted with foreign hybrid grasses and grains, although I've heard it's still possible to find traces of the past here, old seeds blowing in the wind, heirloom fields of native blooms. I hope that's true.

I pull off the interstate and drive along a small road leading to a town the size of a bath mat called Grainfield. The Great Plains have emptied dramatically since the Depression, the populations of many of its towns peaking in the 1920s and '30s and declining ever since. In Grainfield I find the local diner, walk in, and notice that nobody in the entire restaurant weighs less than 300 pounds. It makes me think of a Swiss guy I once met in a hostel in Flagstaff, Arizona. 'All Americans do is eat,' he'd said. 'In my country we eat at home, three meals, and nobody really talks about it. Food isn't a big deal. In America, food is everywhere.' It's true. Americans really do eat everywhere, in their cars, in parking lots, in stores, on buses, in movie lines, in front of TVs, in parks, on sidewalks, while bowling.

I strike up a conversation with the hefty family in the next booth, ask them about Grainfield and the surrounding area, where they live, where the kids go to school, what people do on Saturday nights, what they're having for dessert. I'm overwhelmed by their accents and honestly miss about half of what they say. That's something I like about

Californians, by contrast: they don't have an accent; or at least, their accent is almost exactly like mine. Californians don't believe in this bewildering Midwestern twang, the long 'a's. Even my sister Linda who lives in Colorado has developed this twang, which I find strange since her accent is much stronger than anyone else's I've met in Colorado. She actually says things like, 'Our friends went caaaamping in the caaaanyon.' She has become a true American. Even though our parents moved to Canada after leaving the U.S. when she was 7, she always knew she'd return one day to her homeland. She never liked Caaynada.

When I leave the diner of big people, feeling as if I've just been in a movie set, or perhaps, in America's obese future, out in the parking lot I see something straight out of America's past: a nineteenth-century covered wagon pulled by a team of horses. On the side of the wagon in red paint is written 'THE LORD SAVES, HEAR MY MESSAGE'. The man pulling the wagon steps down, nods his head at me as he tips his hat, and walks toward the diner.

I wonder if he can save those people in the diner from eating dessert. I picture him doing a religious version of manic fitness guru Richard Simmons in there, yanking banana cream pie and ice cream off their tables, replacing the pie with Bibles, doing a little jig.

As I drive away I give my head a shake and think, I really am a foreigner here, at least in this part of the country. I don't even recognise this part of the country as the America I know. Out here in this vast heartland, people have guns and Bibles in their homes; they drive big pickup trucks too fast, don't believe in abortion, national health care, gay rights or even evolution, and apparently, spend most of their time eating. Whenever I'm defending the U.S. to Canadians I always seem conveniently to forget about the Bible Belt and the religious right. When I'm in this part of the U.S. I feel very Canadian, but often when I'm in Canada, I feel American, which means, for one, that I'm not anti-American like most Canadians, who make disparaging remarks about Americans regularly, but I also feel American in that I'm a little more open and expressive and friendly – maybe too friendly sometimes – than most Canadians, more willing to strike up conversations with strangers, more outraged at corrupt politicians than many politically-passive Canadians, maybe even a little too loud sometimes (although this, I think, is the result of my father having always been slightly deaf and not a good listener, so we had to yell to make ourselves heard).

OK, not only is the car making more menacing noises than earlier, but it's now slowing down, failing to accelerate. Suddenly it won't go over 30 miles an hour. The idea of breaking down out here on these Kansas drought-sucked plains fills me with dread. I have to start taking back roads and get off the interstate immediately. What a hellish place for a breakdown. The sun is blasting through my windshield and once again the day is promising sweltering heat while ahead lies a thousand square miles of brown stubble. I wonder how this place came to be inhabited, this place so uninspiring and empty and full of flat fields with freezing winters, sweltering summers and no trained mechanics. In the mid-nineteenth century there were fifty million buffalo roaming these Great Plains. Thirty years later there were fewer than a thousand of them. No wonder this place seems haunted.

I turn off onto a smaller road not far from the Colorado border and within half an hour I'm hopelessly lost. Presumably the only people who ever drive on these back roads are people who've lived here all their lives so nobody bothers putting up road signs. I'm passing towns not on the map. When you leave the interstate in places like this you find yourself in a another world, on a system of unmapped back roads penned in by stalks of corn, tall grasses or cow fields. For a while I don't mind not knowing exactly where I am because I'm still driving into the sun, getting sunburned, still going west to California, but then the road curves to the left and the sun is to my right, then behind me. Suddenly, I'm driving behind a tractor under the prairie sun heading for nowhere. The man on the tractor turns down another even smaller road. I wave goodbye, go on alone, and accelerate back up to my 30 miles an hour, a pace that seems about right for this place. I stop the car and get out. Silence. No bird songs, no animal calls, no human voices, not even a farmhouse in sight. I'm in the middle of a vast continent and I'm lost.

A truck approaches far off down the road. I see its dust before the actual vehicle and it seems to take an unfathomably long time to get to me. If I knew the way, I could drive to California and back and still be waiting for this truck. When it finally gets close, I wave the driver down to ask directions.

'You're wantin' the route west out by old Grady's,' says the old man in his truck. 'That'll take ya a piece down the road before ya hit the main road and then take a left at the dead skunk, and keep goin' and goin' and it ain't far before ya come to what you're looking for... yep.'

I stare at the man for a long time hoping the incomprehensible piece of gibberish he has just spoken may actually start to make sense. It doesn't, so eventually I look down at my map and say, 'Oh, I see. Thank you,' just so he'll drive on and be able to tell his wife he helped a stranger out on the road.

I continue down a series of dusty roads at my new snail's pace and start to notice that the surrounding scenery has grown infinitely more absorbing since leaving the interstate. The landscape is much the same – farming country divided into fields, the occasional house, small hamlets, and evidence of religious zealots – but everything has taken on a new life. This may be partly due to the speed I'm driving – more of a horse's trot where you can actually see the world up close, the way the pioneers would have seen this land. When the railroads were built here, people experienced for the first time the conquest of horizontal space – the rapid succession and superimposition of views, the unfolding of landscape in flickering surfaces as passengers were carried swiftly past it. The view from the train was not the view from the horse. It compressed far more motifs into the same time. And it left less time to dwell on any one thing. The soul, some Arabs believe, can only travel at the pace of a trotting camel. Perhaps they're right. All around I'm beginning to see a sudden vivid countryside rolling away endlessly in varying shades of mauve, cream, copper, gold and blue. I turn a corner and the road stretches out forever to the horizon, one field yellow with wild mustard and the next, blue with flax. So this kind of prairie still does exist, I think. Hawks are whirling above in the immense and hard blue sky, a sky so massive that early settlers, usually women, were sometimes driven crazy and had to run to escape its enormity, run until their lungs burst. There must be something about living under this kind of sky, in this big empty space where people are so few and far away and where the wind never stops. Something deeper must be sensed here. The land is too powerful not to tell a person that this is where you come from, this is where you belong and this is where you should die. We all know deep in our bones that we belong to the earth, are happiest in its wilder fringes, and yet on the interstate I've been missing the beauty of these golden fields and this startling blue sky. I don't mind not knowing where I am. I know what John Steinbeck meant when he wrote: 'I was born lost and take no pleasure in being found.'

I cross the border on the eastern side of Colorado, a terrain much like that of Kansas – it's only the western two-thirds of Colorado that is full of mountains – and stop at a diner in a small town called Arapahoe. The car parked in front of mine has this bumper sticker: 'ALL MEN ARE IDIOTS… I MARRIED THEIR KING!'

The diner is buzzing with life: a line of apple-faced men on bar stools at the counter eating the day's special – a mysterious American dish called chicken-fried steak with fries and gravy – and teasing the bustling waitresses who wear mustard nursey uniforms, and the booths full of boisterous families with children or solitary men drinking coffee and talking to each other across the aisle, sturdy, deeply-etched men who've spent their lives outdoors. The seats are full so I stand waiting to take a table when one of the waitresses, a heavy-set woman with tightly clenched bleached-blond curls, white uniform shoes, and a name tag saying *Cheryl Ann*, says, 'Hold on, hon, we'll getcha set up.' A man wearing a high-riding ball cap seated at the back booth takes his cap off and waves it at me. 'Go on back, hon. That's Troy and he don't bite.' I take her advice and make my way back to Troy who has now replaced his cap and is smiling exuberantly, shouting out a hardy, 'Hey there!' This is the kind of thing that happens when I travel: guys with high-riding baseball caps try to strike up conversations with me all the time. Or perhaps it's me, something about the way I look and act when I'm travelling alone like this. I talk to strangers more readily. I suppose I'm more open, more myself. That's the thing about travelling: it's like peeling away a layer of yourself, exposing yourself to the world so it can expose itself to you.

'Where'd you come from?' he asks when I sink into the vinyl cushioned bench across from him. At first I'm not sure how to answer the question. Does he mean where did I come from just before here, as in Kansas? Or does he mean where do I come from? I decide to tell him everything that matters. 'I'm from Canada and I'm driving out west to California in a broken car and right now my car doesn't want to go very fast so I'm taking back roads… I'm a little lost too.' I gulp down a tall glass of water that Cheryl Ann has poured me. The look Troy gives me seems to be one of confusion followed by solemn compassion. I hadn't been looking for pity but maybe getting some isn't a bad idea. Perhaps Troy could give me some mechanical advice. I notice he has deep-set green eyes, beautiful eyes in fact, almost outdone by his long black eyelashes, and I think that if he wasn't so sun damaged, and maybe if he lost the hat and the T-shirt advertising some sort of beer, he'd be attractive. It's funny to think that any of us could look completely different merely by being brought up in another place.

Cheryl Ann comes back to take my order and jokes with Troy in some sort of coded language. I start asking Troy questions and learn that he works for his father selling machinery and he's planning to move to Denver. When I finish the second glass of water, he says, 'I've actually been planning on moving to Denver for a long time now… years actually.' He looks down at the table made of fake plastic wood. This shy confession to a stranger takes me by surprise, his words having suddenly opened him up like a book of poetry, a whole secret world hidden in the folds of his apparent ease at the diner, with Cheryl Ann, with his quick smile and the familiarity of his high-riding ball cap. Yes, that's it, I think. His admission is a universal truth, mysterious and eternal, yet so simple. It's isn't just me; we all want to go someplace else. Isn't that what we're all trying to do in some way? Head towards the next thing? Isn't Troy's utterance just another way of expressing what Goethe meant when he said, 'We must always change, renew, rejuvenate ourselves; otherwise we harden.' It's bred in our bones, to change, move on, hope for something more. But why can't we be satisfied with what we have, to appreciate the gift of where we are now?

Cheryl Ann returns with my meal, an overcooked omelette next to some reconstituted fries, a blob of ketchup and an adornment of wilted iceberg lettuce. Troy clears his throat. I pick up my fork and nod in agreement with him. Here in Arapahoe, the impetus for getting the hell out is a little stronger than in some other places.

Once out of the diner and on the street, Troy peers deeply under the hood of Marcia, looking for clues, signs of veiled or cryptic maladies, rust. I tell him the car's symptoms, the speeding up and slowing down, the smoking, the lurching, the sudden deceleration, and something new – the gas guzzling, a marked increase in how often I have to fill the tank. I tell him the history of the various parts that have been replaced by various mechanics in various small towns, how none of the replaced parts have helped.

'I've actually considered just ditching it on the side of the highway, or maybe leaving it in a small town for some kids to play with, so they can pretend they're mechanics. I could be free of it. I could hitchhike, or take a bus or train. But it's full of all my stuff and what would I do with it all?'

Again, Troy sets his commiserating green eyes on mine and holds them there. His eyes contain a quality of peace and contentment I seem to have misplaced on this trip. As we stare at each other, I have a fleeting fantasy of going back to his place in his pickup truck and staying for good, of leaving the car behind, of living with him on the edge of town on this forsaken edge of the Great West where the wind beats constantly, sometimes gusts ferociously, and seems to hold some raw power and unleashed force of nature that could, perhaps, meet and free some similar energy within myself. I could stop associating beauty with the colour green and could learn to love the big, sparse, bone-dry, arid clarity of this place. It would be like living on the battered edge of beauty, the edge of two hundred miles of dull horizon that forever promises to lift itself into snowy and glorious mountain ranges if one just waited long enough, learned to love the here and now, this solitary, still emptiness first. Maybe I could do that.

Troy opens my car door, sits in the driver's seat, turns on the engine and pumps the gas pedal. 'Don't sound good.' Then he tunes my radio to a local country music station and grins up at me.

Ten minutes later I'm back on the road, leaving Arapahoe, Colorado in the dust. It was an interesting fantasy while it lasted.

In the next small town, Cheyenne Wells, I find a mechanic who tells me I need a kick-down something or other that I'll have to buy and have installed in Denver. The mechanic refuses to charge me for the half hour of his time I've taken, and as I leave, I watch him and his little son waving goodbye until they become invisible in my mirror. Miles down the road I come across this sign: 'Shriner Pasta Feed!' and an out-of-the-way gas station, not a regular gas station owned by a giant corporation but some sort of co-op private one. A young guy also wearing a high-riding ball cap fills up my tank and when I try to pay, he tells me they don't accept credit cards. I have no cash on me at the moment. When I ask him what I should do, he seems somewhat flummoxed and then says, 'Well, you could mail me a cheque.' I look into his face for signs of something sinister, sarcasm perhaps, but instead, see an element of trust so pure and absolute that I realise I've come across a possessor of an old-fashioned honest heart. This is the way the world used to be, I think, and apparently, out in this seemingly boring backwater, still is. People in the larger world are inured to harshness, but they shouldn't be. This easy trust in a fellow human is surely truer to who we are than the hectic and distant complex arrangement we've designed and call normal life.

I take down his address, vowing to send him money and a postcard, and get back on the dusty road. As I drive slowly onward I'm reminded of my trip to South-east Asia, especially my trip to Thailand, and how the back roads I took there also led me, like here, into the true heart of that country. I'm also reminded of Charlie. Charlie and I travelled together in Thailand. Charlie would never believe in the simple, good-hearted nature of the guy at the gas station who said I could mail him a cheque. He'd think there must be more to the story, that perhaps the guy was hoping for other means of payment. Charlie is a cynic.

Charlie is eleven years older than I am but since he never follows any conventional norms for anything in life, I never notice his age. He and I have always had a special connection, ever since we first met at teachers' college when our class was asked to decorate a classroom door, and the sunny fall day drove both of us outside pretending to collect autumn leaves for the door project when really, we both just wanted to be outside. The rest of our class was inside diligently cutting up pieces of cardboard, measuring, colouring, doing teacher-like things. Neither of us was exactly the conventional teacher type. We joked that substitute teaching sounded more suitable and thought that one day we should get a van with a sign saying, The Roving Subs, and travel across the continent substitute teaching in small towns along the way. Not surprisingly, both of us have done a lot of substitute teaching, and both of us are rovers. In his teens, Charlie discovered something rather amazing: that anyone could travel almost anywhere in North America at almost no cost, meeting interesting people, learning about the world, while having adventures the whole time. He travelled from coast to coast, slept under bridges, hitchhiked, worked at various labouring jobs, and once, in British Columbia, saw bears eating out of the trash. Thinking he should cut down on his food costs, he tried that himself. He ate some discarded Kentucky Fried Chicken which resulted in violent food poisoning, making him realise that the anatomy of humans and bears was quite different. Charlie always thought of himself as a shy loner until his mid-thirties when he went to teachers' college and decided the only way he'd survive the year would be to start smiling at people. In three days he'd made more friends than he had made in the previous ten years. I was one of those friends. When I taught on the native reserve, Charlie taught up there too, eight miles away, across a river. It was a horrendous experience for Charlie also, but he wasn't expecting as much as I was. Charlie's hero is the Greek philosopher Diogenes who came from the cynicism school of philosophy. Charlie knows only three things about Diogenes:

1) He lived in a barrel.
2) In the light of day Diogenes would wander the streets with a lit lantern searching for an honest man.
3) When the conqueror Alexander the Great visited Diogenes, who'd by then become a sage, they talked at great length, and when Alexander rose he told Diogenes that with his great wealth and power he could grant him any wish, to which Diogenes replied: 'Yes, I have a request: would you mind standing to one side? You're blocking the sun.'

I've learned a lot from Charlie, although his cynicism can bother me, which may be why I could never fall in love with him, but only see him as a friend. While I tend to believe in the goodness of the world and its people at large – or at least, most of the time – Charlie believes everything is a scam. We came across several scams in Thailand, but we also came across just the opposite, people with simple honest hearts whose only intentions were good ones. And even Charlie can't deny that.

Chapter 9

Monks on Mopeds

The midnight boat to the island of Koh Phangan was full of German hippies. Not friendly hippies, but people who liked to dress the part. They didn't smile. For such a ragged, dreadlocked motley crew, they took themselves extremely seriously.

I lay awake on the boat's deck for most of the night and let my thoughts sink into the deep purple sky over Thailand. I was thrilled to be in a country I had read so much about, a country so ancient and storied, filled with temples of dawn and northern hill tribes. I recalled what I had seen that day on the train through the southern tip of Thailand: giant Buddhas that sat contemplative in rice paddies, jagged mountains, jungles and rubber plantations.

When the boat reached the island in the morning, I found a bamboo hut to rent on the beach. Over the next ten days I discovered Koh Phangan's outstanding features: nasty dogs that bite your ankles wherever you go, the most delicious food in the entire world (noodles with ginger, chillies, cashews, shrimp in coconut milk, sticky rice), full moon parties where people eat magic mushrooms and fly to solitary planets where conversation is neither required nor even possible, and wandering old men who use their thumbs as instruments of torture.

A Danish woman recommended the Thai massage administered by elderly men who stroll the beaches soliciting willing victims. When the eighty-year-old masseur offered to ply his trade on my body, I eagerly complied, overjoyed at the idea of soothing my aching shoulders which had heaved a far too heavy backpack far too long. Just before he began, I noticed his thumbs. These were no ordinary thumbs, but appendages of astounding proportions, mutated digits, round and flat, the size of dessert spoons. Clearly he had spent his life cultivating his thumbs for the art of massage.

While I lay on the sand, the man with the thumbs prodded and poked his way from my feet up my legs with cruel and unyielding force, even took unnecessary jabs at my knees, showing no mercy at my protests. I had been far less tense before the massage began. He applied his thumbs into the deepest reaches of my body, surely causing irreparable damage to my life-giving organs. By the time he reached my stomach, I was overcome with self-pity. His thumbs forced down into my stomach with such a weight, they seemed to touch the ground beneath me. I couldn't keep my eyes off his face, which was severe, determined and hardened. Clearly, massage was serious business to this man, and flinching was for sissies, and clearly, I was a sissy. When he tried to grab hold of my tongue I clamped my teeth to prevent the intrusion. Then, in a strange and dreadful moment, the giant thumbs were boring into my ears. No one had ever done such a thing and I stopped the thumbs at that point, but not before I heard something pop. Afterwards, I went for a swim in the sea and couldn't get the water out of my ears for two days. The thumbs had carved a small cave in my inner ear for water to sit in, resulting in a painful ear infection that lasted two weeks.

Thailand didn't seem to hold the romance and mystical intrigue I had imagined.

From the moment I arrived in Bangkok I was shoved up against a human tide, jostled by bodies of every description. Every time I walked out of my guest house, I encountered monsoons of activity: human, animal and vegetable. On the streets, I watched people who had fallen into the half-mad gutters of life. Vacant, destitute faces begged for acknowledgement of their existence. Children with rakes for bodies stared at me with eyes bigger than all the world's darkest secrets. Mangy dogs ate rotten vegetables off the roads. I gazed into the rich, brown, beautiful faces of women who sold me combs, cheap soap and pineapples on the sidewalks. I wandered through night markets that sold pig heads, red coiled intestines in glass jars, dripping animal appendages, green leafy vegetable shoots, smoked fish and pyramid mounds of spices. In these markets, every passing scent was either sublime or rank.

Small shops and sidewalk stalls in Bangkok are run by old men with cataracts who have seen too much and give none of it away. They would wrap my passion fruit carefully in yesterday's newspaper, fold all the edges as if it were a wedding present. I watched monks on mopeds, sometimes two to a bike, race down the streets, their saffron robes flowing behind them as they sped through the chaos. Glorious smiles, shaved heads, and Doc Martens on their feet.

Bangkok endures annual floods and an eternal stickiness, a stickiness in the air, in the rice, in the sex sold on the streets. This is the city where men come for sex holidays, whole plane loads of them seeking out the young Thai girls from the hill tribes whose starving parents sell them into prostitution. Young boys sell themselves for movie tickets.

Street life sharpens to a razor's edge on which few can balance.

Bangkok lay smouldering under a blue haze of exhaust fumes and smog: city of perpetual honking horns. Wheels and people are everywhere, all spinning like the city and your head, spinning fast towards the Western world of chaos, Coca-Cola and European cafés.

To cross a street in Bangkok is to risk your life. Pedestrians have no rights. I would always have to wait for a flood of rickshaws and careening cabs, tuk-tuks, bikes and buses to cease and sometimes I waited half an hour. Sidewalks end abruptly with cement walls in your face, and they're full of gaping holes, wide open sewage holes that are gateways to the underworld. I worried for the children and dogs who might slip in too silently. Somewhere in that city, lost souls must wander in the sewers, like filthy fallen angels.

I took a bus north out of Bangkok. I wanted to breathe oxygen again. Just outside a village, I stayed at a guest house run by a woman with too many children to count. Sumalee started working before the sun came up and didn't stop until after it set. She cooked, cleaned, gardened, took care of her children, and, in the evenings, if she had foreign guests, she practised other languages. She loved singing and knew all the words to 'Over the Rainbow'. Although she couldn't be sure exactly, she thought she was close to 35 years old. When I asked where her husband was, she told me, very poetically I thought, that he was experimenting with different hearts.

In the lantern-lit evening I watched the rich communal life of Sumalee's family. As in many non-Western countries, everyone is related and no one is ever alone. Mothers are never isolated and burdened with small, bored children. Children have many mothers, most of them cousins, aunts and older sisters. Social intimacy comes at the cost of privacy, however. Everybody in that extended family seemed to know each other's business. They also seemed to know intimate details about every person in the village.

A week later, I camped in the countryside near a wide glassy river. All night long I gagged from the sickly sweet stench of a burning pile of organic matter and garbage near my tent. I had seen these fires from bus and train windows all over the country. So overpowering were the fumes that I tried to put out the fire, and when that didn't work, I uprooted and moved my tent in the middle of the night. To think I had left Bangkok because of its noxious fumes. Smoke choked even the country skies in an eternal season of burning. Where was the ancient, soft, pure air of Thailand?

In Chiang Mai, I hooked up with Charlie. Charlie and I stayed at the *Be Happy Guest House*, run by an elderly couple who fed us sticky rice and vegetables with fish sauce. After dinner we explored Chiang Mai and discovered the *Be More Happy Guest House*, just down the street. If only we'd known, said Charlie. The next morning when we were eating breakfast at an outdoor restaurant, a little boy came by, holding a cage full of birds. 'Give me five baht and I'll let the birds go,' he said to us. Charlie insisted we not pay the wildlife kidnapper's ransom, and the boy moved on to other tourists at the next table. Later that day, we couldn't help noticing that all over the city, tourists and backpackers, young and old, prosperous and bedraggled, were carrying rolled-up red umbrellas under cloudless blue skies. Since this wasn't monsoon season, we inquired and learned about the You Need Umbrella scam. In this particular scam of the season, tuk-tuk drivers would take tourists to a certain umbrella factory 'on the way' to wherever the tourists wanted to go. Once inside the factory, the bewildered foreigners were given a guided tour of thousands of identical cheap red umbrellas. Outside, the tuk-tuk drivers waited not only for their customers, but for their commission for every umbrella sold. Inside, the tourists weren't allowed to leave the factory until they each bought a cheap red umbrella, although rumours surfaced that a few months previous, some rebellious Swedes had held out, flat out refusing to buy one. They'd had to walk home from the factory, of course, their tuk-tuk driver deeply disappointed with them.

Charlie and I continued north to the city of Chiang Rai, where every second local guy we'd see on the street tried to get us to go on a hill tribe trek. These treks were all the rage. Ride elephants into the past, see hill tribe people untouched by the modern world, they advertised. A Dutch couple, recently returned from one of the more over-trekked expeditions, told us they had walked ahead of their group and arrived at the hill tribe station an hour before they were expected. Through the trees they watched the hill tribe people preparing for the visitors by changing from their ordinary ragged clothes into bright costumes, traditional elaborate hats, and jewellery.

'You see?' said Charlie. 'Everyone has an angle here. You really can't believe a single thing.' Charlie was more jaded than usual, possibly because of an incident which occurred at his guest house in Bangkok, just before I met up with him. Charlie was sharing a dorm room with five other backpackers, one of them a Finnish Buddhist monk-in-training who spent all his time meditating on his bunk bed. Charlie thought he seemed like the real thing at the time, not because he shaved his head and wore an orange robe like the Thai monks, but because he seemed to emanate calmness as he espoused his philosophy of never worrying about anything in the material world. The other backpackers had been having an ongoing discussion about the various Bangkok scams: the diamond scam, the gem scam, the ancient fabric scam, all of which involved naive tourists thinking they were getting a deal of the century on something which turned out to be glass or plastic or polyester instead of diamonds, rubies or heirloom silk. A British backpacker in the dorm had recently been taken by the gem scam and thought he'd have to cut his travels short since he'd spent most of his money on fake emeralds. On hearing their discussion, the Finnish monk would smile serenely and tell them not to bother with such trivial matters, but instead, to laugh at such games. The others would roll their eyes but tried to be polite. When Charlie went to take a quick shower one morning, he left his money belt in the room, since the only person in the room was the Finnish monk in the lotus position in apparent deep meditation up on the bunk bed. Soon after, Charlie discovered his credit card missing. When he called the credit card company some time after that, thousands of dollars had been stacked up on the card: stereo equipment, motorcycle parts, all bought in Helsinki, Finland. Charlie also ran into the British backpacker who told him he'd seen the Finnish monk on the street just after they'd been at the guesthouse, only he wasn't dressed like a monk any more. His head was still shaven, of course, but instead of a flowing orange robe, he was wearing a black leather jacket and spiky wrist bands. The serene Finnish monk had smiled all the way to the bank, and Charlie wasn't laughing.

Rather than taking an organised trek to see the hill tribes, Charlie and I decided to do our own exploring of northern Thailand. We rented a motorcycle in Chiang Rai and set off early one morning into the hills. On the main road north we learned the only law of Thai highway travel: might is right. Every vehicle larger than our motorcycle bullied us over to the extreme edge of the road beside the gutter. We drove on the shoulder – one dead dog and we'd be dead too – and let the wailing, streaking, hurtling highway leave us in the dust.

Soon we escaped the main highway and, on our rickety motorcycle with its sputtering engine, began to follow switchback roads that led into the sky. Thai soldiers had warned us of the danger in the green terraced mountains leading to the Golden Triangle, danger from drug dealers and thieves, communist terrorists and Laotian soldiers who might fly out of the hills to attack travellers at any time. Higher up into the clouds, the mountains became tough and weather-worn, like the skin of the barefoot people who stood and watched us from the roadside. These northern hills were inhabited by ten thousand lives, people eking out their existence in tattered dirt villages that clung to the sides of mountains like bats to cave walls.

When our motorcycle needed a rest, we stopped in a village where we saw a woman smoking opium from a pipe as she breastfed her baby. She looked fifty years old but was probably much younger. I smiled at her and she thrust her hand out toward me. 'Five baht to make picture,' she said. Charlie raised an eyebrow at me when I handed her the money.

Farther up the road we found a Buddha statue inside a cave. The cave was deliciously cold and tranquil after the thick heat of the day. Outside the cave we sat under one of those magical banyan trees which drop their branches down to the ground to take root, forming a spooky dark entanglement below. Monkeys and birds – a pair of Asian paradise flycatchers – were flitting in the branches above. I commented to Charlie how peaceful the place was. 'Yeah, nature's always peaceful if you're at the top of the food chain. For everything else, all these insects and wild animals trying to survive and not get eaten every second of their lives, nature's pure hell.'

I looked at him what felt like a full minute, then said, 'Haven't you ever seen animals having fun? Dolphins?

Don't you think birds are sometimes soaring around up there just because they can?'

'That's only what it looks like to people who want to believe that.' Just then, a monk from a nearby temple came to greet us. He wore biker sunglasses and an orange robe; tattoos laced his forearms. In broken English, he told us about his simple life in the hills and how much happier he was now than when he was young. 'Life is a handful of days, then poof,' he blew on his hands, 'then it's all over.' He laughed and bowed for us as he turned to leave. His jack-o'-lantern robe ruffling in the wind as he walked up a wooded path was a scene of golden beauty. Charlie had to agree he'd been a nice guy.

Charlie and I searched most of the afternoon for the Golden Triangle. Considered by some to be one of the most exotic places in the world, and long a centre for drug trafficking, the infamous Golden Triangle is found at the intersection of the Mekong and Ruak rivers, forming the borders between Burma, Laos and northern Thailand. Road signs were extremely poor and misleading and we got lost several times. So desolate were the roads, many of them ending abruptly into a dead open nowhere, we thought the Golden Triangle must be remote and unvisited.

We rounded a corner and found ourselves on a gleaming paved highway full of honking horns. The first sign of the Golden Triangle was a slick, air-conditioned Japanese tour bus glistening in the sun. I was reminded of Niagara Falls. Cameras clicked incessantly at the small triangular island on the Mekong River. Pepsi and Coke competed for attention like ten-year-old brats. Posters of half-naked Thai women advertised orange pop. A little girl dressed in hill tribe garb asked if I wanted to take her picture for five baht and pouted when I said no.

We fled and got lost again as we headed south, drawn off the beaten tourist track on to smaller, narrower roads. After a while, we found ourselves snaking through a different kind of countryside. An emptiness seemed to clutch hold of the rolling land around us, but it wasn't lonely, or barren. The villages we passed in this new and different land were rich with details of simple, brave, joyful, real lives. The people were evidently not accustomed to outsiders and they stared, waved and smiled as we passed them on the road. A little girl ran when she saw us, and hid behind a tree.

Outside one village, some water buffalo crossing the road forced us to stop and wait. The farmer herding the buffalo ran behind the beasts to hurry them off the road. He grinned sheepishly, embarrassed about interrupting our journey. 'No problem,' Charlie said to the man with a wave of his hand.

'No problem?' said the water buffalo herder. 'No problem, no problem,' he continued to say over and over. He started laughing. He laughed so hard he doubled over and held his stomach. I wondered if this was the first time he'd actually heard an English speaker use the phrase. Perhaps he had heard it once in a movie. 'No problem, no problem,' continued the man. Once his water buffalo had crossed and we drove on, I turned around to see the laughing man running toward his house, probably to tell his family what he'd heard.

Soon after, we realised we were seriously lost. Our map was entirely useless and it was getting dark. In the next village, we stopped to ask a boy the way to Chiang Rai, but he didn't have a clue what we were saying. Frightened, he ran away to his house. An old man came along and didn't understand us either. Soon a gathering of people surrounded us, the lost *falang*s. Repeatedly, we said, 'Chiang Rai,' pointed to our map, pointed ahead and then behind us on the road, trying to discern which way to go. Either the villagers didn't know the way to Chiang Rai or we weren't pronouncing it correctly. Then, we looked up from the map and saw two teenage boys dragging a younger boy by his shirt across the road. Proudly, they deposited him in front of us. The little boy's eyes shone at our decrepit motorcycle. Very slowly, he said, 'Where... you... want go?' The villagers had given us their prize linguist.

The boy pointed the way back for us, and on seeing the boy do this, the whole village pointed the way back for us too. The whole village pointed. It set off inside me a surge of sweet gratitude, an understanding into the magnificence of humanity. The handful of days we're given on earth exploded on the road before us into a thousand shards of light. The way back would be easy to find. The way back would be paved in Judy Garland songs.

No problem.

Chapter 10

I have to call Charlie. I have to remind him of our trip to Thailand, of those people in the village. I have to tell him about the guy at the gas station who said I could mail him a cheque. I have to let optimism reign all the way to California, keep the faith that California is where I'm meant to go, just as I believed it was that very first time, when, yet again, the kindness of a stranger pointed me in the right direction.

That day thirteen years ago, after I'd almost frozen on the picnic table in Oregon, the businessman who'd picked me up had wanted to take me all the way into California but since it was getting late, I said it would be fine if he dropped me off in Grants Pass, just north of the California border. In the pouring rain, he stopped in front of some dreary little motels, and after our day-long revitalising conversation, I suddenly felt panicky about getting out of his car. The problem was money. I had a cheque with me from the Alberta lodge but hadn't been able to cash it back in Canada for a stupid banking reason so had been living off the little cash I'd made waitressing in Oregon. I didn't think I could afford a motel. I recall knocking at the office door of one of the motels and telling the woman I only had seventeen dollars and if it wasn't enough for a room I could chambermaid. She sent me away feeling thoroughly dejected into the rain while her malicious dog barked at me. I felt a sudden empathy for hobos and realised this is how they must feel all the time, cast out of society, the essential impact of life's cruelty constantly bearing down on them. I crossed the road to another motel, on the verge of tears, then looked up through the downpour to find what seemed exactly like a vision, like a glowing angel in the rain. An East Indian man wearing traditional white cotton pyjamas was standing outside a door of the motel and holding up an umbrella. 'Come,' he said. 'Come quickly. Get out of the water.' He looked to be about thirty and was smiling and slight with warm, penetrating brown eyes. I explained my situation to him, although I can't imagine what I said, what my plan was, or if I had one at all other than a vague notion of finding a job in California. He invited me into his room which he was renting by the month, and then gave me a steaming bowl of curried rice. I know we talked for hours, mostly about India, as I asked him one question after the next about his village and family and which parts of India I should visit some day. He let me stay the night in his room, and the next morning when I left to hitchhike the remaining few miles to California, I felt I'd had been saved a second time – first by the businessman and then by this Indian man – perhaps by an ancient god for weary travellers, or simply by the compassion of a stranger. In any case, I took it as a sign I was headed the right way, to California.

Yes, I have to call Charlie and remind him about the goodness in the world. Mostly, I have to talk to a friend. Marcia is crankier than ever and every half hour or so sounds as if she's going to conk out completely and all my dreams of California sputter out the exhaust pipe in puffs of black thoughts like: I don't think I have the energy to start a whole new life some place new; or, what if California is full of those smug Westerners who think they live in Xanadu?

What about earthquakes? But then suddenly, Marcia surges forward and carries on as if nothing is wrong at all, and I'm back to singing show tunes out the window, or imagining working in California at a job where I can teach, write and travel, a job where I can take cappuccino breaks with my new work friends, and every so often we're sent off on a travel assignment, to Borneo perhaps, to write about the struggles of the indigenous people. Come on Marcia, you can do it. We're getting there!

Today I seem to have crossed over an invisible line, have left the Midwest behind and entered the West, where the land and air are even drier, the skies bigger, and the horizons wider, where pickup truck drivers raise their hands to wave 'howdy' and instead of high-riding ball caps, they're sporting cowboy hats. Their accents change too, and although you can't see them, you know their feet are covered in the rawhide of cowboy boots.

I keep looking to the horizon for them and suddenly, there they are: the Rockies, craggy and jagged and white with snow. Snow seems impossible in this heat. I want to drive up a mountain and roll in that snow, eat it, throw it at my car. I want to climb into the mountains and peek down into their secret hearts.

Colorado: the word still jumps up and holds magic for me. I first came to Colorado when I was a shy seventeen-year-old, having finished high school early in Ontario and wanting to go somewhere for a year before starting university, maybe even staying longer if I liked it. I'd heard of other people my age going west to work in Alberta, but Boulder, Colorado sounded more enticing. I must have been impressed by *Mork and Mindy*. Since I was born in the U.S. I could work there and had all kinds of fantasies about what exotic jobs I might find: a river raft guide, a park ranger, a beginner ski instructor, an Outward Bound leader – something daring and outdoorsy that I wasn't in the least qualified to do but that I'd be hired for on enthusiasm alone.

I got my first job the week I arrived in Boulder: a waitress at Chuck E. Cheese Pizza. Chuck E. Cheese is an American restaurant emporium specialising in bad taste, not only of the pizza, which is lousy, but in the décor which is designed mainly for kids' birthday parties. I'm sure I would have loved it at age six myself, getting to tear around with my friends from one thematic room to the next, watching the mechanical Elvises dance and sing Happy Birthday. On the Friday night of my first week at Chuck E. Cheese, I was told to meet the manager at 10 p.m. at the restaurant where I'd dress up as a giant furry mouse, the Chuck E. Cheese mascot, and go downtown with him to Boulder's Pearl Street pedestrian mall to a bar called the Blue Note where I'd be expected, as the giant furry mouse, to interact with strangers and try to get them to give me money for charity. The costume was one of those extravagant Disney-type affairs which made me not only completely unrecognisable but stifling hot. The tiny eye holes in the mouse's mouth made peripheral vision impossible and even walking was a little difficult at first. I remember stumbling into the dark moody bar thinking, hey, I'm only 17 and the drinking age in this state is 21. Would they ask a giant mouse for I.D.? Once inside, I looked around at the mixed crowd, the older men lined up along the bar, a clump of overly-perfumed office women on a girls' night out, the preppy university guys and the preppy university girls in their Levis and Lacoste polo shirts. I remember looking down at what I was wearing and thinking, wow, this is *so* not cool. The Chuck E. Cheese manager nudged me out into the crowd and although I felt like an idiot, I realised that the costume made me anonymous – nobody even knew if I was male or female under all that fabric and fur – and besides, I didn't know anyone in town yet anyway, so what did I care? The crowd seemed to take to me, or rather, to the giant mouse, and at around midnight, they formed a fervent circle around me on the dance floor and clapped and cheered as I performed some sort of giant mouse dance. I remember twirling all over the floor feeling completely free. A week before I'd been living at home with my parents. Here I was almost 2,000 miles away in a place I'd never been, out on my own for the first time in my life, dancing with good-looking guys, being handed free drinks. So what if I was dressed a little funny. This is what it means to be an adult, I thought. This is what it means to be a traveller. I love this!

I never did get one of those outdoorsy jobs. I liked Boulder too much to leave, although I did go into the mountains to hike, ski, explore and travel as often as I could. In the summer I went on several extended backpacking trips and even a six-day river rafting trip down the Colorado River through the Cataract Canyon in Utah. But Boulder was where I found my heart and, eventually, a job I liked, one where I wasn't required to dress as a rodent.

Nothing in my life had prepared me for a place like Boulder. It was a utopian wonder. The college town of 95,000 usually seems to be on the top ten list of the best places to live in America and it's easy to see why. Boulder embodies everything from American life that is ideal, joyful, worldly, conscientious, progressive, deserving of fondness, and wacky. It's Jimmy Stewart's Bedford Falls with an edge. Other than all the intellectuals, environmentalists, social activists and Buddhists, it attracts a lot of eccentrics: New Agers, Deadheads, topless women, mountain men down from the mountains for a falafel and a bath, someone called Naked Guy, and the 'Q-tip' people – a cult of survivalists living in the nearby mountains who dress entirely in white with little white turbans. You see them occasionally on the streets of Boulder and they really do look like giant Q-tips.

Boulder gets more sunshine than any place in the country. Everything always seems green, fresh, fecund and smells of giant blossoms. Brightly painted houses are surrounded by magnificent well-tended gardens. Magnolia trees filter sunlight along boulevards. A greenbelt protects the city from suburban development and the mountains sweep right down into people's backyards, so close you feel as if you could reach up and touch them from anywhere in town. You can take a walk from your house and, depending on where you live, find yourself all alone in the mountains – with perhaps a herd of elk nearby – within ten minutes. Beautiful people practise yoga in the parks. They also jog and ride their bikes on trails all throughout the town's foothills and race madcap handmade contraptions across reservoirs, run an annual marathon called the Bolder Boulder, and like to celebrate holidays extravagantly. They also eat organic. The pedestrian mall downtown, one of the most successful pedestrian malls in North America, leads straight into Boulder Canyon and, from there, straight into the mountains. The mall is always brimming with life: buskers, jugglers, musicians, balloon artists, tarot card readers, a guy who can curl his lanky body into a 20-inch plexiglas box, and Zipcode Man, who can pinpoint exactly where you live when you holler out your zip code. The mall is also full of cheerful people strolling or reading books or talking at the outdoor cafés and restaurants. Everyone is beaming with health and everyone is a little too attractive, sometimes so much so that you crave to see just one ugly person walking down the street. I once met an Ontario couple who told me they moved to Boulder but had to leave because everyone was too happy. 'They all looked like they were on Prozac,' they said. 'It was too much. We're used to seeing regular people who eat French fries and go to Tim Hortons doughnut chain and smoke. People don't do stuff like that in Boulder. It's unnerving.'

It's true. Walking into a park in Boulder where couples are strolling hand in hand or running through the woods, kids are turning cartwheels, teenagers are playing Ultimate Frisbee, and old people are doing t'ai chi or attending Chautauquas and drinking pineapple-coconut juice can set you off balance. You wonder if this kind of happiness is sustainable. You wonder if the people who live there are happier than the people who live in Buffalo or in Hays, Kansas. You suspect they are, and it doesn't seem quite fair. On the other hand, most of the people who live in Boulder come from someplace else, have had the gumption to get up and look for a better place, have left the French fries and Tim Hortons, the smoky bars and crappy weather behind, making it one of those cream of the crop places you come across almost always in scenically gorgeous settings.

I wonder now why I didn't stay for good. It must have had something to do with those good-looking people all over town – they *are* a little annoying. Maybe I left after a year because I missed a certain friendly familiarity of my hometown of Guelph, however unlike Boulder it was.

And here it is approaching ahead, Boulder the Beautiful, although each time I've returned since that first youthful year, I've noticed what many of the locals used to complain about, that Boulder has changed, that 'the yuppies drove out the hippies' because it has become so expensive to live here. It also seems a lot busier than before, with trendier more expensive stores downtown. Now there's a Gap and a Starbucks on the Pearl Street mall where before there was a local bead shop and a retro-clothing store.

However, when I drive into town it's clear that Boulder is still an electrifying and stunningly gorgeous place. I walk down the Pearl Street mall and see it still has the same small-town feeling only now even more trees have been planted – peach and Linden trees, ash, honey locust and a cypress standing in a bed of pansies. Exuberant flowers are everywhere as are public art, sculptures and fountains. I see that the people are still beaming, the runners still beautiful and the eccentrics are still, well... eccentric. I even spot a familiar face, one of the mountain men from years ago who has the same faraway look in his eyes, although now his beard is longer and greyer. I also see an electric car parked at its own special electric car spot complete with a battery hookup on the boulevard.

I decide to visit friends of my parents, Bob and Judy Rothe, whom I stayed with the first few weeks I moved here when I was seventeen and always stay with whenever I'm in Boulder. When I arrive at their place in a quiet treed neighbourhood of nice houses in the south end of town, I see their front lawn is filled with about fifteen very blond teenagers setting up tents. For years the Rothes have taken in exchange students and these ones appear to be Scandinavian. In the summer, Bob takes these groups of kids backpacking, mountain climbing or river rafting and for the days they're in Boulder, they camp on the Rothe's front lawn.

The Rothes welcome me in, warmly as always, ask about my trip and update me on their latest news. That evening I return downtown to meet my sister Linda and her husband Steve who live north of Boulder in Fort Collins. I haven't seen Linda in at least two years and it's great to see her, especially after so many days driving alone through the heatwave where I've hardly had a real conversation with anybody. I still feel a little shell-shocked from the long drive but euphoria is starting to set in. An evening breeze feels unbelievably foreign and sublime, and after the parched Midwest, I can't get over how green Boulder is. We're sitting outside at a Russian tea house and Linda, Steve and their friends are discussing the best Thai restaurants in town. A friend of theirs tells me his brother, who lives in Denver, has the same Ford Bronco I do and the brother is handy with cars. He calls his brother on his cell phone and asks if I can take my car to see him the next day. The brother agrees and I write down directions to his Denver suburb. I'm doubtful, as nobody so far has figured out Marcia's problem, but I'm also desperate. When it gets dark, we walk around the corner to a parking lot to watch *The Rocky Horror Picture Show* which they're screening outside against a giant white wall. A sizeable audience has already gathered, most of them dressed in the Rocky Horror garb and ready with their bags of rice and toast to throw during the film. Some of them have brought along not only lawn chairs but old-fashioned sofas, lamps and lazy-boy recliners to replicate the mood of a living room.

Just half an hour into the famous cult movie and already I'm fascinated with the straight-laced looking, middle-aged group of women in front of us who have obviously seen this film fifty times and know all the right lines to shout. When the character Janet in the movie walks through the rain, they yell, 'Buy an umbrella, you cheap bitch!' What makes this especially intriguing is that these women are dressed like my mother with tidy conservative haircuts and sensible shoes. All except their friend, a woman who has to be in her late fifties and is wearing a black teddy, garter belts, a pointy bra and fishnet stockings. She's not what you'd call svelte either, and I wonder what it is that made her dress up and not her friends. Something about the black pointy bra must speak to her, offer her a new identity. I watch her closely as she shoots her water pistol, laughs, and yells out 'Asshole!' to the character Brad, and can't help noticing that through all her black fishnety tangle of garters and make-up she still resembles a woman who lives in the suburbs, has three grown children, an academic husband and several bridge lady friends. I suppose none of us can hide from who we really are.

The next day I get lost in the heat of Denver trying to find the house of the Brother with the Bronco. In a driveway I see a girl skipping rope, talking to herself, probably counting how many times she can skip, trying to beat her own record. I'm touched by the look on her face, the determination, that human compulsion to keep going even when we're hot and tired. When I finally find the Brother with the Bronco's place, he's disappointed I have the mini version of his vehicle and after ten minutes, tells me the kick-down something or other that the last guy recommended won't help at all, but I need a new tail light. Other than that, he offers no advice.

Dejected, I head back towards the mountains, fantasise about dumping the car in an A&W parking lot for good, the keys swinging in the ignition, and walking westward, uphill, into a place with a name like Soda Springs Mountain or Whispering Pines Gulch or Wild Horse Valley.

Instead, I drive to my sister's place in Fort Collins. On the way, I spot a bumper sticker which cheers me up: 'MY KID HAD SEX WITH YOUR HONOR STUDENT.' The thought of spending time with my sister also cheers me up, although it also makes me a little nervous. She and I don't exactly have a lot in common. In fact, I've been told it might be difficult to find two people in North America more opposite than the two of us. I think back ten years ago to our trip to Jamaica, how that trip crystallised how different we are. I haven't thought about my Jamaica trip in ages. I think I travelled better back then than I do now, lighter, not bogged down with heavy luggage and dilemmas and notions of how I ought to be or where I should go. I just went.

Chapter 11

Jamaica

How my sister and I could even for a nanosecond have possibly thought we could travel together, could actually get along as travelling companions on a trip, is something that baffles me to this day. We must have been drunk on eggnog.

It was Christmas in the late eighties at my parents' house and an hour earlier she and I had been arguing about Reagan and his support of death squads and contras in Latin America. She loved Reagan. But since it was Christmas and we were both home for the holidays and hadn't seen each other in a while, perhaps we were feeling some rare sisterly love, some dangerous and misguided festive camaraderie. My sister and I had never gotten along very well, not since I'd entered the world four years after she did – an act for which she never seemed to forgive me. In personality and how we saw the world, we were poles apart. To give an example, after returning from my lengthy trip to the South Pacific and South-east Asia, she had asked me where I stayed when I travelled. I told her I camped or stayed in hostels or guest houses or sometimes with friends or families. 'Then how do you get your exercise?' she had asked, genuinely puzzled. I was puzzled myself until I realised her meaning. Where could I possibly get exercise other than in the exercise room of a fancy hotel? Surely not from lugging a backpack through the hot countryside for miles, or from climbing a mountain, or hiking, or swimming in the ocean or in New Zealand lakes.

Obviously, travelling had different meanings for each of us, as did a lot of things. Inexplicably, we had come from the same parents, had grown up in the same house, had been stimulated by the same cultural offerings of the seventies, a time of cut-off cords, baby-doll dresses, bubble shirts, Polaroid cameras, and parents discussing Watergate; had watched *The Partridge Family*, *The Brady Bunch*, *The Love Boat* and *Mary Tyler Moore* together. How could Mary and Rhoda not have affected my sister as they had me? We'd grown up on my mother's new fad Adelle Davis health food where brewer's yeast and wheat germ were sneaked into every dish. Most importantly, we were both redheads, which used to mean something back before red hair became fashionable. Being a redhead used to mean you had to stand tough against the world, not only against teasing boys, but against everyone who expected you to be quirky, who expected you to be Pippi Longstocking. My sister and I should have been sisters-in-arms for this one feature alone. But evidently, we'd reacted to our upbringing in two very dissimilar ways, causing her to study economics and then electrical engineering, join MENSA, move to the U.S. and work for a big computer company, and me to study international development – a programme centred on how the rich nations had systematically and historically screwed the poor ones, a programme without much chance of employment.

I'd found out about January seat sales to Jamaica, only $250 for an air-only open return ticket, and I was planning on going by myself, perhaps even staying the winter to teach in a Jamaican village. 'I'll go with you!' said Linda, after I'd announced my plan to her and to my mother that snowy afternoon in the kitchen while Bing Crosby sang 'White Christmas' in the background from my parents' teak hi-fi stereo. 'I could go for two weeks!' My mother looked up from the piecrust she was rolling. All three of us studied each other without speaking, all of us aware of how disastrous such a trip could be, how unprecedented and curious.

'Well... really? You'd want to come with me? I guess that could be... I guess it could be fun. Great!' I don't remember much of the conversation beyond that, the logistics and the planning we must have discussed – we'd obviously broken with reality at that point – although I do recall my father muffling distinct chuckling noises from downstairs.

Early one morning shortly after New Year's, we stood in the snow on my parents' driveway waiting for the airport van. I noticed my sister's suitcases. She had two of them, not regular-sized suitcases, but overstuffed top-of-the-line, colossal suitcases on wheels which could transport the entire contents of several households in certain less fortunate countries. I, on the other hand, had one small knapsack which would fit at my feet on the plane. Perhaps I was being extreme in my under-packing, but I'd already discovered what a burden too much luggage can be, how week after week you end up hauling all kinds of stuff you never use, always thinking the day might come when you'll actually need that down-quilted vest, that tent, the chess board someone gave you at the airport just before you left. The heavy-duty flashlight that's always sticking into your back you only flashed one night in Wales months earlier, and all the extra-large batteries it needs are starting to corrode your underwear; the wool sweater you bought in Scotland you've only worn twice and as the months pass, it begins to smell like soggy sheep. As for the multi-coloured wool leggings, you don't have an earthly clue what you could have been thinking to have bought those from that French 'artisan' woman. Had she hypnotised you? Were you going for a racier, slightly demented look when you bought them or were you just demented?

Since Jamaica was hot, I wouldn't need many clothes, or even a sleeping bag, and I'd read you could rent tents cheaply on the beach. Anything I really needed I could buy there. As for my sister, I decided not to ask what was inside her giant suitcases. I'd find out soon enough.

If you live in a climate like Canada's, it's always a shock after a short plane ride to step out of one season into another, to leave behind the words *blustering*, *bitter* and *wind chill*, days steeped in darkness and a pale, heatless sun, and step into the steamy red fervour of the tropics. As soon as you walk off the plane you feel enveloped in soft, languorous, sensual heat. The heat feels so foreign you don't know what to do at first: start sweating and complain you're overdressed, or rip off your Canadian clothes and run and skip under a sun you've forgotten existed, a sun which is, you begin to recall, an integral part of your solar system.

The Montego Bay airport officials seemed as relaxed and breezy as the weather. Everyone was in a festive, celebratory mood. This carnival atmosphere always seems pervasive in warm countries and the only possible explanation for this is climate. How can people not be cheerful in the sun? Generally speaking, cold climates create cold people with Viking genes who have to walk fast and furiously through winter gales, who are too cold to stop and chat on the streets. Winter is a time of chilled surliness as the days move deeper into darkness and the cold drives people further apart. Winter makes good workers: fast, efficient, busy. We have to work hard to heat our homes, to eat. We can't just step outside and pluck mangoes off a tree any time we want. When springtime finally arrives, we come out to celebrate the return of the sun on our faces, the budding green trees, and, if we remember what our friends look like, we can chat again on the streets. But after all those freezing months, are those few blissful spring days really worth it? I often wonder. When we get the chance to escape the winter even for a week and fly to the tropics, or perhaps, go to California in February, we see what's really going on: not only is the sun warm and shining now but it has been that way *all year long*. The people aren't huddled tense and shivering under a bitter slate sky, nor are they scraping ice off their windshields. Even if they barely notice the sun because they're so accustomed to it, that doesn't mean it's not affecting them, lending them an ease and joyful saunter when they stop to talk with friends. I wonder, is it just inertia that prevents us from leaving behind winter climates and living in more sensible places, or is it something more? Perhaps all of us are attuned to the natural environment in which we were brought up and those who come from a land of four seasons need the seasonal cycles to measure our lives by, would miss winter and the coming of spring and fall if they were gone. Though I think many of us could get used to a gentle sun-drenched climate and would be willing to forgo six months of grey gloom and cold.

We took a taxi-van to a nearby hotel which Linda had booked for the first night. We'd agreed we'd only stay there that night and find something better the next day. 'Better' to me meant a hut on the beach or perhaps a campground. 'Better' to Linda meant a Hilton resort. I think each of us had hoped to convince the other that her way was better and this would be obvious when we arrived in the country. Once Linda saw the bamboo beach hut, or once I saw the hot tub at the Hilton, we'd see the error of our ways and thank the other for seeing the light.

It didn't work like that.

The hotel we stayed in that first night had a noisy and useless air conditioner so not only was the room hot and stuffy but it sounded as if the Concord was trapped in the window. Both of us were happy to leave the next day. Because of that air conditioner I figured Linda would agree with me and prefer to sleep to a cool evening breeze and the sound of the surf in a simple beach hut. But she didn't like this airy fairy idea – so unplanned, primitive and dangerous-sounding. We decided to take a walk through Montego Bay to find another form of accommodation.

Montego Bay is Jamaica's second largest city and since it's a city it has a lot of roads, which by the afternoon, when we left for our walk, had become very hot – unlike the beach with its breezes and swaying palms, I kept saying. Still, Linda was convinced we'd find a nice place to stay in Montego Bay and I'm sure such places exist, mile after touristy mile of them along a stretch of beach somewhere. Only, we never found Resort Row, and I must admit, I wasn't particularly looking for it. Instead, I led my poor sister straight into the heart of a slum. I didn't mean for this to happen, not consciously anyway. At first, we were just walking through town, being followed by a Jamaican woman named Angela who kept trying to sell us things. Angela had crinkled, purple-hued skin, a straight slim back and serious, small eyes. She'd spotted us as soon as we left the hotel and never stopped mumbling from a few paces behind us: 'You want aloe rub? You want T-shirt? You want reggae tape? You want spicy beef patty?' Finally, she hit on something of interest: 'You want hair plaited?' Since it was hot and I have a lot of hair – in the heat, it's like looking after a Chia pet – I let her braid away. Getting your hair pulled into all those tiny tight braids really hurts, surprisingly. I thought it might be like a scalp massage but it's actually more like torture. When she finally finished, however, my head did feel a lot cooler. I paid her and we continued on, Angela still behind us, murmuring 'Braid your hair, Miss,' to Linda, who wasn't interested in a stranger messing with her hair, especially not when it ended up looking like mine. 'I guess it's OK if you like the bohemian look,' said Linda.

We strolled through the colourful city streets full of markets, bars, little shops, and banks, watching women play dominoes on the sidewalks and boys shooting marbles. The architecture was a mix of gingerbread wooden houses and shacks, interspersed with modern, somewhat dilapidated buildings. We wandered around for a few hours, hoping to find the heart of the city and perhaps a tourist information booth. At one point, Linda said, 'Have you noticed we seem to be the only white people around?' The further we walked, the rougher the area became until we realised we were deep in a very tough neighbourhood. We'd crossed some invisible border into a shantytown where feebly built, impossibly small shacks were all that separated a family from living on the road itself. Some of the dwellings were hovels with broken walls where we could look directly into their lives. The people we passed gave us cold hard stares, except for the ones trying to sell us things. We soon had an entourage shouting at us. 'What do you want to buy?' 'I sell you anything.' 'You like to smoke?' 'You want room? I take you to room.' Finally, Linda, wheeling her two heavy suitcases, stopped in the middle of the street and demanded I lead her out of there. This was Linda's first time in a developing country and part of me was feeling sorry for her for ending up in such a derelict neighbourhood when all she wanted was a resort vacation in the sun, but another part of me wanted to show her what poverty looked like. I knew she'd never seen poverty, or even given it much thought, and I felt it was time she did.

'This isn't so bad. This is what most of the world looks like,' I told her. 'And I don't know how to get out of here anyway.'

Linda fumed some distance behind, calling out that she'd never travel with me again. The crowd of hawkers temporarily stopped trying to sell us things as they watched us argue. Finally, I said that since it would be dark soon, what we needed was a room for the night, and tomorrow we'd find a better place. One of the hawkers piped up that he had a room for us, just around the corner.

We followed the man down a dirt road until we came to a ramshackle house with a front yard full of running children, chickens and a goat. The man called out to a woman sitting on the front step who immediately came rushing down to greet us, a tiny woman with a face that looked like it might have one day been a precious piece of pottery but had broken and been put back together. Her cotton dress hung off her shoulders as if still on a hanger. With a warm hand she touched my arm. 'Me Miss Mary. I show you room.' Linda looked dubious but I suggested we at least take a look. Miss Mary led us around the back where we walked up a path that came to a little shack. A flock of children followed, curious at the unexpected guests. Miss Mary pushed open the shack's door. Inside was an old dresser and a double bed. In the bed was an old man. 'Out, out!' shouted Miss Mary at the old man, her arms flying in the air. 'These girls stay here tonight.' The old man, taken aback, but clearly not prepared to argue with her, sat up, a little dazed, and nodded. He coughed heavily, smoothed down the bed covers, and left.

We stayed the night. I'm not sure why Linda agreed to it. The night, however, was not a good one for either of us. It started with the noise of a roaring crowd at a soccer match, a match which must have been taking place very nearby, followed by what sounded like a riot on the street after the game. The row seemed to last for hours with hollering and shouting, blaring music, laughing, cackling and the occasional scream. Linda swore she heard gun shots but I told her it was probably fireworks, even though I wasn't sure about that. Then we heard a noise much closer by, under the bed. 'That sounds like a rat!' Linda was right. It did sound awfully large. I told her it was probably just mice, which didn't seem to comfort her much. I dozed off for a while but soon awoke to the sound of the dresser being dragged across the floor. I looked up to see Linda barricading the door. When she returned to bed she took both her giant suitcases with her and placed them over the length of her body to act as bulletproof shields for the rape and murder attempts which surely were imminent.

'So that's why you brought those giant suitcases.'

'I'm leaving tomorrow. I'm taking the first flight out of here back home. I'm leaving tomorrow.' She repeated this much of the night like a mantra, and, in the morning that's exactly what she did. She left. We saw each other off at a taxi stand. She was on her way to the airport and I was on my way to Negril Beach. As I was sitting in my taxi before it left, Linda started snapping pictures of me so she could have 'the last documented proof of my life' since she was certain I'd be killed in less than a week. I waved goodbye as our driver pulled away until all I could see of her was a small speck of a person standing in the middle of the road, taking one last picture of her doomed sister.

Jamaica's taxi-vans are notorious for being over-crowded and mine was no exception. Even though our taxi was packed beyond capacity, the driver kept stopping for every person who held out a hand along the road. I soon had on top of me a Jamaican woman of abundant flesh and enormous breasts who thought it was the funniest joke in the world that she was squishing me. Despite losing circulation in one leg, I loved flying along the bumpy ride to Negril, passing cane fields, fertile mountains, wooden huts with corrugated roofs, fishing villages, children waving, and the occasional glimpse of the turquoise sea. All this was accompanied by the good-humoured passengers who laughed easily and took life merrily, had a zest and affection for life unparalleled in northern climates. The sun poured down on a dazzling world of indigo blue and fairytale green, a world brimming with tropical abundance – the cries of birds and uproar of insects, extravagant blossoms, giant white lilies, wild red orchids and jasmine drenched in scent. In all directions, wild beauty was shrieking with life. The Jamaican wind whipped back my braids, the giant laughing woman crushed my body, and the glory of the earth radiated around me. If only Linda had known about this. She was missing this privileged moment, lush, vivid and fleeting, when the two of us together might have been swept up into this blue-green island world that had been here all along.

When we arrived at Negril, the pile of us spilling out of the van like gushing water, the driver called out to me, 'A hope yu like yu trip a Jamaica!' and sped away.

Negril was founded by European and American hippies and by the time I was there it had gained a reputation for hedonism and a swinging nightlife. Yet it had a small village atmosphere with many cheap places to stay and several campgrounds dotting the beach.

All the bamboo huts on the beach were full so I found a little guest house run by a family in the village, up a hill and on a dirt road, just a few minutes from the ocean. Then I went exploring and fell into the friendliness and relaxed stride of Negril immediately. Locals and visitors strolled the beach and market, smiling at everyone they passed. They drank pina coladas at beach bars, ate salt fish, ackee and moist fleshy fruit. The Jamaicans had an easy languor. No one was in a hurry and everyone had something to sell: fried plantain, aloe rub, starfish, curried roti and braid your hair miss, vegetable patties, soursop juice for the 'stiff bamboo', bush doctor cures and necklaces, conch shells and coloured shells, beads, Bob Marley everything and everything ganja: cake, tea, leaves, omelettes. All the music in all directions was reggae. It was a law they told me, that all music had to be reggaefied, Elvis, Christmas carols, pop music. Most of it was unbelievably bad but managed to lend a mood of celebration anyway. 'Can you believe they're turning U2 and David Bowie songs into reggae!' laughed the tourists.

A Jamaican girl who lived next door to my guest house befriended me one day. She was on her way to buy fish from someone she knew with a fishing net and asked me to come along. Her name was Marcy and she lived with her mother. With her child's soft face and lithe body I assumed she was about thirteen or fourteen and was shocked to learn she was nineteen and the mother of four children. Her current boyfriend, she told me, was probably cheating on her. Marcy and I spent the day together, walking, cooking and playing with her kids, and she insisted on re-braiding my hair since whoever had done it, she said, obviously didn't know what she was doing. She liked to giggle. Being around her, I felt fourteen again. Late that night, however, I woke up with a start to a more accurate reality of her life. From the window of my guesthouse, I overheard the unmistakable shrieks of a girl whose childhood lay forever lost: 'Tek it out! Tek it out!' Marcy called this over and over like a prayer hobbling up to the stars. Her cries haunted me.

I made many acquaintances during my stay in Negril, especially dreadlocked Jamaican men who were constantly approaching me, men with regal English names: Nobel, Clarence, McPherson. I'd been warned about these men, how they're only after white women, but most of them seemed to be poor, harmless, uneducated, sweet men trying to survive using whatever they had, in this case their tangled nests of hair, which, for inexplicable reasons, some women find appealing.

Every evening I'd watch the sun dip into the sea, the sky bleeding as if it had been stabbed, and listen to palm fronds rattling in the breeze. Afterwards I'd usually find a live band at a reggae or calypso bar on the beach where I'd dance for hours under the stars. It was something of a dream, my Negril days on the turquoise bay, but I wanted more. Even though I was relatively new to the traveller's life, I knew a beach vacation wasn't all I was looking for. That's why when I met Joan and she invited me to stay with her, I jumped at the chance.

Joan was a full-size Jamaican woman with generous hips and a curvaceous, assured body which seemed incongruous with the shy expression on her face. She had Hershey syrup eyes which warmed when she asked me to try on one of the straw hats she sold. She also sold T-shirts, necklaces and colourful shorts at one of the beach stalls of Negril's market under the trees. I guessed her to be in her late twenties or early thirties but it was hard to say. After we'd been talking a while and I'd told her how I wanted to see more of Jamaica's countryside, she said, 'You come stay with me and my family in my village. You like it there. It's by the river. My kids would love you.'

I took the bus with Joan to her village of Little London the next evening. The highway east from Negril crosses several miles of swampland before emerging onto the vast Westmoreland Plain with its cane fields, pastureland and small villages. As we approached Little London, the roads narrowed and curved, becoming thick with voluptuous vegetation. Blossoms swirled off branches, and as night fell quickly upon us, the tropic's stirring scent combination of palm oil and jasmine filled my nostrils with an unfamiliar longing.

From the bus stop, we walked down a dirt road under a sky dripping with stars, then went down a country lane until Joan stopped in front of a wooden shack lit up from within by the dim glow of lanterns. We stood for a moment in the quiet night, looking upwards. 'Sometimes moonshine lights it all up instead of the stars,' she said, then pointed to the house. 'That's where I live. Come.'

Within seconds of walking through the door I was surrounded by at least twenty people, half of them children. It was a sudden flurry of commotion in the little house as relatives rushed to shake my hand and kiss me, one girl calling me 'My Lady', giggling. I met Joan's three kids and her brothers: Glen, Graham and someone who I was sure said his name was Shirley. I met cousins, nephews and nieces, and then, from another room, arched over a cane yet entering like royalty, came Miss Sylvia – Mamma to the rest of them. The others cleared a path for her as she shuffled towards me with her arm outstretched, smiling as if welcoming a long-lost daughter. A toothless vision of timeless beauty, and clearly, the head of the entire household, Miss Sylvia had what can only be described as wisdom in her face, a face that I noticed immediately was fully prepared in its openness to look directly into mine.

Like many in the family, Miss Sylvia didn't speak much English – she spoke the Jamaican patois – but we seemed to communicate nonetheless. 'Me run tings here,' she told me proudly that evening, and I could see that indeed she did. Everyone revered her. In the days to come I'd learn that not only are the elders of Jamaica deeply respected, but the women of Jamaica hold the real power. I came to believe that Jamaican society, desperately poor, dispossessed, wracked with economic instability and violence, is kept from some terrible and final dissolution by the courage and nobility of its women.

That night I slept in a bed with two of Joan's little children, Tracy and Vinard, and realised for the first time that sleeping in a bed with children gives one fanciful, child-like dreams, something I'd notice again in Fiji a few years later. Just before the sun rose, the shrieking of fifty insane roosters began rousing the world, and Joan entered the room through a curtain, slapping little Tracy awake: 'Git up! Git up!' I found Joan's abrupt wake-up technique alarming but would soon learn that a Jamaican child in the countryside is expected to do chores much of the day: making beds, washing clothes, preparing food, cleaning the house. Not wanting to appear lazy, I jumped up out of bed too, ready to help with the chores. After all, what was I doing there anyway?

The children took me to the river that morning, showed me how they washed clothes with a washboard, and laughed when I did it wrong. Later, we went to visit Miss Sylvia who lived alone in a small shack near the river. She was cooking rice outside over a fire and offered me a bowl. It was difficult to guess her age. She carried herself with such noble grace, it seemed she must have been living since the last century. Her bones were just barely hiding beneath the surface of her translucent skin and cataracts filmed over her green eyes. She wore a big straw hat and smiled the entire day as if she found the world perpetually amusing. I looked into her deeply etched face and thought of how as our bodies shrivel, we become our faces. Our bodies shrink, crumple, lose their robustness, while the face gains distinction and beauty. How sad that we don't see enough old faces in the youth-crazed West, I thought. Surely some ethical damage occurs when the faces of old people aren't on view, or their faces have been tucked, pulled and made-over, preventing wisdom from seeping through the cracks. It seems dishonest to keep hidden what becomes of our true faces. Our souls must notice what we do with them.

We live these long and magnificent lives to develop lines on our faces, much like the world itself lives to develop lines on its face, and we should never be afraid of how that face looks.

I wondered what Miss Sylvia's life had been like. I wondered what became of her husband. Was he dead or had he just left one day? Already I'd noticed the odd lack of men in the countryside. It wasn't as if there were no men, they just disappeared into the background, drinking Red Stripe beer on the curbs and watching women stroll by with baskets of laundry or the day's food on their heads. The women seemed to do all the work, took full responsibility for the children, and managed the entire household. The men seemed adolescent. Fifty per cent of Jamaican households are run by single mothers and each child in the families I saw seemed to be fathered by a different man.

That afternoon I met Shirley again, Joan's oldest brother, who lived by himself in a hut next door to Miss Sylvia. For some reason I found Shirley to be a fascinating figure, not just because of his name, or the way he dressed – yellow and white stripped pants that were a foot too short for him, a screaming bright floral shirt, and a headband that looked suspiciously like a J-cloth – but because of his innocence. 'Tell me where you live, Miss Laurie,' he said, his voice betraying a craving for worldly things. 'Tell me which way Canada is from here.'

I thought about which direction north would be. 'There, Canada is that way.' I pointed north.

Shirley knotted his forehead in puzzlement and said, 'No, that be where Aunty Charlene live, in Grange Hill town. You don't live by her.'

We stood staring at each other for what felt like a full minute.

'Well, way beyond where Aunty Charlene lives. Canada is another country, way beyond the water, in North America, north of the United States, not part of Jamaica. Jamaica is an island.'

His eyes widened to alarming proportions, his face filling to the brim with wonder at this news. Perhaps we all do this on some level, I thought, experience ourselves as the primary centre of the universe. Shirley was just taking this tendency to extremes.

'Wait here, Miss Laurie.' Shirley disappeared into his hut and soon came running back with a tattered world map taken from an old National Geographic. We unfolded it. The kids and Miss Sylvia gathered around as did some passers-by from the road. Immediately the map created bewilderment. It took a while to establish the basics of what was continent and ocean, what was Jamaica, the other Caribbean islands, and what was Africa, from where these people's ancestors had come.

Gazing at the map with my new friends, I felt as if I were seeing the multi-coloured display of countries for the first time. Suddenly it seemed miraculous that we all exist in this floating blue world on islands big and small, islands spread across this worn map that was causing such wonder and disbelief. The map seemed to communicate its magic to some degree in all of us, as if a foreign vibration were quivering through the air. Finally, Shirley shook his head. 'No, Miss Laurie. I think you fooling us.' Miss Sylvia looked at me suspiciously, and for a brief moment I thought maybe they were right in their suspicions. Theirs was a geography uncomplicated by facts, lines of latitude and tropics of cancer. I recalled how I'd once memorised all the capital cities in Africa and how this never proved useful in real life. Here, all these people knew was their small turquoise island and still their eyes shone with the things they had seen.

On Sunday nights in the Jamaican countryside, people celebrate and go to 'town', which in Little London meant walking up and down the road to watch everyone else walk up and down the road, and maybe, if people were brave enough, they'd look in the window of the ramshackle roadside bar at the crossroads to see what unspeakable events were occurring inside. Some of the men would even enter the bar, giggling, while their girlfriends and children watched from the windows. Everyone, including the children, got dressed up in their finest clothes for the big night out, and the women and girls spent hours doing each other's hair.

As we set out on the road, the children clamoured to hold my hands, some of them skipping ahead in excitement, eager to point out to me who everyone was. We walked for miles. The women don't really walk, they meander, they mosey, while the men swagger. We stopped often to admire each other's hair and clothes, to chat and laugh, until the stars came out, and we came to the crossroads bar.

Joan's cousin Melba was a wild card of whimsy, a ham, a trickster, a woman of ecstatic enthusiasm for everything she encountered, and she explained to me on the walk that she was determined to go into the bar that night for the first time in her life. In fact, she'd been planning it for months. Her sisters and cousins didn't believe she'd do it, and either cheered her on or tried to discourage her. 'Oh, no, yu cyan go in dat place! Dat place evil. You don't know what happening in there. The women bad in dat place.'

We stood outside the little bar gazing through its dusty windows like street urchins. I felt ten years old and wondered why we didn't just go inside, not that it looked very appealing. I would rather have kept walking further into the soft warm night under the stars. Still, I was curious about the bar. It was dark inside with just a few red light bulbs hanging down to illuminate the faces of the ten or twelve men inside, mostly young men, who sat on stools drinking beer and watching the empty dirt corral of a dance floor with an anticipatory air. Music blared, but evidently, nobody was ready to dance. In a corner of the bar, I noticed three women in mini skirts laughing amongst themselves.

Melba stood outside the door looking resolute, although just as she was about to open the door, I thought I saw a shadow of fear darken her face. Finally, she shouted at us, 'Mi gawn!' and walked inside.

The rest of us resumed our positions by the windows. The men inside were clearly surprised by Melba's sudden entry, calling things out to tease her, things I didn't catch. She made her way towards the line of men while the women and the children next to me either laughed uproariously or were shocked into silence. Clearly this was an unprecedented event.

We watched and waited for something to happen and finally, something did. A slow song began to play over the jukebox. The song was 'Unchained Melody' by the Righteous Brothers and I recall that it thankfully was not a reggae version of that old tune. Melba stood up and walked alone towards the dance floor. The men at the bar cheered her, as did those of us outside, but very quickly, we grew quiet. I think at first we all assumed she was trying to impress one of the boys at the bar and we speculated on who he might be. It soon became clear, however, that the boys at the bar had nothing to do with Melba's intentions that night.

Once she reached the middle of the floor, Melba stood still for a moment and I noticed that something miraculous was happening to her face: it was opening up like a flower. Then, gradually, her body began to move, slowly at first, around and around, with her arms outstretched as if reaching for something beyond what she'd find in the bar, on the road, or anywhere in the village. She twirled and swayed perfectly in time to the music, eventually throwing in inspired and unconventional versions of ballet, modern dance and even an occasional head thrust from the tango. She was ethereal, as if she'd had dancing lessons from God, creating another world not only for herself, but for all those who watched her. We stared at her with a sense of awe bordering on the religious. Melba, who people thought was merely a jokester, had become a beacon of light, hope, colour, erotic spirit and whirling brown arms. Never had I seen anyone with such a storm of beauty, like a hurricane, a volcano, a flaming comet.

And then, as soon as it had started, it was over and the jukebox began playing a reggae version of a Phil Collins song. Melba came back outside. She didn't say anything and neither did we. We all walked back along the road, a road that now looked strangely altered. I'm not sure if anyone else felt this way, but to me it felt as if we were walking through a different world, a world that was from some golden age of human happiness, attained sometimes by children, but rarely by adults, as if the world was resplendent with promise and hidden mystery, as if it were just beginning. I suddenly felt as if my own life was just beginning and I'd just learned everything I needed to know.

I had to leave Little London soon after that because I burned my leg. Joan's brother Graham had taken me on his motorbike through Cockpit Country, a succession of wild wooded hills stretching mile after uninhabited mile where we passed mango and lime trees and birds exploding into the air on sapphire wings. On the way back, he let me drive. On a small dirt road, Graham shouted something over my shoulder that I didn't catch, so I slowed down to hear him. Of course, as always there was the question of communication. He spoke both the local patois and English, but he didn't speak English in a style normally associated with the language, and even when I stopped the bike entirely, I still couldn't make out what he was saying. Thinking perhaps he wanted to drive again, I got off the bike. As I was doing this, I happened to put my calf directly down on the hot muffler, a muffler not covered by any sort of protective plate, and I burned my leg. Stupidly, I was wearing shorts that day. Graham told me not to worry. He immediately unscrewed the oil cap, pulled out the oil dipstick and proceeded to apply dirty hot engine oil all over my burn. 'This good fe yuh,' he said proudly. Did he think dirty engine oil had magical curative powers? I yelped in agony. The burning oil felt even worse than the burn itself. It had all happened so fast. If only I'd thought to put on aloe vera which grew all over the place, or even cold water from a nearby stream. Burning myself confirmed in Graham's mind that women shouldn't drive motorised vehicles and the last thing he said before we walked into Joan's house was, 'Remember, Miss Laurie, is yu kawz de accident.'

He was right that it had been my fault, but regardless, it also meant that the next day I had to leave and go back to Negril to get medical treatment. My leg had gotten much worse overnight. I was sad to leave Little London. I'd miss the family, especially all those sweet kids who continually made their way into the world, and I spent my last morning taking pictures of them, promising to send them copies. I hoped to return to Little London after Negril, perhaps to volunteer teach, but knowing how one place always seems to lead to the next, I couldn't be sure.

I decided to stay at a beach campground in Negril where I rented a tent for a dollar a day. I loved sleeping so close to the ocean, the sea surrounding my sleep, the pounding surf invading my dreams. On the coast, I felt engulfed by tropical rhythms and a pearly orange light. One afternoon as I was walking along the beach, I passed a man who reminded me of a young Robert De Niro: thick brown hair, a shy smirk that either meant mischievousness or intelligence or a combination of the two, and narrow questioning eyes. It occurred to me that it's unwise to compare regular people with movie stars since a regular person can't possibly live up to someone who has clever lines written for him, but I said hi to him anyway and he said hi back. We each kept walking. Then, we each turned around, as if we realised we might be passing by something that looked like fun, or casual distraction, or the question 'Who are you?' which might, later on, lead to a pina colada.

His name was Richard and he was a journalist from Philadelphia. He'd been told about his resemblance to Robert De Niro before. Ten minutes after meeting we were drinking pina coladas at the nearest beach bar and discussing variations on urban travel myths. We also discussed Jamaican politics, Jamaican male chauvinism and Jamaican food, which made us hungry.

On our long walk down the beach towards Joe's Irie Diner, I learned that Richard had recently broken up with his live-in girlfriend, and this trip was his way of trying to forget her. I kept stealing glances of Richard and the further we walked and the more he talked about his life as a journalist, the more handsome he became. He seemed so knowledgeable and worldly, while I, only just beginning to discover the world, had much to ask him. Just as he was telling me about his motorcycle trip through South America, however, we ran into Miss Monica, and because of that chance meeting, I never did find out about the rest of his motorcycle trip, or get to know Richard the way I thought I might.

Miss Monica was a very old, hunched, smiling woman with a cane and a filigree of crow's feet at her eyes. She stopped us on the beach, asked our names, then went digging into her woven basket, saying she had something that may be of interest to us. I thought she'd show us beaded necklaces, or maybe a seashell shellacked miniature pet with plastic eyes that I'd buy out of sheer guilt. But instead, from her woven basket she produced something that looked like a large piece of banana cake wrapped in wax paper. 'It's the ganja cake. I make it every morning. I eat a piece of it myself every afternoon. Only two dollars.' She thrust the dark heavy piece of cake in my hand. 'Tek it! Tek it!' Miss Monica's eyes burned into mine with a curiously fierce passion.

I wondered if this was how children felt when confronted with drug dealers – the pressure is overwhelming. 'I don't know,' I said. 'I don't like to smoke the stuff myself. How do I know how strong this is? And...'

'This just a nice dessert. Its makes you laugh, feel happy, very mild. Makes the sunset redder.'

'Well…'

'Tek it!'

I'm not sure whether it was the cane she kept stomping in the sand or the fire in her old eyes, but Miss Monica was much too good a drug pusher for me to refuse. I bought the cake and must admit the purchase seemed a lot more interesting than any shell souvenir would have been. Richard declined, explaining those days had been over for him since one night years earlier when he'd smoked hashish in a Moroccan bar and woken up the next day, mysteriously, in Algeria.

We continued on to the beachside restaurant where Richard ordered lobster, and I decided that instead of eating dinner, I'd eat my ganja cake.

Only half an hour after eating the innocent-looking dessert, the strangest feeling began to creep over me, literally, as if something were crawling up the back of my head, an electrical surge of power, tingling at first, and then much stronger. The surges persisted as Richard was telling me a story of travelling through a desert in Africa. Suddenly I broke out laughing even though the story wasn't funny. It was his moving mouth that was so hysterical, the fact that words were pouring out of his mouth. I looked down at the sand and noticed a crab scurrying by at a furious pace. The crab seemed to be running sideways yet going forwards and I knew then for certainty that these remarkable alien creatures had to have landed here from another planet, just like the spores of mushrooms. Loudly enough for all those at the restaurant to hear, I pointed at the crab and shouted, 'Alien! They're all aliens!' I looked at the giant tree beside our table and nearly keeled over when I realised the tree had an actual soul that I was seeing. It wasn't just a tree, but a living, breathing, thinking, feeling creature who was fully aware I'd just discovered this and was trying to tell me something. 'What? What?' I asked the tree. I could see its shimmering aura. I looked at Richard's lobster and was appalled that those animals had been swimming just moments before, truly alarmed that they were going into Richard's mouth which was also pouring out words, although by then, Richard wasn't talking so much as gaping at me in horror.

I couldn't stay seated and felt compelled to walk along the shoreline. It seemed to take forever to get there, as if I were on a treadmill, even though the ocean was less than forty feet away. Richard followed closely behind me. Suddenly, patterns began popping out at me: the pattern on the upper edges of my mother's cat eye glasses that she wore when I was a baby, followed by the exact design on what must have been my baby spoon. All those swirls on the spoon and on my mother's glasses I must have studied intently before the age of one. They'd been imprinted on my brain and were now resurfacing with disturbing persistence. I could almost reach out and touch them, and I couldn't make them go away.

Walking on the sand, I was overcome with the feeling that there is no such thing as linear time, that everything is the perpetual present, everything existing at once in a single flash of intensity. My thoughts were jumping from frame to frame, thought to thought, with no memory of how I'd arrived at each moment. The thoughts were flying far too fast to hold on to, to process. Words were wholly inadequate. In fact, I wasn't sure if I was forming sentences at all, although I had a sense I was having a conversation with Richard.

I arrived at the edge of the ocean with its shimmering green surface, the sea lapping gently under the moon. The moonlight sparkling on the water was the most real thing I'd ever seen, fragile and pulsing with life, and I was flabbergasted it had travelled all this distance through the atmosphere to shine on my skin. 'I'm not separated from the otherness of things,' I realised with elation, although whether I said that out loud or not, I didn't know. All I knew was I was getting a secret peek into another world that had been here all along. I kept thinking that this was like Plato's allegory about the people living in the cave, the people who believed the shadows on the cave walls were the reality because they couldn't see the real life that was making the shadows. In the cave they were chained to their limited view of their world, not realising there was something beyond outside the cave. On this Jamaican beach, I realised, I was getting out of the cave, no longer seeing the shadows but what makes the shadows, the reality behind everything.

I also realised Plato must have been on drugs to have thought that up.

Staring at the ocean I felt overwhelmed by ancient memories of a universe forgotten for eons. The moon and stars were bursting out of the sky, thoughts were flaming through the atmosphere, and the wind, alive and amused, was breathing sea salt into my lungs. Everything was familiar, yet everything was new. I felt all the light of the entire galaxy beam down on me, and I reflected that light back until I was glowing like a human-shaped star.

I was as high as a kite.

For a while, I was visiting my childhood, lost after so many years, where the touch of water was as electrifying as it was when I was four. I continued to look out at the sea for what could have been either five minutes or an hour, and then gradually, something truly frightening began to happen: I felt as if I were entering the throbbing heart of the earth itself, deeper and deeper into the soft and flaming core of the planet. The moment seemed to take up my whole life.

I'd now plunged into much too broad a spectrum of reality and I'd had no idea it was that immense. I wanted out. The reality became overwhelming, all powerful, and I longed to get back to everyday life, back to the everyday surface of the earth where so little reality is allowed. Later, I read that Aldous Huxley had the same experience on his famous mescalin trip: 'Anything rather than the burning brightness of unmitigated Reality – anything!'

I walked further along the beach, trying to grasp each thought, but the thoughts were whizzing through me at lightning speed. Did Miss Monica really say she ate this stuff every day? She had to be 83. I passed a reggae show at a beach bar and although normally I would have ventured over there, at that point, the idea seemed absurd. Richard kept asking me questions: Are you disconnected from your body? Do you want some iced tea? Do I still look like Robert De Niro? A woman in her forties, Swedish perhaps, approached and began spraying me with a storm of words. She spokc at some length, the words growing harsher and more guttural. I couldn't comprehend a thing she said. What she was doing or saying was a complete mystery, even with my grossly heightened perceptual advantage. I stared at her for several moments, trying to be normal, but was too high to make it work.

I walked on. I wanted water. Never had I been so thirsty. I came to an almond tree and threw myself under it while

Richard went off to find me a drink. Looking up through the branches of the tree I was absorbed in its inner workings, its shining leaves, twisting limbs, and multitude of textures. Until that night I'd never really *seen* a tree before, probably not since I was one or two, too young to be able to label it a tree. Now, like an amazed baby, I was back in the world of pure perception, where things aren't subordinated to a concept: that's a tree, that's a house, that's a person. I was seeing, as Aldous Huxley described, 'the miracle, moment by moment, of naked existence'.

All I could manage was to sit very still. Even looking down at the sand for too long was dangerous as I became lost in every extraordinary grain. Then, from behind me, two young Jamaican boys approached, asking if I'd like to buy peanuts. I said no thank you, but after that, more peanut boys appeared, and then more, every few minutes, an occurrence I found deeply unsettling. I kept whipping my head around to look for them and more kept coming. 'Peanuts! Peanuts!' they called, their voices alternately clanging in my ears, then fading with the sound of the surf as they continued down the beach. I felt very afraid. I've glimpsed into the abyss, I thought, and it's full of little boys selling peanuts.

Finally, Richard returned with a large bottle of water which I devoured.

'What's happening to you?' he kept asking.

'Too many thoughts, too many thoughts. Sorry about all this.'

He tried to tell a story but I couldn't make sense of it. Finally, when he realised his story wasn't being absorbed, he stopped and said, 'There are more planets in the universe than grains of sand on earth.' The enormity of this practically shut down my mind.

After a while, I began to run along the beach and eventually found the campground, where I fell into my tent. Staring up towards the sky, I began to drift backward in time, back three years to my twenty-year-old self, then back to my seventeen-year-old self, and further back, to every year preceding that until I was very young. I recalled with exact precision how I looked, felt, and what I thought about at all those ages, even what my clothes looked like, my various haircuts throughout the years, who all my friends had been. All of our selves remain hidden inside us as we age, I discovered with surprise. And then, I felt as if I were going back even further, beyond this life, and into the womb itself, which felt very much like the centre of the earth where I'd been earlier that night. Suddenly, I came to an explosion of flaming brilliant colour and blinding light like the sun itself – the point of conception perhaps? Should I ask my mother about this? Jesus. At that point I thought surely I was dying, never to return, and must have fallen into a deep sleep. I dreamt of my mother reading our hometown newspaper with an article and a picture on the front cover about a girl who'd gone to Jamaica and died of a marijuana overdose administered by an octogenarian with a cane.

The girl in the picture looked happy, though, as if she'd had a pleasant vacation.

I was amazed to open my eyes the next day, amazed to be alive. I hadn't died after all, and was incredibly pleased about this. I stumbled out of my tent, groggy and elated, and went searching for as much pineapple-coconut juice as I could acquire. At the market I ran into one of the local Rastafarians with one of the old-fashioned English names – Winston or Emerson or Winchester – and he told me he'd heard I'd met Miss Monica and asked me how my night had been. I tried to describe some of my night but didn't know where to begin. He interrupted. 'God gave us the sacred plant so we can see more of the world. The sacred plant allows humans, trees and animals to communicate. It's our translator.' I understood what he meant. If he'd told me this the day before, I would have thought him the world's biggest flake. The thought occurred to me that perhaps now, after my enlightening night, I'd be considered a little out there myself.

After finding my pineapple-coconut juice and sitting down on the sand, a friendly, middle-aged couple from Ohio came by. The woman stopped and looked down at me. 'Oh, we remember you from last night, dear. You were the girl who spent fifteen minutes telling us about the virtues of the colour green.'

I had no memory of that discussion, or those people, whatsoever.

I thought I should leave Jamaica as soon as possible after that. My leg was badly infected and I was worried about gangrene, and besides, I'd seen enough of the place, and in fact, enough of the entire universe, to last me the rest of my life. It was time to leave the fabled little island that would from now on, for me, glow with a kind of supercharged emerald and luminous light that might be difficult to diffuse. I needed a paler, winter light, and perhaps, a sudden rush of cold air. Most importantly, I had to tell my sister about all she had missed.

Chapter 12

My sister and I have two different versions of that Jamaica trip: she saw it as her dangerous brush with the Third World, her near-death experience, her insight into how reckless her little sister is, while I saw it as the trip that contained the trip of a lifetime. Since that January night on the Jamaican beach all those years ago, I've never looked at the world in the same way, always knowing somewhere at the very back of my mind that everyday reality is just a drop in the ocean of all there is, and if I really want to *see* more of my world, I have to hit a stop button, go into slow motion, and start looking around. Although it's always astonishing what I find that way, it's never quite the same as under the influence of those hallucinogenic plants. I do believe that Rastafarian man was right when he said those plants are here for a purpose.

Other than a wild drug trip, my Jamaica vacation was another of my youthful epic journeys where I found myself in direct contact with human happiness, like that night walking back along the road after Melba had danced in the bar. I was good at finding that back then. Is it just easier to find in your twenties?

I'm hoping to find it again in California.

I saw the world through a child's eyes after eating that ganja cake but, strangely, this is also the way I often see the world while travelling, just not to that extreme. When you travel your senses are fully open like a child's, especially when everything you come across is brand new, demanding all your focused attention. Time slows down, stretches, as everything takes on an added clarity, a depth, with colours brighter and landscapes more vivid. This is how things seemed to me that night in Jamaica, but many times I've felt something close to this unaided by hallucinogens: in the desert of Morocco; in the Sumatran jungle, floating over the coral reef in Fiji, times where I was fully immersed in a single moment, where the whole universe seemed to be contained in a single place, and I was taking it all in. These moments have seemed timeless, richer and more vibrant than routine moments in daily life, and always contain a contented knowledge that life is sublime. They've also stirred something inside me that seems oddly familiar, something I must have felt a long time ago. I'm just not sure when.

I'm travelling at this moment so should be taking it all in, these new surroundings, but this is a little difficult to do driving through the suburbs. Actually, as I drive around Fort Collins on the way to my sister's place, I can't help thinking of the future, of California. I wonder if my love of California is like a drug-induced vision. Will I wake up one morning after a few years of living there and think that the greens aren't so green any more, or observe that I no longer hear the ocean's roar? Will I think, isn't this just another place like the last place? This place just has a different crazy landlady downstairs, or that's just different scenery out the window. How much of my California dreaming is similar to that rush of a new love when we don't initially see the reality of a person or a place? Once we get used to something, it becomes ordinary, perhaps like a euphoric drug wearing off.

I've always been a sucker for a new place, something other than normal, but I can't helping noticing something many people find obvious, but seems to be taking me a lifetime to figure out: somewhere else is always more beautiful, or at least, seems that way. Whenever I move to a different place, in the beginning I'm always bowled over with its newness and physical beauty, and when people have come to visit from somewhere else, they always comment on how lovely that place is, how green and lush, with such deep snow, or big trees, or such clean air. But that's because that place is new to them. Where they live seems lovely and enviable to me (unless they happen to live in, say, Detroit). After a while, the shine always wears off what was once 'someplace new' and becomes something different: it becomes home. But since home is what I'm looking for – it is, I believe, what everyone's looking for – perhaps once we've finally found it, we have to look for the shine in the everyday. It has to be there; it will just take more looking.

I've finally found my sister's home, and it's a gigantic one overlooking a golf course in a gated community outside Fort Collins. Since I'm early and my sister isn't home from work yet, I park the car on the pristine white driveway, sit on her front steps, and return to thoughts of her in Jamaica, how much she hated the place. It's not as if she doesn't like travelling. She travels a lot, just in a more conventional manner. For instance, she lives in Colorado and has come home many times over the years to visit us in Ontario, yet she has always flown, has never even once driven over the land separating her new home in Colorado from her hometown in Ontario, has no idea how the land gradually changes as you go west, how it becomes drier, loses its green, its lushness, how it flattens from rolling hills to wide open spaces of endless golden plains and colossal skies, then rises again. I find this incredible. She has never taken this trip I'm taking now, this trip that all those pioneers took, even though she has lived out here for fifteen years. She has never crossed the Mississippi by land. She has never seen the Badlands. Everyone who goes to the Rockies should see the Badlands by moonlight, to get a taste for what's to come – the real mountains – further west.

I think she developed her distaste for road trips on those camping trips we took in our Ford Falcon. She was so embarrassed by that rusty old station wagon that whenever she was in the car being driven around Guelph and passed someone she knew, she'd duck down so nobody would see her. She always liked the character played by Eva Gabor in *Green Acres* who flung her furs around, wore diamonds and wanted to be a jet-setter. On our camping trips, my sister refused to enter the outhouses, saying she preferred to develop her bladder muscles.

Those camping trips, though, were the only times I remember my sister and I actually getting along, maybe because our regular friends weren't around. In Vermont, she once pulled down a tree branch containing a bee hive while I stood right beside her. When the branch flung back up, an angry line of bees flew out like storm troopers, chasing us as we ran screaming into the car. I got bitten on my knees and she on her lip which swelled like a balloon. When she saw how miserable I was, she seemed kind of sorry and gave me her frozen orange baseball sherbet for the swelling. Another time, in Prince Edward Island, we tramped through the campground field and found a candy store. We only had a dime and she wanted to buy sweet tarts and I wanted to buy a candy necklace, so she said we should flip for it: 'Heads I win; tails you lose,' she said. I agreed – I was only six – and she let me win anyway and buy the candy necklace even though I had no chance. I wonder if she remembers that. I wonder who she really is.

This is the first time I've been to my sister's new house. I'd already heard it's palatial, but I had no idea the house would be so enormous. The house is a Tudor design made of stucco, and actually looks very similar to most of the other giant houses on the street. It's just Linda and her husband Steve living here – they have no children, although Linda said they have two indoor cats.

Even though nobody's home, I'd love to go inside. When I open the screen door, I find a friendly note and way to find the key. Once inside, I'm immediately immersed in fabulously cold air and the soothing sounds of a fountain by the door. I have a lot of fun exploring the three-storey house, room after room, walk-in closet after walk-in closet, even the three-door garage – one of the doors, the small one, for a golf cart.

Upstairs on the top floor, I find a room full of exercise equipment, and many extra rooms full of stuff – clothes, Barbie dolls still in packages, skis, photo albums, tape decks, tennis racquets, videos, Christmas decorations. The basement feels like another house. At the far end is a second kitchen, and there's a giant living space with a large screen television, DVD player, a computer, stereo equipment, plush couches, a dart board and book shelves. There's also a fourth bathroom, an extra bedroom, and a room that seems to be just for the cats. I could get lost in the basement alone.

When she returns home, Linda is shocked that I'm driving such a derelict car and urges me to fly to California instead. Although the plan makes some sense, it seems too inconvenient and expensive, and besides, I've already made it this far and feel fixated on making it to the end, to the California shore, with Marcia.

For some reason when I'm with my sister, I always feel more Canadian than I do in regular life, perhaps because she seems so incredibly American, especially with her new accent – an accent even stronger than Steve's, even though Steve grew up in Chicago and she grew up in Canada. At dinner, we argue about gun control and public schools.

This arguing feels so familiar, going back years to when we were kids, although back then we didn't just argue; we got into terrible fights. Since she was four years older, she always scared me, and sometimes I still feel a little nervous in her presence. A remnant of being six, I suppose. I was always trying to escape from her, hide in the bushes, flee to the woods, run up to the field to play with friends, sleep in the backyard. Her domain was inside the house, so mine became the outdoors, which soon began to feel like home to me, peaceful and safe. All these years later, here I am still seeking the outdoors, still sleeping outside and, in a way, still fleeing. She's still in a house, now a very large one. A large house and material things have always been important to her. I try to recall how our differences began, what we fought about exactly. What do any kids fight about? I'm sure I teased her about things as much as she bullied me. I wonder if we'll always be at odds like this. Linda interjects my thoughts by telling us that a staggering forty per cent of Americans don't believe in evolution.

'What? Who are these Americans? Why don't I meet them?'

'We don't really meet them either,' says Steve, 'but they must be around. They're just not the kind we end up getting to know.'

'They're not even teaching evolution in some states any more,' says Linda. Actually, I don't remember learning about evolution in Caaynada.'

'Of course we learned about evolution in Caaaynada! All those diagrams of human-like primates gradually walking straighter, using tools, losing body hair until they finally turned into homo sapiens. We studied that year after year, in grade school, in high school biology!' How can she not remember? How can she not remember her own childhood? 'You just forget. You seem to have forgotten a lot of things.'

'Well, I remember those horrible boys being mean to me when we first moved to Guelph. Those teachers didn't do anything to stop them.'

I suddenly see Linda in a different light. That must have been really hard on her, to have had to move from a place she liked to come to a place where she was bullied. It seems to have affected her whole life. She even moved back to the U.S. because of it, because Canada never felt like her home. I shouldn't be so impatient with her. When I was a kid, she was so much bigger than I was, and all the bullying she got from those boys she took out on me. But now she's not a bully any more at all. She's a nice person. I finally see that. She's a nice person who was bullied as a kid, and even though our politics and values are completely different – I actually suspect she votes Republican – her intentions are good. She's honest and kind, the virtues that really matter.

After dinner, when we're downstairs watching TV, I think about those forty per cent of Americans who don't believe in evolution and wonder if I moved to this country, would I have arguments with people about Adam and Eve? I've never come across people with these beliefs in California, or when I lived in Boulder, but I'm sure they exist in all parts of the U.S. I guess it must be like Steve said; they're just not the kind of people you end up getting to know.

That night, they put me in the guestroom downstairs where it's so cold from the air conditioning that I actually have to open the window to let in a warm breeze, completely forgetting about the expensive indoor cats which have never been outside and have been trying to get there for years. The next morning, both the cats are missing. Linda has left for work and I confess to Steve what I've done. We search the golf course, making poor Steve late for work. Two hours later, we find the cats having the time of their lives, running, chasing and basking in the sun. They don't seem too pleased to see us, although it's always hard to tell with cats.

I decide to leave after a short visit because I'm increasingly anxious to get to California, and I also don't want to get into any more arguments. As I walk outside, the maid arrives in a new Buick. I think that says a lot: my sister's maid drives a Buick. When I back out of the driveway, I notice Marcia has left a small oil stain on the previously spotless driveway. I feel like the guest from hell. I phone my sister from a mechanic shop and we have a laugh about the cats, although at first she thinks I set her cats free on purpose, trying to make a statement. Although she and I live in different worlds, we can always find something to laugh about, which is probably the best thing siblings can do.

At the mechanic shop where I get the new tail light, the owner, a long bearded man with thick glasses and a weirdly high-pitched voice, looks down at me while I'm reading a map in my car. Noticing some freckles on my legs, he says, 'So do your boyfriends connect the dots?'

I look up from my map. 'What's that?'

'Because it would be fun to do that.'

I gape at the man for a few seconds, then say, 'Do your girlfriends run away screaming?' After my tail light is installed I don't bother asking him for advice on Marcia. I don't want him touching my car.

The narrow road I take west from Fort Collins heads directly into the mountains and is full of ruts, causing Marcia to rattle and make occasional thumping noises. I'm still crawling along at a jogger's speed, especially uphill. Soon, I'm driving through mountain meadows on winding back roads with views of snowy peaks, wild alpine flowers, herds of grazing elk and forests of ponderosa pine, aspen and fir. Mountains are everywhere, the road winding through them, twisting along their bases, following their swift cold streams. The mountains are massive, their crests of snow splicing clear into the cloudless dome of blue sky, making it dark cobalt. Whenever I'm in the West, I always wish I could come along in the night and steal just two or three of these overlooked mountains and put them where I come from, where they'd be an overwhelming source of inspiration and activity for people accustomed to flat land. Who would notice a few missing mountains out here where there must be ten thousand of them?

The American West of the past used to be a national hobby, in that it was a place to visit but not to inhabit, a land seen as backwards and crude. Now, not only do people dream of living in the West, they're moving here in record numbers, they're giving it its own cuisine, they're decorating with it. The West is nature in wild extravagance, completely different in feel from the rolling countryside and forests of the tamed East. The sheer grandeur of the West is what takes people by surprise. Wallace Stegner wrote that scale is the first and easiest of the West's lessons, while colours and forms are harder. I've travelled all over the West, in all the states, on countless back roads, and still have only seen a small fraction of it. As I drive today I fall in love with the West all over again, with the smouldering purple reds of ancient rock, the lost mesas, the cliffs and cloudbursts roaring down unnamed canyons, the brilliant light of the high, dry mountain air, with the pure hopefulness of the West, its infinite and aching vacancy of pure space. One can drive for hours with no sign of human life, the scale of time forgotten. I could be passing through the world as it existed millions of years ago, through a geological time before humans were even an idea, a thought on the wind, before the far-fetched incident of animal life began.

I pull over several times to hike along streams and trails or up slopes of pine and juniper, craving with all my being to keep going upwards. At dusk I find a place to set up my tent in a grove of cottonwoods beside a mountain stream. It always takes me a while to adjust to the fact that the dryness of the West prevents the onslaught of mosquitoes, so it's actually possible to sleep outside without a meshed screen between you and the world. In the dewy East, no sane person could sleep outside without a tent unless it's winter, early spring, or late fall; in other words, when it's too cold for camping. In the summer, the black flies and mosquitoes are always violently angry at you, as if you've slighted them in some way.

I yank my sleeping bag out of the tent and sleep on a ground sheet. Soon, the singing of ten thousand crickets enlivens the night and all is dark except for the stars which are like cut glass and falling down just out of reach of my fingertips. Somewhere nearby, an owl calls.

A certain ecstatic state of mind always grips me when I sleep outside in a place like this, when the sky is ablaze with the mystery of shimmering worlds, mine and an infinity of others. I take a deep breath from this glorious star-laden Western night, inhaling faith in my future, exalted in the timeless arrangement of the elements, and I know that this is the way my life should be.

Something loud crashes through the middle of the night, something next to me in the bushes. I'm in such a deep sleep that I try to convince myself I'm dreaming, but I know I'm not. I force myself awake and scramble into the back of Marcia with my sleeping bag, hunker down to spy on what might be out there, but it's too dark to see anything.

In the morning I look for bear prints, mountain lion prints, something ferocious. All I find are the scraggly claw prints of a raccoon. At least he didn't get at my almond butter, I think with satisfaction. I begin another day's slow drive meandering through alpine meadows as the morning breeze slips off the Rockies and butter-coloured sunlight fills me with something that feels like promise.

In the mid-afternoon I reach Steamboat Springs, a ski resort town, and pay to swim in an outdoor pool of boiling sulfur springs. What I'm really excited about is the giant waterslide next to the pool which I've been anticipating since I saw it advertised on a road sign hours ago. I wait in line and slide down, giddy with excitement at my new life here in the West. I keep on sliding until the place closes, and I protest with the other people when they make us stop: just one more time! we shout. The other people are all under twelve. In fact, I'm the only person on the waterslide who wasn't driven here by their parents.

I spend another night camped in the mountains and think about how I'd love to stay longer in Colorado, to see more of this land that vibrates with these rich reds and purples, to walk longer and higher through the lonely blue slopes and evergreens. I've often thought how refreshing it is to be completely removed from the trappings and enticements of modern culture – advertising, TV, movies, stores, newspapers, magazines, fast food, all the modern conveniences. It can clear your mind and set your spirit free. But I don't have to be on the other side of the world to do this, in places like Indonesia or Fiji. I can do it right here in the Colorado mountains.

I know the American West is greatly romanticised. So much of it is being paved over and lit up. Antigovernment extremists hide out in remote cabins, hunters kill wildlife for sport, and gated communities separate the rich from the rest of us. Yet in parts of the West you still can't pick up a single radio station. Sometimes, whole stretches of country are straight out of a Maxfield Parish painting, pulsating under an immensity of sapphire sky with only the most far-off whipped cream clouds as ceiling. You feel yourself expanding towards the very roundness of that Western sky and you feel that this is where you should stay for good.

I've now left the Colorado mountains and am in Utah, driving along Route 40 towards Salt Lake City and Great Salt Lake. Gradually, the green of Colorado gave way to red rocks and now to this dry, eerie country of lavender cliffs and maroon buttes. The loneliness of this land is obvious from the map, a web of just a few roads connecting tiny towns in the vast white space. The heat has returned, and once again I have burned cheeks from the sun slashing through my windows.

I've travelled through other parts of Utah on previous trips: places with an uncanny cracked beauty, intricately carved, with cones, spires, bizarre monoliths, arches, old sea floors, petrified sand dunes, long-gone volcanoes and countless canyons that lead you deep into the past. You can find secret doors to lost worlds by following gorge after gorge, landscapes of giant red eroded stone carved by time into primeval serpentine shapes. A crazy wind sculpts the rocks and lone trees into grotesque humans, animals, space creatures, and when you're near them, you wonder if you're still on your home planet. I was once in a place south of here called Goblin Valley and hiked through Wild Horse Canyon. The trail wound and twisted its way along a dry river bed through a deep chasm that grew narrower and narrower the further I walked. Finally, the canyon was less than two feet wide yet it shot straight up hundreds of feet. All I could see above me was a slender crack of a blue afternoon. No room was left on the trail for walking so I had to straddle the narrow passageway with my feet on either side of the canyon walls. This wasn't flash flood season, when one could die in a matter of minutes in a sudden rainstorm, but I couldn't wait to get out of there. I felt as if I'd walked down into another time through an ancient ghost-ridden earth.

I pull into a town called Roosevelt and find a diner on the main street. When I order their summer special, 'Hardy

Cold Gazpacho with Cornbread and Iced Tea', my waitress is particularly talkative and friendly. Since I'm the only customer at the moment and she seems bored, she returns to my table after she's chatted with the cook and stands leaning against the booth. She's what people would politely call solid and her cheeks are many shades of pink. 'Guess my weight!' she says within seconds of introducing herself. And then, without giving me time to reply, thank God, she says, 'I've lost sixty pounds in the past two months… Guess my age… Thirty-nine!' I tell her I would have thought much younger. 'Everyone says that! I just left my second husband and my new boyfriend's Mexican – you know, brown skin and all, and there ain't nothing wrong with that. It's what's in your heart matters.' She pauses, as if contemplating this for the first time. 'You should stay around here and go to the high school dance tonight if you want to have some fun. It ain't far, just up Creek Canyon Road and around the bend… you know where that is… then you're just down the road to the high school…' As she speaks her face is softly exploding, as if she's still in high school herself, still excited about what tantalising sins and intrigues the night may hold for her. I try to imagine her in high school. Perhaps she was shy and awkward then, teased because of her weight, and has now decided to relive those days and do it right this time. At 39, she is no longer fat, but pleasantly plump and assured. When I leave, she follows me to the door, asking again if I'll go to the high school dance. I tell her I probably won't make it and she looks a little surprised. 'There'll be lots of guys there,' she tells me. 'I know most all of 'em.' Her voice rattles on as I say goodbye, as if she's terrified of the silence that will settle when I'm gone.

It's on my way out of Roosevelt that I see him. He's standing on the side of the road with his arm and thumb held straight out perpendicular to his body, smiling, with short sun-bleached hair, navy backpack at his feet, wearing a clean white T-shirt, like a guy doing an impression of the perfect hitchhiker. As soon as I see him I know I have to stop – it wouldn't be right not to after all the hitchhiking I've done – but another vehicle has just appeared out of nowhere, from behind, and is also intent, it seems, on picking him up. I take a quick look back to check out my competition and see a shiny silver van full of people, all heads and skinny arms and tanned legs sticking out, comic books and Taco Bell wrappers on the dash. They have music blaring, some sort of retriever dog, and at least two kids. I guess they could be more *fun*, I think, but who'd want to travel with a big dog pouncing everywhere? The hitchhiker looks at both of us, back and forth. Then, he walks towards me, leans down and rests his elbows on my open passenger window. 'Hey there. This never happens. I wait hours with nobody stopping and now two cars stop for me at once!'

'Yeah, that's, you know, how it goes, Murphy's Law, or something,' I say stupidly, because I'm actually shocked at how good-looking he is – most of the hitchhikers I've passed look like Charles Manson – and after all this time on my own and not talking much, I kind of forget how talking is done.

'Where are you headed?' he asks.

'Salt Lake City, then California after that, pretty far.'

'Great. I'm going to Salt Lake City.'

I'm not sure if I'm disappointed or relieved that he's not going all the way to California. 'Great! Get in!' I say, a little too enthusiastically. 'That van looks really chaotic.'

'Yeah, kind of crowded.' He waves at the people behind us as he gets in my front seat. They've all emptied out of the van and seem to be rearranging their seating, standing outside puffing up pillows, letting the dog sniff the ditch, stretching their legs.

'They're Mormons,' says the hitchhiker. 'I can tell. When you live in Utah, you can spot the Mormons. It's all

Mormons around here.' He looks over at me and then says, 'Oh, are you Mormon?'

'No! Why? Do I look it? How can you spot a Mormon?'

'They just have this very family way about them. They're too perfect or something, on the surface.' Then he adds, 'No, you don't look like one.' He flashes me a smile straight from Hollywood and winks.

'Oh, that's good, I guess.'

'Well, not fake-looking is what I mean. You look more natural. I mean, a female Mormon would be all kind of, you know, done up, and wouldn't be driving a car like this alone with all this camping stuff, all these maps all over the place.' He picks up a map and looks at it. 'Kind of looking like she comes from somewhere else. They're very, I don't know, organised, stay-at-home, churchy types, married with kids and all that.'

'Oh, all that. Well, some day I'll be more like that, not the church part, probably not the organised part, and not the all-done-up part… probably won't drive a big family van either… I like kids, though.' I don't know why I add that last part. 'So you must have grown up with Mormons if you come from Utah.'

He stretches his tanned hand out to shake mine and I notice his large deep eyes, fiercely brown and bold, betraying a spirit that would dare a thousand Mormon devils. 'Neil. You?' I tell him my name. 'I'm not from here originally,' he says. 'I've been living in Moab. Moab, Utah. I rock-climb.'

'Rock-climb! In Moab!' I tell him about my rafting trip through Utah when I lived in Colorado, how the rafting trip started in Moab.

'Yeah? I used to be a river guide down there.'

Oh my God, I think, I have a river guide in my car. A river guide. River guides are always gorgeous. I think it must be a requirement for the job. 'You don't do that any more? Whenever I've gone rafting I've always envied the river guides. It seems like a dream job.'

'Oh, I don't know. Some of the people we took down were a pain in the ass, always complaining, afraid of this and that. Not everyone, though,' he adds, remembering I'd just told him I was one of those people myself.

'So now you live in Moab and you rock-climb. Do you teach it or something?'

'Well, that's kind of why I'm going to Salt Lake City. I just left Moab. Now I'm gonna try something new.'

'Like what? Be a Mormon?'

He looks over at me and hesitates before laughing. 'Well, no, not a Mormon, but maybe go to school, get a real job, meet different kinds of people, see if I like it there. I'm not sure yet actually. I just thought I should try moving to a city for a while.'

Suddenly I have a flashback to a lonely Oregon road thirteen years ago, to the businessman who picked me up in the rain, only now *I'm* that businessman and this guy is me. He's me! He's who I was: 21 years old and not knowing what to do or where to go next. I could tell him something, give him advice. But what?

'Well, there's a lot to do in the world, lots to see,' I say. 'There are just so many choices. It was probably easier back in the old days when most people lived their whole lives out wherever they were born, in their village or on a little farm. They did what their parents and grandparents did. Only a handful would have left.'

He relaxes back into the car seat. 'I would have been one of those,' he says.

'Me too,' I say as I gaze over at him, at his young bronzed face polished by the sun and wind like a carving. We look at each other a little too long for people who just met, for total strangers. Yet he's not a stranger. I know him, at least, I think I do. 'I guess the world needs people like us,' I finally say.

'Yeah.' He laughs and unzips his knapsack. Christ, now would be the part in the movie where he pulls out the knife. But no. It's a cell phone. Maybe I don't really know him after all. He starts dialling but can't get a signal. 'I'm trying to call my friend in Salt Lake City. He should be home by now.'

'Oh, you're staying with him?'

'He doesn't know it yet. So why does the world need people like me?'

'I just mean that the world has always needed people who go out and try something new, have new ideas, break away from the status quo. That's the only way anything moves forward when you think about it. You're doing the right thing, to be travelling around like this. That's all. At the end of your life, when you look back, you'll want to know that you followed your passions and laughed enough and were good to people, that you weren't just putting in time, that you were true to yourself.' I clear my throat, not sure where I'm going with all this. Suddenly I feel silly, giving him advice that's probably obvious. Or is it obvious? I should listen to this advice myself.

'So what are you doing tonight? We could find something to do,' he says.

'Oh, really? Well, I'm just driving through,' I say, taken aback.

'I know it's not exactly a thriving nightlife in Salt Lake City, with the Mormons and all…'

'Oh, it's not that. I just don't feel like being in a big city right now, all the traffic and the roads in this heat. I want to get out fast and drive to Great Salt Lake. You know, the lake you can sit on.' He nods. I wonder why I'm saying this, other than the fact that it's true, because it could be fun to stop here for a while, have an adventure. I just don't feel like it for some reason. I'm sure I would have ten years ago. 'Have you ever wanted to live in a teepee?' I ask.

'Maybe when I was ten, why?'

'Just wondering.'

I drop him off in a suburb of Salt Lake City where his friend lives. 'Well, so long!' I say as he gets out. 'I hope you find what you're looking for!' How cliché, I think. I could have said something more memorable than that, something from a Tom Robbins book perhaps, like, 'Those who shun the whimsy of things will experience rigor mortis before death!' I should have said that. He waves and shouts out, 'You too!' in response to my parting remark. Me too? Gee, I guess I really impressed him with my sage advice. Oh well, I guess *'I hope you find what you're looking for'* is a fine thing to say to anyone, like the Hindu greeting 'Namaste' – *I bless the spirit within you*. In fact, maybe *'I hope you find what you're looking for'* is the perfect salutation for Americans, traditionally rootless people always in search of something new.

I wonder, though, do people like us, the hitchhiker and me, ever really find what we're looking for?

In Salt Lake City, where the Wasatch Mountains look like a paint-by-numbers backdrop to the entire city, I get caught in a traffic jam on my way to seeing the Mormon Tabernacle downtown. The Mormon Tabernacle is the historic dome-shaped auditorium where the Mormon Tabernacle Choir sings, and is so acoustically sensitive that a pin dropped at the pulpit can be heard clearly at the back of the hall, 170 feet away. Built in 1863, it was a marvel for its time in both engineering and acoustics. I spot the Tabernacle miles ahead jutting up incongruently next to the tall city buildings and once at its step, expect to see a white-robed choir file out and start singing. I notice people on the busy streets look unnaturally wholesome and smile more than they do in most big cities. On a searing hot smoggy day, this doesn't seem right. I have a creepy feeling I'm back in the fifties in a *Leave it to Beaver* episode, making me wonder what these Mormons are up to. In the intense heat of the day and with all the smog and traffic, I feel like getting out of the city as fast as possible.

I leave the city and drive eagerly to Great Salt Lake, a place I've never been. My dad once showed me a black and white photo of himself reading a newspaper while sitting in the salty lake, looking as if he were levitating, suspended abnormally between water and sky, and ever since then I've wanted to try reading a newspaper on top of the dead lake myself.

The parking lot near the lake is packed with cars. I change into my bathing suit in the change room of a large pavilion which displays old photos of people sitting on the water, smiling for the cameras, much like the picture of my dad. When I walk towards the lake and see it for the first time, I'm awed by its metallic surface, shimmering silver turquoise like a mirror, almost blinding in its intensity. I was expecting white sandy beaches, but surrounding the lake are mud and salt flats, and small salt loving plants. A sign warns people not to dive from any height as the dense, heavy water gives so much resistance it can cause neck injuries. The proper procedure, says the signs, is to wade into waist-deep water, take a sitting position, keep the face up, and cautiously extend the legs.

You can actually taste salt in the air. It's not exactly a refreshing swim – the salinity of the lake can be as high as 25 per cent, second only to Israel's Dead Sea – but I trudge out there anyway carrying a newspaper. All around me other tourists are taking pictures of themselves trying to sit on the water. The newspaper trick would have worked if a little kid hadn't started splashing and gotten my paper soaked. I really can feel myself sitting on the water and I'm amazed, although it's not something I'd want to do on a regular basis.

I take a shower, change back into my shorts and top, then decide to head back to the lake with my camera because I really should have a picture of myself here, just like everyone else has. A friendly elderly couple from Montana take my picture as I'm thigh-deep in the water, and afterwards, they invite me to join them at a nearby picnic table where their grandchildren are gathered, slurping lemonade and tearing apart peanut butter sandwiches. I spend the next hour or so with the family and realise how much I've been missing human contact on this trip. I even go back into the water with the kids, with my clothes on. It's over 100 degrees so I keep expecting the water to cool me down, but it actually does just the opposite. Luckily the showers are blissfully cold.

Despite the shower, I still feel as if I'm covered in a film of salt as I continue my drive west towards Nevada. For the next two hours my eyeballs are violently assaulted, burned actually, even with my sunglasses, because of the extreme white glare of salt flats lining the highway for a hundred miles.

In this heat, the Great Nevada Basin feels like geographic purgatory between the Rockies and the Sierra Nevada. Ahead of me is a road that stretches endlessly into a desert where the approaching cars look like burning balls of fire, where oil slicks shimmer and rise in the heat and then disappear as I draw nearer. The landscape is bled of all colour and seemingly, of life, although I'm sure that's not true. Early white explorers once called this land 'Digger' country because the native Indians of this area dug for roots and grubs and ate larvae and crickets to survive. It's amazing they survived in such harsh, unforgiving land. They must have been master omnivores.

As for the white pioneers on their way to California, those who'd survived the desert of Utah still had another 355 miles to walk following the Humboldt River, which begins in grass and cool rippling water and ends in the bone crusted wasteland that is now western Nevada. There, the pioneers encountered a phenomenon that most of them had never seen. The Humboldt River slowed and turned a yellow milky-green, a sure sign that it was impregnated with alkali. Their cattle that drank the water died and the people that boiled it got dysentery anyway. By this time, since they'd left in the spring, it would be August and 110 degrees in the shade, and nerves began to snap. People went mad. Something else gave out that the people who knew about it dreaded to mention, and those who didn't know, discovered too late. The river itself, foul as it was, dribbled and spread into a fetid marsh and at last, dried up under the burning sun. This seemed impossible. Never had the pioneers seen rivers that simply evaporated and left a scum.

Many of those pioneers died in this wretched desert, and it occurred to some charitable people as they staggered along that you couldn't write home to a dead person's family that he or she had died nowhere. They decided to create place names, and wherever the trail turned or there was a new vista, they marked a stick and planted it, and word got back to Edinburgh or Paris or Chicago that the son, the daughter, the wife, the fiancé, had died in Endurance, Nevada, or in Fortitude, in Hell's Kitchen, in Desolation, or in Last Gasp.

Driving through this desert in a crappy car is bad enough – and right now, Marcia has decided it's that time of day for some lurching and decelerating – but I can't imagine those poor pioneers walking across here or plodding their way with covered wagons. What incredible determination and will they must have had, holding that much faith in the Promised Land of California. I wonder what sort of dreams they had for their new home. Salman Rushdie wrote that 'The effect of mass migrations has been the creation of radically new types of human being: people who root themselves in ideas rather than places, in memories as much as in material things.' All these memories left behind on this trail leading west, thousands of them lost to the dust over the years. I wish I could pick every one of these memories up, polish them off, and hold them like precious stones. They'd have so much to tell me: Go West! Or, don't even think about it! Or, get your car fixed NOW!

As I head to California, I have my own memories to pick up also, and in this severe heat, I recall other travels when all I wanted was to be cool, perhaps because I come from a cool climate, where, for half the year, the dark hand of winter clutches the land. Perhaps this need for cool air on my skin is ingrained in me, and these hot places can never truly feel like home. The temperature right now is 102 degrees. I don't know how those pioneers stood this desert. But at least they had each other for company. At least they could chat as they stumbled or rattled along or their wagons broke down. Driving alone in a car through the U.S. is such a profoundly different way to travel than what I'm used to: backpacking through Third World countries, which, although a little difficult at times, at least allows for encounters and friendships with people of my kind. In this present state of misery, however, I do recall one trip – Sumatra, Indonesia, where I just went a year and a half ago – which was more than a little difficult. But was Sumatra really so bad? Perhaps there was some spark there I've forgotten, some small and fragile moment needing to be recaptured.

Chapter 13

Sumatra

On my trip to South-east Asia, I visited Bali, and on that luscious little island filled with spirits and sweet smelling offerings to the world beyond, I fell under the impression that Sumatra, the vast and wild Indonesian island to the west, was where I really should be, and lingering in Bali was nothing more than a hedonistic fantasy. At least this is what a German traveller named Bruno tried to tell me the evening of my twenty-eighth birthday in Ubud. I was attempting to watch *The Silence of the Lambs* on a large screen TV with some other Bali-loving travellers at an outdoor café, and Bruno kept interrupting. 'This is not real travel. This is too easy,' he shouted over the voice of Hannibal Lecter. 'This is too nice, these movies, batik clothes, all this squishy fruit, these happy Balinese people always smiling at us. Now Sumatra, that's a real place. You'd hate it there. Women can't travel alone in Sumatra. It's awful, terrible. It's nothing like this at all… You should go.'

'Can you pass my fruity drink over this way? And why would I want to go to a place like that?' I asked.

'To see it,' said Bruno. 'And to see yourself in it,' he added, as he stomped off, to the delight of everyone at the café, into the sultry Balinese night. I turned back to watch Jodie Foster run through the woods, but couldn't help thinking Bruno might be right. There I was like a typical tourist in Bali, I thought, gorging on melons and coconut all day, watching movies almost every night. Bali might be close to paradise, but it wasn't exactly challenging.

Bruno's words must have found a place to lodge and grate somewhere in the back of my mind because five years later, in the midst of my life in Guelph – teaching, writing, and having just met Andre but thinking he probably wasn't right for me – I found myself once again headed for Southeast Asia, this time with the intention of taking a boat from Singapore to wild and difficult Sumatra.

I'd heard that the island of Sumatra was a tough place for a woman to travel alone but other than that, much more rugged, remote, mountainous and ethnically diverse than other parts of Indonesia, full of unusual flora in the rainforest – including the rafflesia, the world's largest flower – and an astounding variety of rare animals: tigers, clouded leopards, wild pigs, elephants, sun bears, monkeys and orangutans.

But for the most part, this is what Sumatra was like: awful, just as Bruno said it would be. I seem to be drawn to places with too many agonies and too much passion, so different from Canada, which is clean, cold, efficient, well-mannered and lacking. In travel I often find myself looking for hardship, even danger, so that I might feel the life in me more deeply.

After 36 consecutive hours flying from Toronto to Boston to New York to Anchorage, to Seoul and, finally, to Singapore – Korean Airlines had given me a very convoluted route – I was more than a little tired, despite the melatonin pills I'd been popping. The Korean Airlines flight attendants didn't believe in hydrating their passengers. Whenever I asked for water the flight attendant would look at me as if I'd asked her to disrobe and half an hour later would return with a Dixie cup half-full of lukewarm water. If you're on a journey that spans time zones, land masses, days and nights on big and small planes, and vast oceanic distances, a glass of water doesn't seem like much to ask for.

Singapore was moist, hot and smelled like lilacs. The Westernised city-country is surprisingly green and it's true what they say about never seeing anyone spit or chew gum on the orderly clean streets for fear of being fined. It rains a lot in Singapore, averaging only six hours of sunshine a day. People like to shop in big neon stores and air-conditioned malls, eat fast food and drink outlandishly priced iced coffee, and for the most part, the whole city seems sterile and boring. Only much later, when I was in Sumatra, would Singapore seem like a dream city I couldn't wait to see again.

Indonesia is a vast chain of more than 17,000 islands and I was on my way by ferry to one of those islands, Batam, a small and dirty island of scattered fishing villages, between the Malay peninsula and Sumatra. To get to Sumatra from Singapore you can fly or take a ferry, but you can't take a ferry directly because nothing is direct in that part of the world, so I had to go via Batam. On the bumpy ferry ride I met a man from Batam who told me I could eat dinner with him, spend the night, and the next day could catch the early morning ferry for Sumatra. I was elated and told myself how much friendlier Indonesia obviously was than Singapore. Assuming I'd be staying with his family, I asked if he had a wife and children. He said he had, but we wouldn't have to meet them. 'But I'd love to meet them,' I told him.

'No. We go to hotel instead. Much better there. They have nice hotel on Batam, small but nice.' He paused for a moment when he saw my doubtful expression, then added, 'You can trust me. I'm a seaman.'

Perhaps my elation had been premature. I told him I'd find a place to stay on my own and went back to reading my book about the history and geography of Indonesia. Sumatra has over forty million people, I read, more than all of Canada's thirty million. Much of Sumatra is covered in dense forests and jungle. A pamphlet I'd found on boarding the boat said, 'In Sumatra, wild pigs are likely to charge at you with firing eyes out of the dark. Watch out for wild things!'

My night in a small hotel in Batam was not a good one. I slept fitfully, dreaming of childhood friends I hadn't seen in years, as I always do when I travel, and I dreamt that someone was knocking on my door and calling my name. The knocking got louder and the sound of my name, mispronounced and whispered, infiltrated my dreams and, finally, broke through the surface, waking me. I bolted upright into the muggy heat of the room. 'Lo-wy, Lo-wy,' whispered a man's voice. I looked around, confused, sensing chaos, a disorder of things. I looked up at the old wooden ceiling fan and thought it might fly off at any second. What was I doing in this dingy room on the other side of the world all by myself? 'Lo-wy, Lo-wy.' I tiptoed over to the door.

'Hello? What's the matter?' I asked.

'It's me. Your friend.'

I wasn't aware I'd made any friends here and suddenly I had a fleeting yet overwhelming sensation that I was lost at sea and completely alone, as if I'd left all my people behind somewhere, which, I suppose, I had. 'You mean the seaman?'

'Yes! Of course! Your friend. I want to talk to you. I want to tell you about my travels.'

'It's four in the morning! Tell me tomorrow!' He scratched the door and made a feeble whining sound. Finally he left, but only after I was forced to yell at him, and I wondered if I'd have to turn into a raging maniac to get by in this country, or at least, become more aggressive somehow. I'm not very aggressive in my normal life.

In the morning I woke up with the singular thought that I had to get to a cooler place as soon as possible and that once I arrived there, everything would be sublime. Seamen would no longer knock at my door in the night and I'd find a quiet place to rest my head and feel cool air on my skin, although not like the cool air back in Canada just then, which was well below zero. I checked in my travel book again to reassure myself about the climate of the mountain town Bukittinggi in West Sumatra where I was headed. It seemed impossible it could be cool there since it was so cruelly hot here, even at such an early hour. But Bukittinggi, a university town just south of the equator, was supposed to be 'nestled in the mountains', 3,000 feet above sea level and surrounded by volcanoes. There were to be musical taxis, horse carts, regal women walking sedately under parasols, banks of flowers and cafés. The town was also supposed to be clean. Magical Bukittinggi, cool, breezy and exotic, was my destination, my solitary focus. All manner of unpleasantness in finding it would take a back seat. Getting there would involve a boat ride to Sumatra, followed by some bus rides on notoriously bad roads, but I calculated I'd be breathing in Bukittinggi's cool mountain air by late that evening.

I stepped out into the blinding sun. It was so hot and humid you could swipe your hand through the air and end up with a palm full of water. I tried to stay in the shade and walk slowly as I headed for the ferry terminal, trying to look inconspicuous to all the men and boys staring at me and shouting out, 'What's your name? Where you from?

Where you go?' At first I answered them and even smiled but quickly had to revert to my previously learned travel mode of giving what I call the Royal Gaze which the Queen gives to everyone she passes on her royal tours: smile but give no eye contact to any individual, only a general glaze as if you're looking through them. The Royal Gaze works well on small islands in Indonesia.

Already there was a great crowd lined up on the docks waiting for the ferry, an old fishing boat so rickety I was amazed that so many of us were to travel so far in such a derelict vessel. The passengers all seemed to be Indonesian – there were certainly no other tourists – and they were all laden with enormous sacks and bundles and small children, all in a state of turmoil induced by the adventure of travel. The moment the gangplank came down a frantic rush ensued to secure a seat on the boat since the seat capacity, I assumed, was insufficient for the number of us. I soon realised, however, that the passengers were rushing to find a seat which wasn't broken. I banged my head going from the dock into the boat, which didn't seem like a good omen to start a journey, but I was happy to find a seat with a view outside, even though the seat itself was ripped and wobbly.

The boat began to fill with people. Some of the women started cooking right away on little gas stoves in preparation for the five-hour journey. Women were surrounded by children, the smallest tied to their bodies with sarongs, while the men all sat together, separated from their families, laughing and talking amongst themselves, smoking sickly-sweet-smelling clove cigarettes and filling the boat with smoke. The men also did a lot of spitting on the floor since they chewed betelnut which stained what was left of their teeth a bright scarlet visible whenever they smiled. Many of the men were holding hands. Touching in public between members of the opposite sex is strictly taboo in most Muslim countries but touching between the same sex is very common. It's not unusual to see pairs of middle-aged men or teenage boys strolling happily down the street arm in arm. This isn't sexual, just a healthy display of the basic human need for touch, but I found it interesting that they could be open and naturally healthy about one form of public display and so unnaturally repressive about another.

As we pulled away from shore, waving goodbye to the people on the dock, I took out my journal since I hadn't written anything since Singapore. As soon as I put pen to paper, the man across the aisle came over to sit next to me and watch me write. I continued writing, trying to describe the scene out the window. Soon the man's head was mere inches from my journal. I'd seen this kind of thing before. Indonesians, along with many Asians, neither share nor sympathise with the Western preoccupation of personal space. Privacy is a foreign concept. I tried to tell myself that his head, his hair, actually, which was practically falling on my lap, was no big deal. He's just curious. Perhaps he has never seen English written before. Soon two people in front of me were also scrutinising at close range the oddly shaped letters and the journal itself. Perhaps I'd known at one time, in previous travels, how much we take our own personal space for granted, but I'd forgotten how it feels to have your privacy stripped from you. In any case, I had to resign myself to the fact that from now on, nothing I did could be private. And, just so the man next to me knew how this felt, I stared deeply into his ears. Not surprisingly, he didn't seem to care.

My curious onlookers' attention waned when the overhead video began to play a slapstick movie made in Taiwan. The main character was a man who chased naked women throughout suburban neighbourhoods and got into all kinds of trouble, an Asian version of Benny Hill.

All those jiggling bare breasts and giggly women surprised me. Islamic Indonesia is strict in some places, I thought, but perhaps out at sea, anything goes.

Three hours passed. The sea was rough, the air on the boat stifling, and so many people were openly staring at me that I felt like making faces at them. I tried to sleep to escape the oppressive atmosphere but my seat was only slightly more comfortable than a plastic McDonald's chair.

The boat began to make stops at several small islands and at each one, hundreds of islanders, ragged and weather-worn people seemingly cast adrift from the world, came to line up along the frail wooden docks to stare at us. I watched the dark, intensely still faces of the people and the wide eyes of children gaping as if they'd never seen strangers before. I stared back at them in dismay, looking straight into the open jaws of their lives. One little boy in particular struck me, his face registering nothing at first until his gaze lit on me, the white face of a woman from far away, and I could sense the telescope of his attention try to focus, make sense of this alien being who was staring back at him through the boat's window. I smiled and waved but this seemed to confuse him more. The boat pulled away as we continued to stare at one another, and finally, he smiled back, a world of interstellar light created between us in an instant, only to vanish in the next.

Five hours after leaving Batam, I looked up through the hazy heat and saw Sumatra on the horizon. The land looked like a sleeping giant at first, low-lying and full of secrets, but as we drew closer I began to notice dilapidated river houses on stilts, decrepit stretches of docks, fishing boats, and beyond the docks, buses and people all massed together like one giant pulsing life form.

At the port I went in search of a bus to take me to the city of Pekanbaru where I could catch another bus to Bukittinggi. When I finally found the right bus, it was so packed full of people, I didn't dare get on, but stood outside staring at it in disbelief. The driver was squished over to the extreme edge of his seat with the side of his face pressing against the window. Surely he wasn't actually going to drive that way. He pointed to the bus beside him, which, when I investigated, also looked beyond capacity, at least three people to a seat, many of them encouraging me on even though there was no obvious place for me. Space doesn't have the same significance to much of the world as it does to protected Western limbs, and when it comes to buses in Asia, the number of given seats is irrelevant, the space adapting to the number of passengers.

I gave the driver my ticket and stood in the aisle, clinging tightly to an overhead rope as the bus roared off, spewing black smoke into the crowds. Soon, some men on the back bench began rearranging themselves and indicated for me to join them. They'd made room for me. I accepted their offer and, thankfully, sat down in the back corner beside the window where I was so cramped I had to keep my knees up against my body, the seat in front of me and its occupant's head mere inches from my face. Next to me on the hard little bench sat five small men, all smoking clove cigarettes and looking at me with intense curiosity. I nodded and smiled and tried to open the window. The heat and cigarette smoke were suffocating; the window was stuck and I assume, not meant to be opened, ever, because all the men glared at me as soon as I started touching it. This happens on buses in Asia, this inexplicable closed window phenomenon, even here on the equator at sea level where the earth is about as hot as it ever gets and a little breezc couldn't possibly hurt anyone. We drove at breakneck speed along a muddy road through dense tropical shrub, occasionally passing villages of shacks and impossibly tiny children running in rags. The man next to me fell asleep on my shoulder. I stared out the window, unable to move for the entire four-hour trip and not even wanting to because of the heat. I felt worn down already and I'd only just arrived. This was what Bruno must have been talking about, this challenge of a difficult and untamed place, this breaking point of what was bearable. Why had I come?

Pekanbaru was the ugliest city I'd ever seen, lying flat and maimed like a broken arm of humanity. At the station I waited for my Bukittinggi bus, my saviour, and was told it would leave in half an hour. I soon realised, however, that there were no timetables, no schedules. Buses simply left when they were bursting at the seams with passengers and the man who'd told me half an hour told me that only because I wanted to hear it. I went outside for some air where I was swarmed by at least fifteen children who appeared within minutes from surrounding streets. I asked them their names, got to hold a baby, and when I took their pictures they squealed whenever the camera flashed. Suddenly Sumatra didn't seem so bad after all. When my bus was finally ready, I almost hated to leave.

I usually love bus rides in developing countries, the bumpy joy of rattling along, the strangeness around every corner, the excitement of the passengers at the pure joy of living – we're off! – the cacophony of music, the occasional goat onboard, the narrow jungle roads. As I boarded, and found myself in the exact same spot as the last bus – the back corner on the bench, this time next to five teenage boys – I reminisced about my bus rides in Morocco through the Atlas Mountains where the passengers clapped and sang for the entire journey, or the bus rides in Fiji where I watched big hairy men dressed as women, or a bus ride in Malaysia where a woman next to me cooked an entire meal at her feet on a little stove, or another bus ride in Malaysia where the woman next to me vomited into her sari and held the contents there for the rest of the trip. Perhaps not all bus rides were ideal. But this Bukittinggi bus had potential because we'd be hurtling over spectacular steep mountains of tropical forest as we made our way west.

Our bus was the usual ramshackle collection of rusty metal filled with people and their various cargoes of bundles, boxes and babies. As we drove through the outskirts of the city, fumes billowing beneath us, and headed into the mountains, it became obvious that much of the road was under repair, and the unrepaired stretches were in atrocious condition, perhaps impassable in places. Stretches of the road had suffered severe demolition from heavy vehicles and wheels had left gouges, ruts and potholes. The bus had no suspension and the back of the bus, where I was, suffered the worst of this bone-jarring journey. The driver must have thought he was in a race, flying around corners on what was often just a single-lane road, his only concession to safe driving being an occasional honk of his horn. I was relieved to note, however, that despite the bumpy ride over treacherous terrain, none of the passengers nearby was vomiting, a practice Indonesians are known for on buses. To accompany the entertainment feature of being thrown around as if on an amusement park ride, a speaker directly over my head began to blare whining and nasal Eastern music at full distorted volume. Occasionally, an old Lionel Richie hit was thrown in for variety.

As the hours passed we cut a swath backwards through time into the roughest country imaginable, jungle-covered mountains, mud houses with crumbling walls clinging to cliffs, and deep steamy canyons. With every mile the trappings of the twentieth century lessened as the surroundings became wilder. On a torn piece of paper, the teenage boy next to me sketched a tiger, leaned across my lap to hold the picture up to the window, and shouted something like, 'Roar!' I laughed with him and his friends, hoping we'd catch a glimpse of a tiger lurking in the jungle beyond. I was in wild Sumatra, where gruesome traffic deaths were an hourly occurrence and where pigs charged out of the bush. Some neglected part of my brain stirred from the exhilaration of being a stranger in a faraway land and I realised this must be what I came for, to cross over to the unknown.

It grew dark as we penetrated deeper into the jungle and I felt as if I were leaving my old life further and further behind, that I was as secluded from the world as I'd ever be. We jolted over the mud road, the bus raging through the night like a big clumsy animal. As the road became rougher, so the driver's attack on it became more zealous as he charged headlong into the potholes. I'm sure I spent as much time airborne as in my seat. Next to me, the boys chain-smoked clove cigarettes, talking amongst themselves, and often watching me and giggling. They spoke a little English, and, thinking I'd try to save their young lungs and mine, I told them that in North America, it was no longer cool to smoke. They seemed to find this fact fascinating and I think actually believed me because – coolness being the reason teenagers smoke in the first place – they didn't smoke for some time after that. Later, down the road, we all jumped in fright when a loud bang fired beneath us. This could only mean that bandits were shooting at us, or, we had a flat tyre.

It took over an hour to fix the tyre. All the men got off the bus to see the flat tyre for themselves, leaving me, by this time the only female passenger, alone and finally with enough room on the bench to sleep. Eventually the men and teenagers returned, a heightened sense of gusto and camaraderie surrounding them after what I assumed was a group effort in the repair, and the bus resumed its mad course.

Hours later, we stopped at a bustling all-night market in the jungled middle of nowhere. I wondered how such commotion and frenzy could occur in this remote place at such a dark hour. Staring out the window, I felt as if I were dreaming, my surroundings as dense with strangeness as the jungle itself. I got off the bus, walked straight through the open stares of people and their curiously wide-awake children, and bought some bottled water, spiky red fruit and pistachios. Like many midnight markets it was full of people chatting and eating, wandering dogs, and enticing tropical smells, but since I had no idea how long we were stopping, I rushed back to my bus so it wouldn't leave without me. Cracking pistachios and waiting for the bus to leave, I watched people out the window as they laughed, gossiped and bargained with merchants, as children chased each other, darting around wheelbarrows. A circle of men were engaged in a heated debate, their voices rising up through the crowd, while some women looked on in pride at the antics of their rambunctious kids. I thought of how humans the world over are essentially the same, our bodies bright sparks of wilderness evolved over millions of years, wholly made to absorb and discover the earth and each other. Finally the bus driver returned and we tore off again.

At the next night market, I got off to stretch my legs for just a few minutes and had to run back when I saw my bus pulling away. I made it just in time. It was nerve-racking not speaking the language, not knowing what was going on, but I soon learned that my fellow passengers didn't always know either. The bus driver was leaving the stops on a whim. At one market, he only stopped for a minute – luckily I stayed on that time – but two of the teenage boys on the bench had gotten out and didn't make it back before we took off. The other three boys began shouting at the driver. The driver slowed down, hesitated for a moment as if he were going to relent, then changed his mind, yelled something back and stepped on it full throttle, continuing his obsessive rage into the darkness and leaving the two boys forsaken back at the stop. Perhaps he really was in a race. For me, this meant I now had considerably more room on the crowded bench and could lie down. But as I drifted off into a peaceful, if somewhat back-breaking haze, I did feel sorry for the boys left behind and wondered what they'd do.

Remarkably, two hours later, when we stopped again, the same two forsaken boys reappeared on our bus, next to me as before, and to this day, I have no idea how they caught up with us. In any case, I was impressed, even if it did mean having to sit up on the bench again, squeezed into the corner, and tired beyond comprehension.

'*We're gonna have a party, all night long. All night, all night long, all night...*' Lionel Richie sang overhead, mocking me.

We continued on into the night, forging across an island that was discouragingly large, approximately the size and shape of California, but without California's pleasant roads. A video at the front had been showing kung fu movies with no sound. When the kung fu finished, the driver's assistant, a man wearing a little suit jacket, put in a Chinese porno and turned to the enthusiastic passengers with a toothy smile. I looked around at the passengers. The unsettling awareness came over me that not only was I the only woman on board in the middle of a jungle at four in the morning, but I was a foreigner who nobody in that part of the world would notice missing, and I was, like the actress in the movie, white and friendly – although certainly not as friendly as she was. What if they wanted a real-life reenactment? Some men on the bus turned around to watch for my reaction and giggle nervously. They also giggled at every sex scene, these Muslim men who were evidently far less fundamentalist than men in other parts of the Islamic world. I considered leafing through my guidebook to see if they had any advice, tips for the foreign woman who finds herself surrounded by forty horny men in the jungle. Tell a joke? Fake an epileptic fit? I soon realised I had nothing to worry about with these shy men. The movie had lousy acting, a feeble plot and some very odd squealing scenes which didn't seem natural. This was entertainment to divert attention from the bus ride, I told myself. I looked over at the teenage boys whose eyes were glued to the small screen. They'd started smoking again.

Just as dawn's first light was stirring the rising mist, we entered the rolling, high country of the Minangkabau in West Sumatra, whose green hills and valleys are dotted with ornate, finely carved wooden houses with roofs shaped like buffalo horns. After eleven hours on the Bus of Death, Debauchery and Discomfort, we were at last arriving in Bukittinggi, my dream town, and I was too dog-tired to care.

In the taxi to town I was nearly delirious with fatigue. The driver dropped me off at a guest house but since it was just 6 a.m. I had to wait for the place to open, and sleep in the lobby. An hour later, when they told me they were full, I felt like a vagabond, trudging my weary body outside again searching for a place to sleep. Bukittinggi was waking up, this lively hill town bustling and ready for a new day, but I would have to wait and explore when my eyes were open.

Across the street, I spotted another guest house, a small white-washed building with a courtyard shaded by palm trees, and, in front, a particularly exuberant jasmine bush next to the vacancy sign. A sign below said 'Abdullah's Good Guest House'.

Abdullah was a small wiry man with a small wiry moustache, with eyes so black and tiny they seemed steeped in a dosage of the world's darkness. He tried to hide this in his smile, as if his true character could be contained in the curve of his lips and straight little teeth. I wasn't fooled. I'd met others like him, although not often.

When I arrived, he immediately hid the broom he'd been sweeping with and waved me over to one of the tables. 'Come, my friend, come, come.' He sat across from me and began to inquire, in order of some logical relevance to him I suppose, the details of my life. It felt like an interview to see if I were worthy of staying there. I was in that state of exhaustion where the world has suddenly become absurd and I recall the conversation sounding something like this:

'How big is your Canadian city?' he asked.

'So big a person would have to sleep for days if she walked across it.'

'How was your schooling?'

'I used to fall asleep in class.'

'What did they teach you about Indonesia?'

'That you're a kind, hospitable people who take people in and let them rest.'

'Are you married?'

'No. I'm too tired to get married.'

'Are the other Canadian women like you?'

'Yes, every one of us... although some are more job oriented, early risers. I like my sleep.'

'Why did you come to Bukittinggi?'

'I can't remember. Something to do with finding a cool quiet place to rest my head.'

The questions continued in agony until finally I told him it was urgent I slept or I'd collapse on the ground. He said the rooms were all full; however, one would be free in a couple of hours and until then, I could sleep in his room.

His room, like all the others, was off the courtyard, small, dark and, with the curtains closed, a little dingy. Interestingly, it was full of maps and books, even an old geography book about Canada with pictures of mountains and lakes and happy couples hiking in the Rockies, circa 1965. I fell onto his hard little bed and fell asleep within seconds, only to be woken seconds later. Abdullah had entered the room and was tiptoeing across the floor, rummaging through shelves, ruffling papers, all the while, mumbling to himself. I kept my eyes shut, thinking he'd soon leave, but then I heard his footsteps beside the head of the bed and then, no sound at all, as if he were just standing there. Finally, he bent down to whisper, 'My friend, are you sleeping well?' I should have known this wouldn't work. Too politely, I told him, yes, thank you. 'I forgot to ask you,' he continued, 'Why are you travelling alone?'

Bukittinggi in those first days was everything I'd hoped for and more. Most importantly, cool air was at last caressing my skin which rejuvenated my entire being. I wandered the town to get lost, taking in the surrounding scenery of volcanoes and mountains, the magnificent architecture of elegant high gables and soaring upswept roofs, the vibrant life on the narrow cobbled streets, the colourfully dressed women in their caftans. It was a city of conversation. Cafés were full with townsfolk, old and young, discussing, laughing and gossiping. As in most of Asia, nightlife is street life and lasts well into the morning hours. After all it took to get to Bukittinggi, I felt like staying a long time. In fact, I wondered where I'd ever find the energy to make the trip back.

Pasar Atas was a large and colourful market filled with unrecognisable fruit, intoxicating spices, stories, shouts and shrieks of children with long hair and dirty feet. The market seemed medieval with its bright tents, men in skullcaps and women in shawls, charlatans, magicians, chanting Muslim holy men, snake-oil merchants and acupuncturists. I gorged on the fried noodle dishes of *nasi gorang* and *nasi padang*, but stayed away from the dishes of fried intestines and lungs. I also stayed away from the dogs, both the kind that tried to bite my ankles and those served on platters. Sumatrans love to eat dogs, especially black dogs. For breakfast I ate a delicious local specialty, *dadiach campur*, a mixture of oats, coconut, fruit, molasses and buffalo milk yogurt. At a stall selling second-hand English books for tourists I tried to trade the best-selling novel *The English Patient*, which was also currently a hit movie. The man who ran the shop scowled and refused it, telling me only someone studying medicine would be interested in a book with that title.

One stall sold nothing but lingerie and I got caught up in a crowd of women who were examining the merchandise with extraordinary intensity. I happened to need a bra at the time and as soon as I made my interest known, the gathering of women surrounded me like a flock of gulls, merchants and shoppers alike, all waving bras in front of me, all saying, 'Try it, try it!' One woman offered me a red bra, imploring, 'Try it to match your hair!' Another swung a black lacy number in front of me. 'You like? Put it on!' Then she set it back down, suddenly blushing with embarrassment. An elderly woman tried to foist on me a shiny purple bra with a distinct push-up feature. Despite the wide range of colours, I noticed all the bras were tiny and padded, none of them right for me. The two women who ran the stall, a mother and teenaged daughter, pointed to a curtain behind them to show me their dressing room. 'Come, come,' they demanded. Somehow, I became swept up in the frenzy and followed their orders, walking towards the curtain and taking three bras with me. The mother and daughter sales team followed me inside, which I found a little odd, but not as odd as the two other women, mere shoppers, passers-by, bra-pushers, who also came into the dressing room. Inside the crowded room, all four women tried to help lift off my shirt. The teenage girl produced a measuring tape from under her caftan and began measuring my waist, rib cage and chest. The women made a lot of ooohhs and aaahhhhs as they assessed, scrutinised, giggled, and talked amongst themselves. I was poked, prodded and even pinched. More bras were brought in. Just outside the curtain stood the flock of women, shouting out questions to the insiders, with an occasional, 'You like it, Miss?' thrown in for me. Inside, the two women infiltrators were forced out as two more came in to replace them, eyes shiny with excitement at finding themselves thrust into the dark room watching a foreigner's breasts. All the bras were too small, which was understandable given the small statures of Asian women, but they insisted on trying to find me the right fit. Orders were shouted for more sizes. Finally, after strapping on me every colour, shape and style offered and squabbling over various attachments – front or back closures? – the women found a silky mocha-coloured bra which they deemed to be perfect – too beautiful, so good for you! – and even though I wasn't convinced, I bought it anyway, not being able to bear the thought of their faces if I walked away empty-handed. Besides, maybe they were right about the bra. Maybe a mocha bra was just what I needed.

I escaped down a narrow alley to shouts of, 'Now try some panties! Come back! Some bottom undergarments for you!' That's why I was wary when a woman who must have been in the audience at the bra stall called out for me to stop. I turned around and looked down at a teeny-tiny woman who barely reached my chest. She was dressed in a long green polyester caftan with a white veil over her head allowing only her face to be shown. I imagined that hiding under her veil flowed hair that might reach the ground if allowed its freedom. Her age could have been anywhere from sixteen to thirty-five. She smiled, shook my hand in a surprisingly confident manner and introduced herself with a name I couldn't catch. Keeping hold of my hand, the miniature woman began leading me through the market. I didn't mind. I enjoyed being led. It made me feel less aimless. It also meant I now had a friend, even if I'd just met her twenty seconds ago. We chatted and asked each other all the usual questions until she said, with a childlike excitement, 'Let's go meet my father!'

I wondered if her father might also be a little person, if they'd live in a tiny house with a tiny cat and diminutive furniture. I was disappointed to see that although he was quite short, he wasn't much shorter than the average Indonesian, which is still shorter than my 5 feet 7 inches – I always felt too tall there – and their house, although not large, didn't have a single miniature feature in view. The father, who spoke more English than his daughter, told me about his time in a Japanese prison camp during the war and showed me scars on his arm from his attempted escape. His daughter disappeared behind a curtain and returned with a giant plate full of the most exquisitely decorated candy I'd ever seen. The plate, weighed down from enormous pieces of gooey treats, looked as if it would topple her over. She set the plate on a table and began talking quickly, almost breathlessly. From what I gathered of her broken English, the candy was left over from a funeral and it was bad luck not to finish it as soon as possible or the dead soul, an uncle of hers, would hang around the house causing both her and her father a good deal of grief until all the candy was consumed. Apparently it was the dead person who was host of his own funeral and unfinished food was impolite. Why they couldn't have given the candy to neighbours or tossed it out, I didn't ask. Why the dead uncle would care if people liked his food or not, I didn't ask either. The candy didn't look that appetising. Other than chocolate, which I love beyond reason, most sweets aren't appealing to me in the least. 'Eat, eat!' they said in unison. Together, they pushed the plate towards me, their expressions a mixture of anticipation, thrill and dread. I tried a piece of candy and knew within seconds it was the most foul object I'd ever put in my mouth. The candy had an overpowering, vaguely familiar flavour, tasting a little like incense and a little like rotten garbage. 'It's delicious,' I lied. 'What's in it?' I noticed neither of them was eating the candy themselves. Just then, the prayer call sounded from a nearby temple and the father excused himself, asked me to please keep eating, and rushed out the door. My friend touched my arm and said in the sweetest voice imaginable that she also had to leave for a short while, although not to pray, but to do something else religious on which she didn't elaborate, and would I please stay to enjoy the candy and wait for her return. With a slam of the door, she was gone. The stack of lousy candy, dripping a dark lava-like ooze, sat staring at me, daring me to eat more of it, and I contemplated running out of there and never looking back. I'd take some candy along and chuck it into a gutter for the rats. Except, these were the first people I'd managed to befriend in what felt like weeks in this faraway country. I couldn't run away. Besides, how could I allow an ill-mannered dead uncle to terrorise these kind, little people after they'd been so welcoming to me?

I took another bite. The second piece wasn't as bad as the first. I tried pretending the candy was made of molasses instead of the nefarious toxic ingredients I feared, and found this actually worked for a while. Then the rich stickiness began to get to me so I imagined it was made of something lighter, a flowery nut butter with lots of B vitamins, nutrients I was probably lacking. I kept eating. The candy seemed to be getting better, the strong flavour now strangely pleasant. I started thinking about how Sumatra, like the candy, was growing on me. It just took time to adjust. Maybe I'd find a job teaching English in this town. Maybe I'd meet more locals. And, after I'd explored Bukittinggi more, I hoped to go on an excursion to the nearby Mentawai Islands to trek through the jungle and see people only recently emerged from stone-age isolation.

As I sat gorging on the candies, I realised I was heady with exhilaration, oddly euphoric and energised when sugar usually made me feel lousy. An hour later, when my two hosts returned, I barely looked up to greet them, so engrossed I was with the intoxicating delicacies. My new friends seemed jubilant, although a little surprised, to find me not only still there, but still eating the candies, having polished off over half of them.

When I left the little people's house soon after, I not only felt oddly drunk, but happy to have done a good deed, hopefully kicking the dead uncle out of the house for good. I looked up at the evening sky and imagined him flying off to a loftier place where domestic duties weren't on the agenda. 'Enjoy yourself out there!' I shouted into the cherry-lipped night, and with that, I ran back to my guest house.

My mind was whirling that evening as I strolled the winding streets, taking in the lively surroundings. Eventually, I encountered two Swiss women, shaken up and mad as hell at some local teenage boys who'd grabbed their breasts as they ran by them on some dark steps. I'd noticed this a couple of times in Bukittinggi, these run-by gropings – like drive-by shootings, only tamer – although the gropings hadn't yet happened to me and I felt a little left out. The Swiss women asked me to join them for dinner. We found a restaurant where some other travellers were gathered and we sat at a long table with backpackers of mixed nationalities. As I ate some delicious spicy noodles with coconut milk, revelling in the conversation around me – all of it involving horror stories of Sumatran buses – I realised I was relaxing, having fun. I hadn't realised how stressful the trip had been until I was surrounded by people with whom I could laugh about it all. An English woman, Gwen, had a similar experience to mine involving a late-night bus and a porno flick, but she said that during her movie, she pretended to be asleep and snored as unattractively as possible throughout the entire showing. Jacob from Denmark told us about his recent train trip through China where for six days and nights he'd sat on a crowded third class wooden bench, sick with a nagging illness, while around him, fellow passengers had urinated on the floor because the toilets were locked. I'd almost forgotten that one of the greatest pleasures of travelling is talking about how awful it can be. It was a wonderful night. Hours later, after we'd all become friends, made plans for the coming week, ordered more food and told more stories, Jacob and I decided to hike in the nearby Ngari Canyon the following day.

I met Jacob the next morning at Bukittinggi's famous Dutch clock tower overlooking the market square. He was tall and lanky with eyes the deepest blueberry blue, blonde hair that wisped across one brow, and northern skin that doesn't do well in tropical climates. He looked like a Nordic cross-country skier. Actually, I've never seen a Dane who couldn't be a model in a camping equipment catalogue. The strange thing about Danish people is they don't even seem to know they're good-looking. Instead of being conceited, they're friendly, intelligent, environmentally aware, riding bikes everywhere, eating fruit and nuts all day when they hike, socialising for hours without being on the way to the next thing. Like most Europeans, they also all speak several languages, making largely unilingual North Americans look bad. Most importantly, they're eminently humanitarian. During World War II, the Danish king decided to wear the yellow star of David to confuse and madden the Nazis and almost every Danish citizen, Jewish or not, followed the king's lead and wore the star also. Denmark was the only occupied country that actively resisted the Nazi regime's attempts to deport its Jewish citizens. When the Danes learned of the Nazi invasion, they organised a nationwide effort to smuggle their Jews by sea to neutral Sweden. Within a two-week period fishermen helped ferry 7,220 Danish Jews and 680 non-Jewish family members to safety across the narrow body of water separating Denmark from Sweden. The world could learn a lot from Denmark.

Jacob and I walked to the outskirts of town to the Ngari Canyon, where long-tailed monkeys were said to swing through trees. We stood at the edge and looked down into the voluptuous vegetation, branches twisting and writhing upwards from a blanket of mist far below. The canyon's sheer cliff walls took us over an hour to descend on a steep path and, all the while, Jacob told me about a trip he'd taken to the Amazon, how he'd travelled for days without seeing the sky, how the sun was nothing but a memory, an object of faith through the forest's emerald roof. He saw tumultuous trees and gigantic fronds, fluorescent insects, flowers that bloomed at night and painted birds screeching deafening proclamations. I nearly fell over at the drenching beauty he described. Or was it from his drenching beauty? I couldn't tell. In any case, I felt a little dizzy, but when a sudden squall of butterflies flew right in front of us, I awoke to the dazzling display of life in the canyon. The air that morning was much cooler than it had been lately, a dream of early summer days, a reverie of watermelons and running through sprinklers even when it's not quite hot enough. I could hardly believe we were so perilously close to the equator. We felt fresh, enveloped in the luminous light of the tropics, and we spent most of the day talking about how enlivening travelling was, how we couldn't imagine not doing it the rest of our lives. We made tentative plans to visit, in the following week, the surrounding mountain crater lakes, Maninjau and Lake Toba.

The next day I decided to return to the canyon alone so I could walk to the village of Kota Gadang, known for its silver filigree jewellery, four miles away, on the other side of the canyon. Returning seemed like a simple decision at the time, one not weighted down by any particular sense of fate or foreboding. It was to be a small excursion, a tame adventure. I never would have guessed that something so unusual, so inexplicable would happen to me in the canyon, that the course of my time in Sumatra would change, and perhaps, even I would change, subtly, but to the depths of my innermost territory.

It was much hotter than the day before, and as I walked away from my guest house and up the street, I wondered how well my straw hat would protect me from the equatorial sun. On my way down a road which led to the canyon, as I was looking at an entrance to some caves built by the Japanese during the war, a local teenager, probably sixteen or seventeen, asked where I was going. When I told him, his face lit up and he said was also going to the village of Kota Gadang. I didn't really believe him but since he seemed entirely harmless I took him up on his offer of showing me some points of interest on the way. He said the village was a short walk, half an hour or so, which I knew from being in the canyon the day before, and from my guide book, wasn't right at all, but I'd grown accustomed to the game of exaggeration and so didn't mind or care that our walk would be longer than he'd indicated. His name was Cloudy, which I thought was ironic since his bright, hopeful face, the colour of soft tan suede, seemed to be permanently set in sunlight, a face, it seemed, with little history underneath it yet.

After we'd talked about our lives, after he'd told me about his schooling and his sisters and his belief in spirits, Cloudy and I, once on the canyon floor, grew silent, wandering along together, wading through the high grasses side by side. At one point, he ran down a side trail through some dense bushes and returned carrying two enormous beetles he seemed to know would be there. The beetles were half as large as his hand, things of uncanny beauty, metallic and unearthly, and after we'd gazed at them enough, he ran back down the path to return them. Later, we took another side trail and came to a dazzling hidden waterfall. Cloudy stripped down to his underwear and waded through a series of green, lily-padded pools until he reached the torrents of cooling water. He hesitated for a moment before stepping beneath them, then slowly raised his arms and face upwards towards the source, as if receiving the falling water like a blessing. He shouted something I didn't understand, something for the water gods perhaps, and then he began to laugh and jump up and down as he disappeared into the misty cascades. The sun was becoming a tropical maniac, orange and flaming hot, and I was tempted to strip off my clothes and let the cold water pelt down on me also, but fearing this might break some traditional cultural code, I decided against it. Besides, I wasn't wearing any underwear. Eventually, Cloudy came back to dry off and as we continued on towards the village, we began to laugh and joke and contemplate the unusual ways of each other's lives. We saw monkeys swinging in trees and he told me that monkeys are really the spirits of tricksters in disguise. He enlightened me on some myths of the indigenous orangutan, which means 'person of the forest', of how orangutans carry off pretty girls and how they really can speak but refuse since they don't want to be made to work. Cloudy also talked of ghosts hidden under rocks. I loved his stories and as time passed I felt I could have no better companion.

A couple of hours later, after walking through rice paddies and swarms of dragonflies, after spotting flying foxes and searching for some elusive giant bats supposedly with wing spans of three feet, we arrived at some steep steps which led to the village of Kota Gadang. We'd run out of water by then and were desperately thirsty. In a small café, I bought us some lunch, bottled water and fruit. Afterwards, we visited a little jewellery stall set back in the trees where I bought a silver ring for myself which would tarnish in two days and break in four, and some bracelets for friends. With our thirst quenched, we left the village, happily making plans for an excursion to the equator on Cloudy's motorcycle some day soon.

It was on our way back, after we'd been walking an hour or so, that Cloudy suddenly stopped in his tracks ahead of me and froze. 'Listen,' he said. 'Hear that?' I didn't hear anything other than the squawking of birds we'd been hearing all along. 'The spirits aren't good here,' he announced. 'I think there's a tiger spirit close by.'

'What? A tiger or a tiger spirit?'

'Tiger spirit.'

'Personally, I'm more afraid of an actual tiger than a spirit.'

'No, a tiger spirit is much worse.'

'Why?'

'It never leaves you. We have to get out of here.' We picked up our pace and very soon were running. My sandals kept getting caught in the vegetation and I hated running through the steaming heat. Besides, I thought it was silly to run away from a spirit. I told Cloudy he should go ahead and I'd catch up with him at the waterfall. He agreed and raced into the distance at an alarming speed. Once on my own, I strolled contentedly along the jungle trail, looking up occasionally to watch the rainbow of birds making a racket in the trees. They did seem a little agitated, louder than they'd been before. When I left the trees and came out into the open rice paddy, the mid-afternoon heat felt unbearable with the brazen sun scorching cruelly down on my scalp. It was then I realised I'd left my hat behind in the village. Since it was too late to go back for it, I trudged on, my head beginning to swim with liquid heaviness and the cloying scent of jungle flowers and moist vegetation. I needed to walk through winter for five minutes, its chilling calm, its rational firmness which would never allow tiger spirits to enter its frigid domain. Giant bats whooshed just above my head, scaring the hell out of me. I walked faster.

Time passed. I lost track of it and found myself back in the trees, having reached a point that looked familiar and I realised I'd been there before, only not that long ago. Somehow I'd circled back and was once again at the spot where Cloudy had said he'd heard the tiger spirit, whatever that was. I must have gotten turned around. The birds were louder than ever. My head was dizzy with caustic sun and confusion and I was thirsty again. I tried to quell a rising panic in my chest. I looked down at the trail which had seemed so helpful before and was now so foreign, a traitor. How could it have led me back here? I started to shout out Cloudy's name but the name got stuck in my throat, suddenly afraid to escape into a jungle of spirits. The jungle was all consuming, dark and dense, suffocating the earth in all directions, hanging with great tangles of fronds all massed together, so different from Canadian woods which come on gradually, with perhaps a meadow to lead you in gently. Here I was stunned by the raw power of giant black trees. Suddenly I missed my home, my friends, my family, and I thought, *No one knows where I am right now*. Few could even guess.

Gradually, I started to feel as if I were losing myself, wandering through this strange tropical land where not even the heavy air and its smells had anything in common with any air I'd ever known, wading through a dream trying to find an ending, trying to get away from something, but what? All I could do was keep walking further and further through the canyon into the dream. I eventually arrived back at the rice paddy which looked different now, glowing orange, with crickets strumming at a deafening roar. The sun was thankfully sinking towards the horizon but I began to worry about not arriving in town before night fell. I wondered if Cloudy would be at the waterfall and I wondered if he'd been right about the spirits in that place after all. I could hardly see the trail now in the sudden darkness of the tropics where twilight is a faraway notion. I don't trust the trail anyway, I said aloud as I quickened my steps. I don't trust myself down here. How stupid to lose my hat, to run out of water, to get turned around. I don't know this terrain, I thought. Anything could jump out at me. I'm not so brave any more. I've lost my braveness. The darkness was becoming deep and fierce, pouring into the canyon like spilled black ink. Suddenly there was a numbing sensation on the top of my head and a cold trickle down my neck. Blood drummed in my ears. I stopped. A feeling I can only describe as terror swept over me, rushed through my every vein.

I heard something and realised it was a low whistle. Just ahead, beside the trail, I could barely make out what I hoped was Cloudy's silhouette. 'Cloudy?' He was shivering, shaken to the bone and convinced the tiger spirits had taken me. 'Maybe they did,' I told him. I then realised I was shaking myself. We walked back to Bukittinggi in near silence. When we finally reached the canyon's ridge and heard the familiar beeping of horns not far away, I was relieved beyond comprehension. The town was the same as it was every evening, bustling and bright, with the same stench of diesel and rotting fruit, the same shouts of children in the dark lanes. But I was different. I couldn't explain why but I didn't feel like the same person who had walked into the canyon that morning. I'd passed through something and not found my way out, had slipped off my own centre somehow. Perhaps I just have heat exhaustion, I told myself.

That night I woke up in my guest house with a fever. My entire body was drenched in sweat and I'd had variations of the same dream all night: running through a dark forest, then through streets of my childhood, then through an old grocery store, always in search of grape juice, aisle after aisle, and never finding it, which was oddly similar to a dream Kevin had once told me he'd had while sick in India. He'd dreamt of running through a giant American grocery store searching in vain for the frozen orange juice section. Just as he'd reach the orange juice, it would disappear. It must be some sort of universal dehydration dream, I thought. I stumbled out of bed to find my water bottle and was so lightheaded I immediately fell back down. I tried again and became alarmed at how unsteady and weak I felt. The next morning I was no better, nor the next night. In the middle of the second night, Abdullah knocked on my door, carrying mandarins and a damp cloth for my head.

Days and nights passed by in a trance-like daze. I don't think I'd ever really known what it was to be delirious before, where your waking life and your dreams begin to blur. Abdullah would come in at all hours, always carrying a small glass of water. He would never leave me with water but felt he had to bring it himself in small doses. When he'd put a cool cloth to my forehead, he'd say, 'So sick, my Canadian girl's so sick and all she has is Abdullah to take care for her. No other friends.' I did wonder why Jacob and the others from the restaurant hadn't stopped by to see if I wanted to go for one of the outings we'd planned. And where was Cloudy and his motorcycle? Abdullah was the only person I saw in those nightmarish feverish days. I was glad for his thoughtfulness but also repelled by it. He'd enter the room without knocking, tiptoe across the floor to the bed and just stand there watching me, holding out oranges or water, waiting until I opened my eyes. I'd never know how long he'd been standing there. Sometime during the fourth night, while I was in the middle of a fitful dream, I woke up to see him sitting next to me on the bed, hovering right over my head. 'I've been waiting for you,' he said. 'I've been so worried about you. You're not getting better. Your head is so hot I could cook a roe egg on it.' Did he mean a raw egg? He placed the cold cloth on my head and left, returning a few hours later with another small glass of water, again sitting on the bed, mumbling words in his language until I fell back asleep. The next afternoon he burst into my room, stood above the bed and gave me a long cold stare. I lay there without speaking, impaled on the intensity of his glare, while he continued to study me intently. Finally, he said, 'Who is Dennish?'

'Dennish? Do you mean Dennis? I don't know any Dennis.'

'Yes, he has come for you many times. Why are you lying to me?'

'Someone has come for me named Dennis? What does he look like?'

'Blonde, sunburned.'

I realised he must have been talking about Jacob from Denmark and almost laughed, saying, 'Well, Sumatran, why haven't you let him in?'

'I told him and the others you don't want any visitors. But they keep coming back.'

'But of course I want visitors.'

'No, you're too sick.' He slammed the door and left.

I knew after that it was crucial that I will myself to get better. What must have started out as severe heatstroke seemed to have turned into something else. My fever wasn't going down and the heat and humidity of the room were suffocating. The days dripped by like water torture. I'd wake up not knowing where I was, and when I remembered, I wondered why I was there, why I'd come so far. As time passed I could feel my old self seeping out of me. My days and nights were a hazy confusion of bad dreams, all involving Abdullah, invading my thoughts, appearing unsummoned. Sometimes I wasn't sure if he was in the room or not, or if he'd just crept in as quiet as lust and left again. Still, I sometimes looked forward to his visits in an odd way and felt indebted to him. He was my only friend during that time and I couldn't have imagined going through that illness alone. I tried to get him to talk about himself and his country but he was an expert at evading my questions. When I asked him what he knew about Indonesia invading East Timor he told me he didn't want to know about it. When I asked what he thought of Soeharto, his eyes glazed over as he said robotically, 'I love him,' which was eerily similar to what Moroccans had done when I'd asked them about their king, as if they were terrified not to say that. Whatever lay behind Abdullah's smiling face was carefully concealed. Like many Indonesians, he also was vague and hesitant when he spoke of personal matters, things below the surface. He'd simply smile, close his eyes, feel my forehead, and say never mind.

On the sixth day my fever broke and I felt my energy returning. I was well enough to have a mandi, the Indonesian equivalent of a shower – a large bath filled with cold water which you scoop up with a container and throw over yourself. Sometimes the mandis have fish swimming in them which the people eat at night. The cold water was exactly what I needed to splash off the memory of the past week from my skin forever down the drain. I poured water over my head, washed my hair and was so happy I even sang. Then I looked up to see an eyeball aimed on me through a peephole in the wall. I grabbed my towel and when I opened the door, nobody was there, although nobody but Abdullah was in the guest house that morning.

I wanted to change guest houses that day but didn't feel strong enough to walk through the noisy roads in the sun in search of one, so decided to wait until the next day. That evening I felt an overwhelming urge to make long distance calls to Canada, to hear voices of friends. Abdullah didn't think I was well enough to go out and tried to stop me but I brushed past him. As soon as I stepped into the fresh air of the bustling street I felt hugely relieved to be out in the world again. I had to walk slowly because I was weak and by the time I made it up the hill to a long distance phone, I was exhausted. I couldn't get through to Canada and kept getting the Australian operator. The Australian operator was kind and I wanted to keep her on the line just to hear her accent and talk to her, bridge myself back to the larger world. When I left the phone and walked through the streets, a boy ran by and grabbed at my breasts. Five minutes later another boy did the same thing. They ran away so fast they were lost in the crowds, leaving me with a sudden fury. I now understood why the Swiss women had been so upset.

The next day I gathered my things. I never wanted to see that dingy little room again. Abdullah sulked at my door as I packed, telling me how his was the best guest house in town, asking how I could leave after he'd taken care of me, brought me back to health. 'And I wanted to visit you in Canada some day, in your city that takes all day to walk across. Are you going to find Dennish now?'

'I don't know. I just have to leave. Thank you for taking care of me, Abdullah.'

After I paid him for my stay, swung on my backpack, and walked through the courtyard for the last time, I looked at the jasmine and hibiscus flowers, the frangipani and giant lotus lilies that filled the courtyard like a glorious parade of splashing colours, swooning and flaunting femininity, intoxicating scents. It was the first time I'd noticed how luxurious and well tended the garden was, and, realising that Abdullah was the gardener, I thought of how all the beauty in his garden must also be found somewhere in him. Perhaps no matter how deeply buried or hidden we keep our secrets, they eventually reveal themselves in unexpected ways, swirling up from within.

I wanted to stay in a particular guest house I'd noticed, which was at the top of 300 stone steps near the market. As soon as I walked into my new, lighter and larger, breezier room, I knew, or thought I knew, that I'd found the right place. Surely now things would go well for me. I'd get back on track. I'd just taken a wrong turn somewhere. For unknown reasons I'd been trapped behind a veil of mystery, caught up in some strange destiny. What should have been a journey full of adventure was being compromised by something unnatural, some unpleasant and dark intrusion, something I'd passed through in the canyon perhaps. But that's silly, I thought. I'm not superstitious.

Yet things didn't get better for me after my illness. Something inside me had changed and people seemed to sense that. The run-by gropings were now an everyday occurrence when before the boys had left me alone. I had to start carrying handfuls of rocks at night, especially when I climbed the stairs to my guest house. A group of boys twelve and thirteen years old always hung out on the steps, smoking clove cigarettes and whistling at girls. Imagine being nervous of twelve year olds. It seemed ridiculous, but I was. Fortunately they'd see the rocks in my hand and must have felt the anger and determination clenched in my body. They'd make their whistling noises but were too afraid to go for the grab. The daytime was a different story, however, when my breasts would be clutched out of the blue in the most unlikely places, right out in the open market. Passers-by never seemed to notice, or pretended not to. I also found it harder to deal with grown men when before I had thought them amusing. Each morning as I stepped out of my guest house I had to run the gauntlet of staring men lined up along the streets. I'd prepare myself psychologically for their brigades of hello, where you going?

What's your name? You love me? 'This is a country where the female orgasm is unheard of,' I'd grumble to myself. From all directions I'd be fired with a battery of questions from men who'd walk along with me and wouldn't leave until I answered them. They didn't care what I said either. When they asked where I was from I'd say Saudi Arabia, Jupiter, the circus, fine French cuisine, from Delaware and Winston Churchill is my poor tortured husband, whatever came to my mind, and they'd continue with the next question unfazed. I found it impossible to block out these men. I knew that solitude was not an option in this country but this was different. This was as if they sensed something missing inside me, something essential I'd had before, an inner strength, a happy-go-lucky, get-out-of-my-way stride. Walking through the town and market wasn't fun any more. I hated being a source of entertainment, an oddity, with body parts to seize, hair to pull, an infidel among believers.

I felt the loneliness of solo travel as I'd only felt it once before, that time hitchhiking in Oregon in the rain and not having a destination. Jacob and the others from the restaurant had all left for other parts of Sumatra while I'd been sick, and when I went to visit Cloudy at the coffee shop where he worked, he would hardly speak to me. I didn't know if this was because Abdullah had made up some ridiculous lie about me or if Cloudy was actually afraid of me, afraid I was possessed by some tiger demon.

As I walked up the steps one night to my new guest house, rocks in hand, I thought of how I'd always embraced this kind of travel that mystified me, how so often in travel I'd encountered things unfathomable that in one sparkling moment would become suddenly clear, and true to the spirit of travel, I'd go on. Yet this didn't seem to be working for me now. I had to admit I was no longer the traveller I once was, that fear-nothing girl. Whatever it was I once had, a younger toughness, a self-assured eagerness to explore the world no matter how bad things got, I'd lost. When I saw the boys on the steps, all clustered together like a gang of thugs ready to pounce, I turned around and ran back down, prepared to go home the long way. Only at the bottom did I throw a rock up as hard as I could. 'Take that you loser brats! Take that!'

'Prepare yourself,' announced the German backpacker, when I told him I was leaving Bukittinggi and travelling back to Singapore via bus and boat. What was it with these German guys? So serious all the time. I was at a low ebb, but the gravity in his voice seemed excessive to me. I'd already experienced the bus and boat on my way here. I'd already waded through the murky pools of self despair and unfortunate circumstances and because of this, I felt protected by a shield of bad times. Nothing could possibly bother me any more. There was a way out of all this. After the buses and boats there was Singapore with its shiny buildings, iced cappuccinos and air-conditioned cinemas showing Tom Hanks movies; there were green parks with benches where you can sit and stare and not be stared at and there were shopping malls. Shopping malls all over the damned place. I never knew I liked shopping malls, but I must have all along. I must secretly have loved them.

I ate my last breakfast at the Clock Tower Coffee Shop and full of anticipation, hopped on the bus. The air in the vehicle held me like a sauna but I didn't care. Soon we were passing through the Harau Valley enclosed by plunging cliffs and gleaming with waterfalls. I was disappointed to be passing so much I hadn't explored, so much scenery. Scenery is only scenery when you pass by it. When you're actually walking through it, it's not scenery but part of the world. Later, we had a long view across another valley and I watched farmers driving animals, hoeing, and tending little fires in the fields. People in the fields carried umbrellas against the rain and sun. Gradually, the land turned to dense forest and low-lying mangrove swamp. At dusk, we arrived at the dirty oil town of Pekanbaru where I'd have to spend the night and take another bus the next day.

Near the bus station I found a guest house called 'The Paradise' for reasons that weren't apparent. The owner, an old man in an undershirt, gave me a room smelling like a dead rodent. The bamboo bed held a lumpy stained mattress and crayoned all over the plywood walls was graffiti of naked women. The old man rushed to the room's corner where a tiny TV covered in dust sat on a stack of boxes. 'See? TV!' He switched it on and nothing happened. He quickly turned if off again and came back. 'You like?' It was getting too dark to look for anything else and it would be a short night anyway since my bus left at 6 a.m. 'Yes,' I told him, 'I like.'

Since I didn't want to spend any time in my room, I set off to find something to eat and explore downtown. Walking outside was like going to battle. I had to brace myself against it. As soon as I stepped onto the street I was bombarded, as if the men in that town had never in their lives seen a white woman, except perhaps in a blue movie. Every man I passed barked out a question as I tried to avoid the open sewage holes on the crumbled intermittent sidewalks. An overpowering stench hovered over the city of impossible traffic, constant clanging and incessant honking of horns. Construction work seemed to have halted all over the place leaving huge pieces of broken machinery in the filthy streets, adding to the nightmarish landscape of squalor and despair.

All the ugly words belong here, I thought. But I don't. I'm getting away. This is just something I'm passing through. I'm one of those people deeply affected by my surroundings. I soar where the world is beautiful and sink in Pekanbaru.

That night I set my alarm for 5.30 a.m. so I would be sure to catch the bus the next morning. The sun hadn't yet risen when I walked down the treacherous, pot-holed sidewalk to the bus station, and when I arrived, they told me the bus wasn't leaving until 8 a.m. 'But you said it was leaving at six!' With a face empty of expression, the sweaty man at the counter said he'd told me it left at six so I'd be there on time. Another man behind the counter, chuckling as he spoke, said the bus was actually leaving at nine. I took a deep breath and sat on the bench with some women in floral sarongs. I tried to look on the bright side, the only one I could see being that in 24 hours I might be drinking an iced cappuccino in Singapore on a park bench under a tree. I sat watching the other passengers who seemed to be waiting more patiently than I was. I could learn from these people, I thought. I'd heard of the Indonesian concept called *jam karet* – rubber time – which had to do with filtering frustration out of daily events, accepting what must be. Sweat dripped down my forehead and a cute kid climbed on my lap. Finally, at 10.45 the bus was ready for passengers.

I was lucky to get a seat on the stifling bus since as many people were standing in the aisles as were sitting down. I tried to open my window but when three passengers frowned at me for attempting this, I decided against fresh air. We waited another half hour before leaving and all the while the engine rattled hotly and spewed black fumes beneath us. At last, we were off, only to stop again for no apparent reason ten minutes later. This stopping and starting continued mysteriously for two hours before we reached the outer edge of the city. I began to worry about missing the afternoon ferry to Batam. Already we were seven hours later than I thought we'd be. Then, when we finally waved goodbye to Pekanbaru for good, we stopped at what appeared to be a roadside restaurant where the driver got off, leaving the rest of us to fry in the bus. Was the driver going to eat lunch in there? I looked at my fellow passengers incredulously. They just sat there as sweat poured down their faces. Patience must be inbred among these people, I thought. Why were they so passive? I thought Canadians were passive, but even Canadians would never stand for this. Twenty-five minutes passed as I fumed. 'This suppression of the individual goes against my Western grain,' I said under my breath. I had to do something. Without knowing exactly what I'd do, I squeezed past the passengers in the aisles, got off the bus, and charged towards the restaurant. 'Where's the driver?' I demanded when I walked in. The customers looked up from their food. When I spotted the driver eating from a heaping plate of chicken and rice and drinking coffee with some other men, I stood facing his table, and said, 'When are we leaving?' I pointed at my watch. I pointed back towards the bus full of patient hot people. I would have pointed at him too but I'd read that's rude in Indonesia. As if this wasn't, I thought to myself. As if I'm not acting like the most obnoxious spoiled person in this country right now, raging at this poor chubby driver who probably eats here every day of his lousy life.

Before you begin your travels it doesn't occur to you that the most outlandish glimpse you may catch of any living thing in a foreign land may be the glimpse you catch of yourself. Who was this raging woman? I stared at the driver. He stared back, holding a piece of chicken in his cheek the entire time. Then I smiled sheepishly, shrugged my shoulders, and walked back to the bus. The passengers pretended they hadn't noticed my outburst. The driver came back faster than I think he would have normally, and once again, we were off.

The last ferry of the day for Batam was meant to leave the harbour at 3 p.m. We didn't arrive at the harbour until after four and for once I was glad that Indonesian schedules weren't meant to be taken seriously.

The harbour looked and smelled like a garbage dump. A flood of people stood under the hot sun waiting for the ferry and I was soon to join their ranks. Not surprisingly, there was no place to sit, not even an old wooden bench. After we'd waited an hour they made us walk to a dock some distance away where we were to wait in line again to be handed boarding passes, which seemed futile since they could have simply taken our tickets when we boarded the ferry. Nobody complained. Then they marched us back like cattle to resume our wait on another dock. All around me I felt the sense of a civilisation in decay. Never had I seen such flagrant disregard for human beings, such utter disrespect for human life.

Waiting my turn to go through a cow gate to board, I felt a small tug on my shoulder. I looked down to catch sight of a weathered hand trying to fiddle with the latch of my purse. I grabbed the man's wrist and yelled, 'Stop!' The people around me became unexpectedly agitated and shook their heads at me as if I'd done something wrong. In the confusion I wasn't sure if they were upset because I'd yelled at the man or if they were angry at his attempted thievery. All I knew was that suddenly the crowd of people seemed to be discussing me and my situation as if this whole thing, my entire journey, had been a set-up, as if they'd all been in on it, watching me stumble through the wreckage of this rotten trip, as if I'd been on *Candid Camera* the whole time. Freaking *Candid Camera*! It made me wonder what was going on in this country.

Forget the journey being more important than the destination. As I boarded the boat, the notion of destination seemed more important than ever. Singapore was on the horizon, almost. I'd have to get to Batam first. As I took my seat in the crowded boat I closed my eyes to daydream of a good movie and air conditioning. It was all coming.

A woman lay down in the centre aisle next to me. A child crawled underneath my plastic seat and immediately went to sleep. An old man curled up at my feet and began coughing up phlegm in a manner which suggested a highly infectious disease. When the boat was ready to leave just after dark, the floor had become a human carpet, not a square inch of floorboard visible. The video began to blare the Chinese Benny Hill. The air had grown heavy and still as if the world were holding its breath. I wish I could slip away, I thought, become light as air and fly out of here to a place where I could lie on some unfathomably large cushy bed.

It wasn't long before the storm arrived.

The lightning flared like gigantic roman candles, bursting open the sky, and the thunder was like cannon fire inside our brains. The rain was another ocean emptying out of the sky, a solid wall of water pouring its contents all at once. The whole life force of the sea was heaving itself upwards, waves and crests of foam mounting furiously onto our little vessel as it was tossed around like a toy. I was fairly sure this would be a small news item on page 16 of several foreign newspapers: 'Indonesian Ferry Sunk in Storm – No Survivors.'

A woman handed out barf bags.

I stared out the window at the temperamental sea, the primordial, evil-lurking depths, imagining the poverty of my future, as if all that had potential and possibility inside me was already used up. Whatever spark of independence and anticipation I still had seemed to wither within me. I've come too far this time, I thought. Maybe there's only so far you can cross over into the unknown. I've worn myself down, as if I've passed through the exhaustion of centuries. Finally, travel has done this to me.

I tried to step outside myself, sit quietly, and calmly watch the danger of the situation unfold. It wasn't easy but there was really nothing else to do. The Chinese Benny Hill had gone off along with the dim electric light bulbs and there was no point in worrying about the storm when I couldn't do anything about it. Our craft had slowed considerably. Suddenly the air was refreshingly cool, a strange, delicious sensation I hadn't felt in a while. The passengers were shivering and chilled, not used to temperatures below 90 degrees. It was very dark outside – in fact, there could be no darkness anywhere compared to that darkness. I tried to relax and enjoy myself, resign to the chances of fate, and it didn't feel that bad. Nothing opens up life to new interpretations like the ocean heaving beneath you. Only then do you see this whirling planet of water and dirt for the vulnerable little ball it really is.

As I was considering this, a terrible and disconcerting moment came to pass. A wave of titanic proportions hit us and I thought my world as I'd known it was over. We were going down. My heart raced. For unknown reasons I wasn't sick but almost everyone else around me was. Over the loudspeaker a man was trying to tell us something. A storm of words flooded out, scratchy and sputtering, and even the people who spoke the language seemed confused by what he'd said.

It soon became evident that the boat had stopped completely. I wasn't sure if this was good or bad. Maybe this is what boats do just before they sink into oblivion. I felt anxiety beginning to build like a foregone conclusion. Outside, I noticed some faint lights and thought I heard shouting. I realised we must be docked at one of those far-flung islands where, what felt like so long ago, I'd seen the people lined up, where I'd watched the little boy. I'd since read that one group of these 'Riau Islanders' was called the Orang Laut, people of the sea, or 'Sea Gypsies'.

Full of anxiety from the near-death experience, I stood up with a few other passengers, hoping to disembark. The storm seemed to have passed, although the boat was still rocking in choppy waters. An old man hesitated before opening the door to the outside world, as if he might find what's over the rainbow on the door's other side. When he flung it open, the air that drifted in was fresh and sweet-smelling. From over his shoulder I could see we'd have to make a great leap for the dock which was a discouraging four feet away over the water. The old guy jumped as if he were a teenager, further enforcing my belief that elderly people don't act their age in countries like this, but maintain a youthful strength and agility all their hard-working lives. My jump wasn't as impressive – I took off as if performing the running long jump and stumbled to my knees when I landed, but I made it.

All along the docks, islanders were emerging from their little houses to see what was happening. Their houses were built on stilts right over the water. I started wandering around the docks trying to gain perspective on the situation. I had no idea how long we'd be docked. All night? Two days? I had lost all confidence in trying to see order to these things. In my cynical mood I wondered if I'd ever get to Singapore at all. I was shaky and hungry and felt as if the storm were still howling inside me. All I wanted was to walk around by myself, to think, to calm down, but this proved impossible since I was followed by men everywhere I went, men from the boat, men from the island, men who appeared out of nowhere, all of them shouting out their inane questions. I couldn't lose them. Finally, I walked down a smaller dock that seemed to lead into utter darkness. Maybe I can just hide here for a while, I thought. I crouched down next to a wooden building. Thankfully, I seemed to have shaken off the men, although I could still hear them calling out English words and laughing. I looked up at the sky, longed to see a familiar constellation peek through the clouds, and then, without meaning to, I burst out crying, as if all the tension and alienation that had been building within me on the trip had decided to escape at that moment. The watery blackness of that remote Indonesian island seemed suddenly to contain all the misgivings and mistakes I'd ever known. Never had the impact of life's loneliness and hopelessness crushed down on me with such cruel and unyielding force.

Yet I wasn't alone. Sensing a presence, I looked down the dock where I'd come from and saw something white against the darkness of another building. The whiteness seemed to be someone's clothing and I realised there was a person leaning against a building, just as I was, not twenty feet away. I got up to walk back to the boat, embarrassed to have been crying so close to a stranger. When I passed the person, I looked down to see a small girl. What was she doing all alone out here so late at night? The girl looked up at me, her face deeply shadowed, her liquid brown eyes full of melancholy puzzlement. She didn't look so happy herself. I crouched down and smiled and as we faced one another it was as if something were passing between us, as if we were speaking a language beyond tongues. Her solemn eyes narrowed. She tilted forward and I saw she too had been crying. '*Selamat malam* (Good evening),' I said. She greeted me back and asked a question. I pointed in the direction of the boat, which seemed to satisfy her. I wondered if she'd had a fight with her family and I recalled how as a kid I used to 'run away' to the nearby woods when that happened to me.

She took my hand. I let her lead me along the pathway of docks until we came to what must have been her house, a ramshackle structure perched over the water. A woman's voice called out from inside and the girl said something quick and shrill in response while staring up at me. The door opened and two sarong-clad figures holding oil lamps materialised like Madonnas out of the hut. The women motioned for me to come inside. Still led by the hand of the little girl I stepped into the smallest home for a family I'd ever seen. The family – the two women, two boys and an older man – was eating, seated on woven mats on the floor and circled around a single kerosene hurricane lamp. Beds were partially hidden behind curtains in each of the corners and there was a simple kitchen area along one wall. I couldn't imagine too many foreigners would visit this tiny island – it was just the fluke of the storm that we'd stopped here at all – but if the family were surprised to have such a wild-looking, sun-burnt alien suddenly in their home, they hid it well. They smiled kindly and motioned for me to join them. The man placed some noodles onto a plate and bowed slightly as he handed it to me. I said thank you – *termina kasih* – and began eating the most delicious and spicy nasi gorang I'd had on the trip. They seemed pleased I was enjoying the food and we managed to communicate a surprising amount of information, mostly by sign language and laughing. The youngest boy said his name was Kemas; the older boy pointed at himself and said, Bambang. When I repeated it back, they laughed uproariously as if I'd pronounced something else instead. In their soft faces lit by the flickering lamp was a quality of love so true, so ancient, that I felt as if I were connecting with the life force of humanity, lifted out of my isolation, enriched forever by the simple act of sharing a meal with a family in their home. It filled me with affection not just for them but for all the people I hadn't met in Sumatra, all the millions of families just like this one.

Although I didn't want to, I thought I should leave in case the boat sailed without me. I left some money on a bench as an offering for their generosity and shook their hands goodbye. The little girl, still surrounded by an aura of sadness, seemed upset I was leaving and followed me outside. I wondered what secrets she held trapped in her frightened heart. Perhaps her brothers were mean to her and her only escape was that dark pier. I could get away, could leave this water village forever. But she would probably spend the rest of her life on this island, immersed in the unrelenting timeless poverty of this careless world where so many have so little and so few have too much. I crouched down to her level and held her slight arms. The whole universe seemed to be contained in her eyes. We stared at each other, at the chasm between our bewildering lives, then I kissed her on the cheek. She looked amazed, befuddled, then suddenly, smiled a crooked, delighted grin.

We waved goodbye as I walked in the direction of the boat. She followed, keeping a steady pace some distance behind, silently in her bare feet. The night was now balmy and scented with rain and when I looked up ahead at the boat and saw the stirring of people ready to board, I felt sick. I dreaded getting back on that boat, had no faith left in this country's transportation system, or maybe the faith lost was in my confidence in dealing with it, in being a true traveller. I looked back at the girl, waited for her. I wanted to grab her and flee somewhere unknown and magical, feel the two of us flying away together and floating through the sky, upwards, until we were as carefree as birds, then higher, until we were blazing with wonder and purple intergalactic spiral light, and higher still until we looked back down on earth to laugh and say, 'We've left! Have fun!'

Instead, I kissed her goodbye once more and she kissed me a kiss as soft as petals, and I boarded the boat.

Happily, the remainder of the boat ride to Batam was without incident. I'd lost my seat, so I curled up like so many others on the floor where I slept the sleep of queens. When I woke, dawn was breaking over the sea and we were in Batam. I caught the first ferry to Singapore, a very un-Indonesian, high-speed, air-conditioned luxury liner which would take exactly 45 minutes. I had a cushioned chair which tilted back just like one on an airplane and the overhead video played *Seinfeld*. I was in culture shock heaven. A friendly, well-dressed Taiwanese family, back from a short holiday in Batam – God knows why – practised their English on me. The father carried a briefcase. The mother's hair was cut in straight, expensive lines and halfway through the voyage, she opened a designer picnic basket to give her family rye bread sandwiches with romaine lettuce sticking out of the sides.

When I arrived in Singapore everything was a dream. I thought I'd never seen clean like that anywhere in the world, or green so lush or grass so manicured. No noxious fumes spilled out of cars – I could smell lilacs again – and no men followed, questioned or cackled at me. I found my bench in the park under a tree where I drank an exorbitant but delicious iced cappuccino. An iced cap, the girl in the T-shirt and white hat had called it, laughing. A nice cap! I even went to a mall but after five minutes inside I remembered I didn't like them much after all. I went back to my bench in the park and thought about Sumatra. I thought this: trips don't mean you have to have a good time. All you need to have is a 'time' for its own sake where you see this baffling universe in a different way than you've ever seen it before. Bruno had said I should go to Sumatra to see it and to see myself in it. I'd done that, and even though I didn't always like what I saw in either, it would change me. When we travel we cross borders of reality and strengthen the spirit, face the unknown, escape, get lost, found, see a light and discover something new. I supposed I'd done all those things in Sumatra. What mattered now was finding a place to go next.

Chapter 14

I'm driving at night when the sun can't fry me because Utah today was unspeakably hot, the sun a cruel beast without shape, a howl without sound. Driving under the cold blue moon instead of the sun is more than a relief, it's a celestial miracle that I'll never take for granted again.

My headlights pick out nothing but white lines of highway and murky shadows of a girl on an Indonesian boat. So there was a spark of light in that trip after all, a single moment asking to be remembered. I see now that the easy road isn't the road to take to find that spark. If we really want to find true beauty in this world, the road to find it can be full of ache, wrenching hurdles, heartbreak and potholes. But it's the road we sometimes need, the one I needed to come across that little girl and her family on that forlorn island after the storm.

Although I was just there a year and a half ago, Sumatra seems a world away, another lifetime. In Sumatra I recalled something I've learned before in my travels: I really am a product of my culture. I like it for the comfort, protection and identity it provides me. In North America I'm allowed to be a strong independent woman with her own thoughts and ideas. This wasn't allowed in Indonesia. Travelling in foreign places allows us to see ourselves outside of our culture, to see how much we behave according to our own cultural standards and how much we behave according to our own moral compasses, forcing us to see the human being inside the cultural packaging. I feel fiercely independent in communal places where people aren't allowed diverging opinions and solitude is unknown, but I have to wonder, is this me or my culture? Also, I sometimes think that North Americans, with our tough independent streak, pay for our autonomy with loneliness. In most developing countries, nobody lives alone; and in more primitive societies around the world, not only does nobody live alone, but there are villages where people may know solitude for only a few hours or days in a lifetime, maybe in a hut or on the outskirts, as part of a coming-of-age ritual. The rest of their lives they sleep ears-to-heels with all their relations and apparently like it that way. They wouldn't understand North Americans, so many of us living alone, eating alone, travelling alone. They'd find it unnatural, and perhaps they'd be right.

Alone. It's funny how I think of myself as a social person, how I love the company of others, going out on the town, parties, community events, yet so often find myself alone. All alone here on this dark Utah highway tonight, I can't even get any radio stations for some reason. So I contemplate this, the real lesson of my Sumatra trip: I'm not such an intrepid traveller after all. I had thought I wasn't afraid of anything, was one of those rare genetically mutated humans missing the survival instinct called fear. I was wrong. It wasn't the buses or even those flimsy death-defying Indonesian boats which really scared me. It was myself alone in that dark canyon, utterly removed from all that was familiar, a person without an identity, and worse, a person wondering if and why something was after her. And afterwards, I was aware of that palpable inner shift, barely perceptible but still there, a new vulnerability, as if a layer of my skin had been scorched off without my consent, leaving me far too exposed and open, even to myself. It was as if being alone that far away had caused something deep within me to surface, a part of myself I didn't really know, someone who knew fear.

Yet I kept going, survived, on to the next place. Whenever I'm stuck in a lousy situation while travelling through this life, I should always try to remember that no matter how bad things get, I always seem to come out of it OK in the end. I say to myself, 'This too shall pass,' and, miraculously, it does – except for the times when everything gets worse, like now.

I pull over to sleep in a rest stop where mine is the only car. Although the engine is off and I'm lying down in the back, Marcia continues to making eerie grumbling sounds for some time into the night. I find my flashlight and pull out my California cave journal. Surely it won't be long now before I arrive in California.

Cave Journal

I seem to be retreating deeper and deeper into this beach cove with each passing day. And when the people come by, I retreat deeper and deeper into my cave. Clusters of people have occasionally been coming down to the beach today. It's amazing how quickly I've forgotten about people. It's interesting how they walk straight to the ocean, turn to walk along the shore for ten minutes or so, then leave. This is the pattern when they come with friends. If a person comes alone, there is no pattern. Almost all the people eventually see me up here. They must find it odd to see a girl camped inside the cliff wall. I'm not sure why I don't just go down to the shore and talk to them, act like a normal person. I didn't think I was a hermit by nature, but I seem to be one now. Only one of these people has waved to me. The others have all looked away. I waved back at the man who waved, feeling suddenly conspicuous, and a little ridiculous up here.

These gulls don't like people. They seem to prefer their own inner circle of bird acquaintances, standing together all facing the ocean, or soaring curved white above the waves, calling out to each other, or perhaps, to no other bird at all. I listen for their single piercing call that cuts through the wind, for the ensuing silence magnified by the memory of that single cry.

The people have all gone. I'm still having no luck building a fire. Every day I try to make one and give up. Everything is too soggy here, the wood, the air. I can't stand listening to the radio any more. I bought this radio in San Francisco because I thought it would be company, or stimulation, and I did enjoy it the first couple of days here, but now everything that comes out of it is distracting.

The longer I stay here by the ocean the more the place grows on me and the harder it will be to leave. In fact, I love being alone like this, to be living with the elemental life of wild nature. This must be our deepest religious urge, for our lives to be intertwined with the cosmos, with the mountains, the air, the water and the sun. Watching the sun crinkling over the waves fills me with ecstasy and I realise this is the way my life should be. This is who I am.

Will I be able to fit in when I go back to the regular world? That other world seems so far away. Do I belong there? Travelling alone like this, being so solitary day after day, has set me apart. I don't think I'll know what to say to people any more. Life seems so much simpler here, so basic.

The sun is my consolation. After the cold nights it warms me all day and does spectacular things to the sky and rocks in the evening, a different painting every time. The nights are what I dread. This is November, when night begins at six o'clock.

Suddenly it's black and cold, the sun having deserted me for places further west. Sometimes I wake up in the middle of the night and vow to leave the next day. I'm hungry and thirsty and the cold sea mist fills my lungs with salt making me even more thirsty and damp. I consider what it might be like to freeze to death. But the next morning the sun returns to heat the sand and me and the idea of leaving this place seems absurd.

The ocean has drawn the sun down out of the sky and my world has turned pink. In a few minutes it will be dark and I'll be alone with my thoughts.

The whole Pacific, a quarter of the planet, has now rolled away into pitch blackness and all that's left is the sea's thunder, its waves pounding an ancient beat. I look above my cliff wall to see the sky brilliant with stars, memories of the universe falling down on the beach. I'm alone here, but not lonely. This place is taking me into its dark and powerful kingdom. I'm being devoured by nature. There's no way I'll be able to sleep, not for hours. I'm wide awake, busting with elation, and hungry as hell.

This morning a gentle rain is falling from a grey silk sky, like a winter rain in the desert, what the Navajos called female rain. Even though I don't sleep much here, I feel so awake. I'm letting the earth come to me at its own pace, beginning to see that nature is entirely serene. A James Joyce passage I've just found sums up how I'm feeling today: 'He was alone. He was unheeded, happy, and near to the wild heart of life.'

Jesus. I really have to find that cave again. How did I ever venture out into the rest of my life after that? How did I manage to leave such a serene place?

I've forgotten so much about the person I used to be, that girl in the cave. It's simply unfathomable how many versions of oneself that life keeps offering, how the old versions begin to vanish to make way for the new. I discovered that night in Jamaica that all of our selves remain hidden inside us as we age. Yet we forget so much. Now that I'm older I find a strange pleasure in going back over things, reentering and rediscovering what I once lived. Back in my cave I was either in the moment or looking ahead, wondering what my future would hold. Now I seem to spend a lot of time looking back. And looking back on that girl, I see she knew a surprising amount, like how to be happily alone and at peace.

Maybe that's something we have to keep relearning all our lives.

I sleep deeply under a blazing multitude of stars at the deserted rest stop and wake up at dawn. When I start Marcia's engine, she sounds perfectly fine after her night of grumbling. She only seems to complain after we've been on the road a while, after too much driving. Perhaps she's just getting old. As I set off towards Nevada, I begin seeing road kill all over the place, especially dead coyotes. I've never run over an animal in my life. Surely this is from people driving too fast and too recklessly. I once drove with a friend down the Baja Peninsula and saw a dead horse on the road. It was still there the next day when we drove back, although a little more rotted by then. We wondered how someone could possibly smash into a horse, until we came across a live horse standing in the middle of the road. We had to slam on the brakes and honk to get it to move. A friend of mine once saw some unusual road kill on a remote highway in Africa: the body of woman, flattened like a pancake, almost one-dimensional, the way you sometimes see squirrels. She must have been driven over many times. He said he could still see the bright yellow cotton of her dress. What if someone she knew, her kids, had gone by and recognised her? Human road kill. Some things are simply incomprehensible.

I've arrived at the Utah–Nevada border, at the twin towns of Wendover and West Wendover. You can't gamble in Wendover, Utah, but you can in West Wendover because this is Nevada and gambling is the only way the state can make money as there's nothing else to do in a desert like this.

I've never been in a casino and since it's 98 degrees outside, the air conditioning alone is enough to lure me inside the biggest and tackiest casino of them all. Casinos are always made to be glamorous in the movies, full of gorgeous rich people, but as I soon discover, casinos are the seediest places on earth, full of fat, bored, miserable people who are intent on losing their money to one-arm bandit contraptions that clang and ding and annoy to keep these people hypnotised. One of the most depressing aspects of casinos is how dark they are: no windows. They're designed that way so money-spenders lose track of time. Hours, even days, can pass without their knowledge. The carpets are all hideous, dizzying, with red swirling patterns 'like woven vomit', wrote Bill Bryson. There aren't exit signs so it's easy to get lost, one giant 'gaming' room leading to the next, all looking exactly the same, full of the same unattractive people in Hawaii shirts all mindlessly feeding their money into noisy machines. Nobody seems to be having any fun at all. The people who work at the casinos never use the word 'gambling'. Perhaps since it sounds less sleazy, they call it 'gaming', and correct you if you say 'gambling', as if they don't know what that means.

My hair feels really dirty. I should have washed it in the cold shower at Great Salt Lake. I find a restroom with marble floors, fill the sink with water, and begin washing my hair, as if this is a normal thing to do in a casino. A woman in her sixties who is putting on make-up smiles at me and asks how I am. I suppose washing my hair in here is a conversation starter, a rather intimate act for such a public place.

'Getting lucky today?' she asks.

'Lucky?' For a second I think she has the wrong idea about me, that I'm a showgirl, or even a prostitute. 'Oh, the gambling. No, I haven't tried yet. I just need to wash my hair. I've been driving through this heat. You know how sometimes you just have to wash your hair? So, have you been lucky today?'

She doesn't answer for a moment as she looks in the mirror and applies bright carroty lipstick, occasionally looking over at me. I wonder if she thinks I'm some kind of homeless vagrant.

'We don't mind the heat,' she finally says, pressing her newly orange lips together. 'Well, we don't notice it much with the air conditioning, dear. Gus is losing our money out there, my husband. He usually does.' She shakes her head in disapproval and inspects her face up close in the mirror.

'Oh, that's too bad. Can you stop him? I mean, is he having fun?'

'Oh, sure. Well, when he wins. You don't want to be around him when he doesn't. We're seeing a show tonight. Not Wayne Newton either. I'm making him take me this time. Don't quite know what to do 'til then.' She looks at me through the mirror, raises her eyebrows slightly. I smile but don't say anything, hoping she won't ask me to join her for a drink or something. 'Well, good luck with the hair washing,' she says a little too merrily, the smile gripping her face. 'Bye!' I call after her. As she breezes out the door I'm left with the lingering scents of cheap perfume and the loneliness of a woman who has chosen badly in love.

After she leaves, I study my own reflection in the mirror and see a 34-year-old woman, never married, childless, with a sunburned Celtic complexion, long, wet, tangled auburn hair, shorts and top a little crumpled, and looking very out of place in this chrome casino restroom. Outdoorsy is how

I look, if I'm being kind to myself. Unkempt would also fit. 'I'm driving a beaten-up car and washing my hair in a casino bathroom,' I say to the mirror. To myself, I also say, I'm running away. Why am I running away?

I see a line of phones in a lobby and decide to call Andre. I'm suddenly dying to hear his voice across all these miles. His voice always holds so much enthusiasm for things, like a kid's, like someone I might have sat next to in school, one of those boys secretly in love with half the girls in the class. He's the type of guy who, when you first meet him, speaks infrequently and when he does, your ears prick up, because you imagine any ideas that have taken so long to develop are definitely worth considering. When we first got together, I was so taken with his cheerfulness, his ability to fix things, invent things, like potato cannons which he'd fire off into the neighbourhood, and battery-powered scooters. I thought this was all I needed, someone this fun and strong and happy with his life. I didn't think I needed to talk about the world or travelling or books. I could imagine our lives pared down to pioneer essentials where people need to be dependable and loyal and have a good garden. Over time, we'd develop common interests, which we did, and have. I love our comfort and companionship: going to yard sales, playing with his five-year-old son when he stays with us every other week; canoeing down the river at the end of the street, eating dark chocolate almond bars while watching *The X Files* even though the plot never quite makes sense, laughing about our next-door neighbour Mary Lou, whom we secretly call Mary Louped since she's inebriated all day. I could go back to all that. I could. I just have to think of his muscular tanned shoulders, his strong hands that can fix things, his warm brown eyes that love me, his voice that tells me over and over that he wants to marry me. This world is so difficult and cold and hard to fathom on your own. Things are so much easier with someone you love by your side. If only I could make up my mind about him, let my heart swell, become inflamed, stop thinking so much. If only I didn't wake up in the dead of night from a fitful dream wanting to scream NO! into the room. No, this is all wrong – this life I'm living with the wrong nice man.

If only, like a friend of mine once wrote in a song, they hadn't written the book of love for an illiterate.

I dial, hear two rings, and then, 'Hello?'

What a faraway gentle voice he has. I'd forgotten. 'It's me,' I say.

'I was wondering when you'd call. How are you? Where are you?'

'In a horrible casino, in Nevada. I'm OK, sort of.'

'Come home.'

'Oh God, I'd love to come home right now. That would be so easy. I mean, if my car worked it would be easy, but never mind that right now. How are you?'

'Missing you, and busy.'

'Busy's good.'

As our conversation continues I realise how much I've been missing him, how much fun it would be if he were here right now with me, how we'd be laughing at this place instead of me hating it on my own. It's true that it would be easy to go back home. I could fall right back into that life. He's such a good person, so warm and kind and thoughtful. 'I just have to try out California. I'm almost there,' I tell him.

When I hang up, although I'm sad to be missing Andre, I'm suddenly overcome with a feeling of absolute certainty that I'm headed in the right direction, doing the right thing in going to California instead of going back home. Going back would be easy, but I don't want easy. Easy feels like a cop-out. I'd always regret not trying it out here in the West.

The West, for me, has always been so filled with promise, new ways of thinking, the great and expansive outdoors, clean air, mountains and vistas, healthy fresh food and sunshine, right from when I first moved to Boulder at seventeen, to when I stayed in the cave, to all the other times I've visited California. I've always thought of the West as being populated largely by enlightened people who've come here on purpose, looking for and creating healthy, progressive towns and cities. Back in Guelph, it sometimes feels as if I have wings which can't stretch out and fly the way they're meant to, as I'm hoping they will in California. In California, I'll fly into the warm sun instead of beneath the cold constraining winters of Ontario.

After a few hours I want to escape the casino, to begin my journey across the Nevada desert to California, but that's a journey one only makes at night at this time of year. I have to stay and kill time in the casino until the sun sets. I go in search of a swimming pool and find one on the top floor. I swim, paddle around with some kids, and dive off the board. I haven't done a back dive or back flip since I was fifteen, so I decide to try a back dive and work up to the flip later. I stand at the end of the board on my toes, facing the wall with my arms outstretched, preparing for take off. The kids and some nosy parents are in the water encouraging me. Five minutes go by. I seem to be hesitating. What's happening? I used to do these all the time. I bend my knees, stand up straight again, turn around and look down at the water. A boy is now standing at the other end of the board. He's all wet and skinny and ready to do a cannonball. 'Are you gonna go or what?' 'What,' I say. A mother sitting with her feet dangling in the pool calls out, 'Try a jump instead.' She's right. The kid I once was and her agile fearless body must have skipped town long ago. Finally, I turn around and do a regular dive instead. When I bob to the surface, a teenage girl and her father shout out 'Good for you!' but I can see the pity in their eyes. I used to be able to do that, I want to tell them. I used to do back flips too, and even those inward dives. Where did the old me go? When did she leave? I decide to try the sauna instead. Later, I wander around to see if the casino really is as bad as I think it is.

It is.

In a glassed-in corridor I find a couch where I have a clear view west tracking the progress of the sun. I'm waiting for the sun's daily death, when it will relinquish its fiery burning and spread softly, mauve and gauze-like, over the fading world. Then I can take the last leg of my journey, away from here, to California, and follow the path of my fate. It seems appropriate I have to wait a while longer for this to begin, to push off from this last edge, to contemplate a while more what I've left and where I'm going. For a moment, I wonder if California really is my fate or just another place on the way. I always seem to be on the way somewhere. Perhaps living in California won't be what I envision at all. I think of a story I once heard about a man kayaking in Utah. He came across a lone Hopi Indian on the shore. The Indian's face was painted black. 'I'm waiting here for a vision,' the Hopi man told the kayaker, 'but you're not it.' Maybe California will be like that for me: 'not it.' What are our lives anyway but a continual series of beginnings, settings out into the unknown? Do we ever really arrive? I feel trapped in this monotonous depraved place, not to mention filled with anxiety about driving a broken car across a desert of fearsome emptiness all night. In fact, it suddenly seems like a remarkably bad idea.

Can it be there's a catastrophe waiting to happen out there in that desert tonight, a catastrophe that has been hiding all along in the pockets of this so-called free-spirited pilgrimage? Right now I can identify with a line in a Lorrie Moore short story: 'Sometimes she thought she was just trying to have fun in life, and other times she realised she must be terribly confused.'

I need to rethink what I'm doing out here, on this mad dash across the country towards California, because, right now anyway, it feels a lot like fleeing. Perhaps fleeing has always been an impetus for any movement in the world, even the modern world where people flee winter, jobs, boredom, the rat race and even dictatorships. Fleeing is what many Europeans did in coming to this new land, and fleeing is what many pioneers did in coming out here; they fled their stifling and stilted lives in the puritanical East as they looked with longing towards the freedom of the untamed West. That's the fine balancing act in any move: the fleeing of the old and the anticipation of the new promised land. I think I have my feet caught up in this balancing act, where one moment I feel like I'm fleeing – fleeing a life of settling for the ordinary, the not-quite-enough – and the next moment, find myself longing for all that California provides. But how much do I lose in leaving behind everything I've built up over the years at home? I leave behind my parents, boyfriend, friends I've known for years, a community. I leave behind the Laurie that lives in Guelph, that knows her way around, that has her own work, bike routes, the Laurie who is Canadian, who swims in Canadian Shield lakes every summer. I haven't often identified myself much as a Canadian – thinking I'm more of a world citizen – but here in this casino where the people seem like characters from *The Flintstones*, maybe Canadian is a big part of who I am. Even though there are casinos in Canada, this feels different somehow, alien. Perhaps Canadians just do things a little more quietly.

Americans really are different in many ways. For one, in this nation founded by restless seekers, they're always looking over the next valley. American heroes have traditionally been sailors, cowboys, prospectors, speculators, backwoods ramblers, explorers and vagabonds. In longing for the open road, I suppose I'm fulfilling my American heritage, believing that just down that road, the world is more magical, glamorous, and that's where I need to be: someplace new. But that sounds a lot like fleeing, and instead of sounding exotic, it sounds unstable. Should we really be uprooting ourselves? Shouldn't we stay committed to one place, taking care of the land where we are? Making the community where we live a better place? After all, it has been said that the movement that matters, the work of nature and community, goes on everywhere. But this isn't always true. Some places really are terrible, the land forsaken for concrete, having becoming so unrecognisable as part of this earth that there's no turning back, ever. And some places, no matter how hard you try, you know you just don't fit in.

I certainly didn't 'fit in' in Korea. When I think about my trip to Korea last year, the place I went after Sumatra and Singapore, I think about fleeing, and although I went there full of anticipation, once there, I wound up terribly confused.

Chapter 15

Seoul: Not for the Soulful

If I were to give advice to anyone wanting to teach in Korea, this would be it: DON'T GO!

I bolted, fled, escaped South Korea after just six days, having suffered a series of odd and sinister setbacks. As one Kafkaesque day passed on into the next, I kept pondering what had become of Laurie the explorer? What was going wrong on this trip, first to Singapore and Sumatra, and then to Korea? Had I lost my way somehow? Hadn't I usually thrived on a healthy dose of culture shock? Wasn't I relaxed, open to change, easy-going? Hadn't I always gone anywhere, eaten anything, talked to strangers, taken midnight walks? Korea was the thirty-first country I'd visited. Perhaps my quota was filled. I'd overstepped an invisible boundary and wasn't allowed any more of the world. Although many of the countries I'd visited had been in the developing world, never had I felt even a fraction of the alienation I experienced in South Korea, land of the concrete jungle, cement faces, and fish-jelly popsicles.

After Sumatra and Singapore, I flew to Korea, not only for the adventure of visiting a new and unusual place, but to get a job teaching English and earn some money. On the advice of a friend who'd taught there before, I tried just showing up in Korea without a job, to search for one once I got there. Nobody I'd met had actually tried this, but they all thought it might be preferable to signing a contract before I left for a lower paying and perhaps poorer job. Since I'd found teaching jobs overseas before by just showing up, I thought I'd try it again in Korea.

Flying over the thick brown haze of Seoul towards the airport, I looked out the window and felt sick at the sight of the grey and cancerous mega-metropolis below. The city sprawled out like an oil slick, looking like a war zone from a sci-fi flick. I saw miles and miles of crushed-together, hideous high-rise identical apartment buildings, lifeless, stark and thoroughly dismal. The rain that day didn't help but it *was* ugly.

This isn't a problem, I thought. As soon as I get out of the airport I'll hop on a bus and leave Seoul, as I'd planned. I'll go four hours south, to the city of Taegu, a much smaller city, I imagined, with surrounding mountains for hiking.

As I stood for close to an hour in the immigration line at Seoul's Kimpo Airport, I noticed no other Westerners in sight. When I reached the immigration officer and handed him my passport and immigration form, he held out an impatient hand and said something sternly in Korean. The man was expecting me to present him with something more, perhaps another piece of paper I should have filled in on the plane, something they had neglected to give me. I shook my head and he said the thing again, angrier this time as he slapped his hand to the counter. Since I didn't have what he wanted, the dreadful man pointed me back to the line-up. Lugging with me my ridiculously heavy luggage, I went searching for the piece of paper. No one spoke English to help me. Everyone was Korean and I was quickly realising that Koreans don't speak English. Not even the airport officials. But that's why I was in Korea, to teach English. This is a good thing, I told myself. Eventually, they let me go, but certainly weren't very friendly about it.

I wanted a city bus to get to a central bus station where I could take a cross-country bus to Taegu. Seoul has fourteen million people and I'm not a big city person. At the information desk in the airport I asked which bus would take me to the express bus station. They didn't understand my question. Finally one of them pointed in the general direction of outside and I dragged my bags out into the soup of cold dirty air which actually *hurt* my lungs. Somehow I found the right city bus, and after an hour, it stopped at a gigantic central bus station. Rain slid from the sky in drab afterthoughts. I was shivering, wearing a long cotton skirt, a light jacket, no tights, no hat. Into the massive dirty, noisy bus station, I looked for a sign that said 'Taegu'. Nothing did, nothing in English anyway. That was my trouble. Everything was written in Korean script, a totally different alphabet from the one I knew. I felt five years old. Flipping through my Korean–English dictionary, I tried to say, 'Where is the Taegu bus?' Several bus employees shook their heads but offered nothing more. Was I pronouncing it wrong? Eventually, a woman understood and pointed outside. But where? Outside was big. At least fifty buses were out there. Where could I buy my ticket? She shook her head. Apparently, I couldn't buy my ticket for Taegu in that station. I would have to go someplace else, to another bus station some blocks away. Back into the rain I dragged my luggage and sorry self to find the other station. At the next bus station, after asking several more people, 'Taegu? Taegu?', I found the appropriate ticket counter. Then I went to find something to eat. It had grown dark and I was hungry. All the food sold in the bus station looked abnormally grotesque, but I'm experimental. This food looked strange, though, intestinal, lard-like, fish-eyed and red hot. I felt so entirely ignorant of just about every aspect of Korean life. Everything – people, food and Korean signs – were intimidating and thoroughly unfamiliar. This wouldn't have been bad at all – this is what travel is about – but what made it so uncomfortable was that everyone was staring at me. Was it because they weren't used to Westerners? Was it my inappropriate, too-summery clothing? Nobody seemed friendly, happy, helpful. They only stared – a cold arctic stare, very unnerving. Thankfully, there were only six others on the bus, all of them sleeping, so none of them could stare.

At eleven that night my bus pulled into the Taegu bus terminal. This seedy section of town looked like the red light district. Smaller than Seoul, Taegu has as many people as Chicago. Chicago seemed like a dream city, full of jovial, compassionate people, green parks and trees. Taegu was a neon nightmare. Once off the bus I didn't know where to go and I was cold. I had the names of two cheap hotels but they weren't across the street from the bus station as my guide book had promised. I would have stayed practically anywhere but didn't see a single building resembling a hotel or *yogwan* (Korean guest house). Feeling like a bag lady, I lugged my backpack and two smaller bags behind me on the wheeled contraption I'd bought in Singapore. The few men left on the street were drunk and staggering, reeking of cheap wine, leering at me, asking Korean questions.

'Hotel? *Yogwan*?' I asked people. They just shook their heads, kept walking, not seeming to understand me. I wandered down a street where a tall building stood which resembled a fancy hotel. Inside, I asked the desk clerk in some sort of sign language if any rooms were available. He gave me a card to fill out which was in Korean, but I filled it out anyway, guessing at the questions. When he took my credit card, he looked at it as if I had handed him a rotten fish, then took it into a back room. Five minutes later he returned, threw the credit card down on the counter and shook his head. Apparently he was offended. I had to leave the hotel, the prospect of a warm bed, the safety from the night, and go back out into the street with my mysteriously rejected credit card.

At the next drunk I passed, I said, '*Yogwan*?' He kept wobbling, so I kept following him, saying '*Yogwan*, *yogwan*,' in desperation. I was determined this would be the man who could help me. After a while he stopped and turned to face me, and for a second, his eyes seemed to betray a haunting flash of intensity, of comprehension, almost disturbing in its appeal. He understood me. At last I had communicated successfully with a Korean. I followed him down a few blocks as he staggered along, until we reached a small door in a cement wall which he called a *yogwan*. I bowed to the drunk, which seemed to please him immensely, and walked inside. An old woman asleep on a mat in the little office woke up to serve me. She had me fill out the same card, and I paid her 25,000 won ($40.00 Canadian). When I closed the door of my little room, I closed the door on Korea, and a flow of relief washed through my entire body. I decided never to go out that door again.

When I took a bath in hot water, I noticed that a surprising amount of Sumatran dirt came off me, even though I'd had showers in Singapore. I turned on the TV, switched a dial of channels around, all Korean, and then... David Letterman. David Letterman in a country where no one speaks a word of David Letterman's language? It seemed this was the American military TV station. Even though David Letterman showed his 'stupid pet tricks' for an amazingly long time, it was a terrific comfort to hear English. I went to bed, shutting my eyes against the strangeness of Korea, forcing myself to believe I'd wake up the next morning in a land of sunshine where people would sing to me and point me down a yellow brick road.

That night I dreamt of being blindfolded at a birthday party while kids pushed me back and forth, laughing at my backpack and too summery clothing.

The next morning I woke up, remembered where I was, and immediately went back to sleep, deciding to escape the place for a blissful hour longer. When I left the *yogwan*, I searched the streets for a corner store. I wanted to buy water, food, and an English language newspaper advertising teaching jobs. I had heard such a paper existed. Surely I could find this newspaper in a city of this size. But I couldn't even find a corner store.

Everything felt so altered from the rest of the world, so peculiar. I'd been to many obscure, untouristed places on the earth. This didn't feel like earth. This place smelled different, sounded different. Taegu was even more alienating than Seoul. When people saw me, they not only stared, but whispered to their friends. I wandered around for an hour, looking for something to grasp onto, a way in, or out. The phone books were of course all in Korean script, which made calling a school or university impossible. When my luggage collapsed off my wheelie contraption and all my things spilled onto the street, with books and papers blowing everywhere, I admitted defeat, weighted by a crush of helplessness. This was like a rural Mongolian woman who speaks no English, wandering around New York trying to find a job, a place to live, a situation. What would she do?

People stopped to gape at me as I picked up my papers strewn on the street and that's when it struck me: I don't have to be here. The idea came to me like a gift-wrapped thought. I can head back to the bus station right now, I realised with elation. I DON'T HAVE TO BE HERE! So that's what I did. I headed back to the bus station and got on the next bus back to Seoul. In Seoul I could get back to the airport, go back home to English, to friends, to my old life. I had failed miserably in this mad dash to Korea. So ill-prepared.

A horrendous traffic jam on the highway back to Seoul made a four-hour trip take six hours, but I didn't care. The rest stops on the way were dirty exhaust-fumed strip malls of fast food joints. Almost all of these places sold white popsicles which people were licking and lapping up with almost perverse abandonment. Since I was curious and hungry I bought one. It consisted of homogenised cold white processed fish with a jelly consistency. I threw it in a trash can and bought a waxy chocolate bar instead.

Outside the Seoul express bus station, I went looking for the airport city bus. I spotted it almost immediately, across the street, across eight lanes of traffic. All I needed to do was cross the street, get on the bus, and I'd be on my way to freedom. But the traffic was relentless. I wouldn't make it across with my life intact. For at least twenty minutes I stood there waiting for a break in traffic. Even though that original airport bus had long gone, another was sure to arrive. But a break in traffic never came. That's when something inside me changed, something essential, and I no longer recognised myself. I heard myself shouting into the crowds 'How can you people live like this? I just want to cross the street! That's all I want. Let me cross! This is barbaric!' I no longer cared what people thought. I continued yelling obscenities into the madness of traffic, all the while having hostile thoughts about the kind of world that could turn someone like me into a pontificating maniac. When another airport city bus came along on my side of the street, I jumped on it, even though it would have to go all through its route first to get back to the other side of the street, then back to the airport. For the next three hours I sat on that bus and rode all over Seoul – the unrelenting, concrete massive mess of Seoul – until we got to the airport. It took me hours, not minutes, to cross the street.

Back at the airport, I went to the Korean Airlines desk to see about changing my ticket to get on the next plane to Vancouver. I was prepared to live in the airport, to sleep on its cold hard floors until the next escape plane would accept me. They pointed to a stand-by line where about fifty people were crowded around shouting at each other. It was on my way to the stand-by section that I saw him: James Dean. He came right over and seemed to be equally surprised to see me. Even though we were in an international airport, we were the only non-Koreans around. He was attractive, with a strong build and wavy brown hair. More importantly, he spoke English.

'Hi, where are you going?' he said.

'Home.'

'Where?'

'Anywhere but here,' I mumbled as I kept walking, too frazzled even to talk to the guy. The stand-by line was a nightmare. Everyone was butting up ahead of me. Then he was beside me again.

'You have to be aggressive like they are. Just walk right up there.' Although his voice sounded a little anxious, it had a calming influence on me. He told the airport worker in Korean that I wanted to change my ticket. The airport worker looked blankly at my ticket and told me to go back to the Korean Airline desk.

James Dean followed me through the crowds, which was no easy feat because I walked determinedly, pushing through the throngs with purpose, homeward. Finally, I swung around to face him, to shout out through the muffled roar that only exists in airports. 'I hate it here. I really hate it!'

'Me too,' he shouted back. 'Me too!' He took a deep breath and then his shoulders slouched as if he were releasing years of anguish. 'I'm Eric.' He thrust out his hand, which was sturdy, large and surprisingly warm. He said he was from New Mexico, from Albuquerque, but from other places too, after Albuquerque, and that he'd been teaching in Korea for the past two years. 'I'm not sure why,' he admitted.

'I'm from Canada,' I said, 'and other places too I guess, and I don't belong here.' He told me I shouldn't be fleeing so fast. I admitted it was kind of rash. 'Do you like it here?' I asked him. 'Are you happy in Korea?'

'Well, no, not really, but I'm making money... and... I think I'd be happy if you were here.' He paused, his composure undone in embarrassment. We both watched a small scurrying woman drag an enormous suitcase. 'Oh God, this is what Korea has done to me. It's made me say things like that.'

I burst out laughing. His eyes widened and I sensed a slight collapsing of his height, as if I'd hurt him on some level. 'I'm not laughing at you,' I said. 'It's just that some sort of deeply locked frustration or disappointment or strain or loneliness, something inside me is escaping. I think I'm going through severe culture shock.'

He brightened. 'You are. You shouldn't be coming to Korea alone this way. It's too hard to do alone. I'm still in culture shock and I've been here two years.'

'You are? Maybe you're right.'

'I'm going to Japan right now to renew my visa. I'll be back in four days, on Saturday. Take the keys to my apartment. I'll tell you how to get there on the subway. I live in a university dorm. Look around the city for a job. If you still hate it when I get back, then leave. What have you got to lose?'

'My sanity.'

'I think you've already lost that.'

We continued talking until I was convinced I should stay, find a job. He was making sense. Also, he was incredibly good-looking, smart, and he made me laugh. He was James Dean, only taller.

I took the subway from the airport, even changed subways twice with the help of a young Korean student who introduced himself as Mr Kim. Mr Kim spoke not English but German. My high school German was finally paying off. He was an extremely polite and helpful kid, Mr Kim, or as I called him, Herr Kim, and without him I would have been hopelessly lost on the subway with Eric's directions. I had to take a cab the last part of the journey and Herr Kim came with me, bless his heart. People were helping me. For the first time since I'd landed, I was happy.

At the university dorm where Eric lived, I let myself in and immediately raided his fridge and checked out his bookshelf (that's important, what kind of books guys read). I was starving, having only eaten a chocolate bar that day. I ate his oranges, his orange juice, and a couple of home-made cookies that someone – his mother? – had sent him, and then I cooked some rice. I went knocking on doors to meet the five other teachers at the university. Only one was home, a man named John from New Jersey, who told me he had no confidence in giving advice on teaching jobs, no confidence in giving directions for the city, and really, he admitted, he had no confidence in much at all. Nonetheless, he scrawled me a map of the area of town where there are English language schools –*hogwans* – and told me to take bus #50 to get there. Grateful, I returned to Eric's room. Before going to sleep, I pressed my clothes with the iron I'd bought in Singapore. I turned on Eric's TV and watched *M★A★S★H* and *David Letterman*, then jumped into the warm sheets of the bed, heated from the hot floor – that's how they heat their houses, hot water pipes under the floor – and thanked the god of good sense I hadn't left, and hadn't been so impulsive, after all.

The next morning I borrowed Eric's really cool brown leather jacket, packed my resume, and took bus #50 the wrong way. John was right about his direction-giving. Eventually, over an hour later, the bus let me off in the Chongno-Samga area of Seoul where there is supposedly an abundance of English language schools. First I tried to buy some good shoes but the shopkeeper again rejected my credit card for no legitimate reason other than it was foreign, so I had to buy some cheap shoes instead. I found a large English language school and watched Korean students with headphones in little language labs, like mice. At the administration desk the Korean woman told me in her broken English I would have to apply someplace else, three subway changes away, and there were no jobs for two months anyway. At the next school I tried, in a little basement in a tall office building, the director of the school asked me, even before looking at my resume, whether I would be wearing the short skirts to class. He had hoped I would. He actually wrote this on a piece of paper because I couldn't understand his pronunciation. After looking through his dictionary, he wrote down for me, 'Will you wear the tight skits to class?' Skits! I grabbed my resume back and grumbled something disdainful at him as I left. I tried a few more places, none very appealing, and faxed my resumes for some advertised jobs in the office of a large language school. After that, I found an underground city, another Seoul underneath the streets, where I bought a pair of tights to keep my legs warm, and some oranges. Back on a main street, I realised I was hungry, and when I passed a McDonalds, I found myself rushing inside even though in my everyday life I'd rather eat fermented slugs than go to McDonald's. I thought it would feel familiar in a neon, jubilant sort of way, like walking into the flashy essence of the Western world itself, but it didn't feel that way at all. They didn't even understand me when I tried to order fries, which I figured in a McDonalds would be universally pronounceable. I realised I didn't want the fries anyway and bolted out of there, more despondent than ever.

By then it was five-thirty and I thought I should go back to Eric's place. Both Eric and John had warned me that the university gates are locked every night at 8 p.m. and I didn't have a gate key. Knowing how many times I'd experienced bus traumas in my Asian travels, I thought allowing myself two and a half hours would be about right for getting home. It took me a while to find a bus #50. When I finally did, I flagged it down and eagerly boarded, taking the front seat so I could see where to get off, having carefully memorised the place that morning since all of Seoul looks exactly the same. Seoul didn't seem to have any parks whatsoever, nothing green, not even a little grassy patch, no benches, just buildings, neon and concrete.

Bus #50 seemed to be taking a while to go through its route. I kept waiting for it to cross the bridge we'd crossed that morning. The bridge was a landmark I recognised, a big river, some boats. But where was the river? The bus just kept driving all through the chaotic peopled streets of Seoul, through the staggering enormity of urban unsightliness, on and on with nothing familiar from that morning. After an hour and half we reached a bus terminal, some shanty edge of nowhere, and I realised I was the only one left on the bus. The driver cast me a bored glance and departed. I ran after him, desperately, and said 'Fifty?' as I pointed at our bus. He shrugged and walked away. Just then, another bus #50 came along so I ran onto that. Surely this #50 would take me back to where I got on it that morning. Another hour and a half went by. Twice, we passed the same gigantic Lotte Department Store. Again, we ended up at that same hateful place at the end of the line where I had to switch #50s. Had I missed my place? But we hadn't crossed the bridge. Another hour. At one point, I scrawled on a paper the number '50' and showed it to the woman behind me, who nodded her head. But in Korea, did nodding up and down mean 'yes' or 'no'? Nodding had meant 'no' in Fiji. My brain started to crack open. I was getting frantic, another transportation nightmare, bus purgatory. By then it was well past 8 p.m. and I'd be locked out of the university gate. A nagging thought kept pressing on my brain with disturbing regularity: I HATE THIS COUNTRY! I'd go home the next day.

'Shoon Shee Day,' I said to the driver. That was the name of Eric's university. The driver shot me a dirty look. I said it again, this time with a lump in my throat. He barked something at me in Korean, but what else could he do? Neither of us spoke a word of the other's language.

A crazy man boarded the bus. Immediately, he began screaming at the driver. On and on he raged, who knows about what, and the driver shouted back at him. I'd read that Koreans are hot tempered, but this man, I think, really was insane. When the crazy man punched the driver on the shoulder, the driver stopped the bus and turned off the lights and engine. Traffic and honking horns built up behind us for two blocks. I was enjoying myself. The crazy man's unbridled hostility seemed to be coming from the depths of my own despair. I let my frustration ream out in waves through the crazy man. As his tantrum continued, I calmed down. Unfortunately, it all ended when an old woman walked up to the front with her cane and pushed the crazy man off the bus. The driver, pouty after being punched, started the bus again, and off we went, along bus #50's deceitful route.

'Shoon Shee Day,' I cried out again. I must have said that twenty times. Like a lunatic, I kept throwing it out every time a new person boarded the bus. The rest of the time I was thinking: wow, this is a really bad dream. Will I keep riding around on bus #50 for the next twenty years?

I could do a lot on this bus in that time. I could learn Korean. I could read the classics. I could shout obscenities out the window... 'Shoon Shee Day!' I called out again. Finally, a girl who looked twelve but was more likely a university student, boarded the bus and when I called out the university's name to her, she came to sit beside me. 'Shoon Shee Day?' she said. I nodded. From her purse she produced a little book through which she immediately started rifling. In very broken English, she said the number '143'. There is a God. I was to take bus #143, wherever that was. By this time it was nine-thirty and I was a mess, could hardly catch my breath. I felt ten years old, the way you feel when you've been somehow wronged and sympathy only makes you want to cry, completely let loose and make a total fool of yourself. And that's what I did. As soon as the girl told me '143' and I got off the bus, I burst into uncontrollable sobs on the street. I still had no idea where to find bus #143. I was completely lost.

Then something strange happened, that inexplicable phenomenon known to all distraught travellers that somehow saves us from ourselves, from death, destruction, or simply, from taking the wrong road. There I was, crying, wailing, shaking on the crowded, cold sidewalk, and out of nowhere, this Korean guy appeared. I don't know if he'd been on my bus or if he just happened along. All I know is the guy spoke English – the only Korean in all of Korea, population 43 million, to speak English, and there he was comforting me, pathetic me, with his arm around me, saying everything would be fine. 'Don't cry, please don't cry.' He looked so distraught I thought he'd start crying himself. Introducing himself as Mr Kim (another Mr Kim!), he told me he was going to help me. I stared into the calmness of his large benign face, at the unadulterated compassion in his eyes. Suddenly, I felt as if I'd been transported into a kinder world where people care about what becomes of their fellow humans. I wouldn't curl up in a cold lost lump on the sidewalk and cry all night. I would get back to Eric's lovely little dorm with his mother's cookies, the TV with the English language station, the warm bed.

And I did get back. Mr Kim even insisted on paying for a taxi. He even walked me to my dorm. The gate wasn't locked after all, and at my door, he bowed, smiled and thanked me, thanked me for what exactly I have no idea. I'm the one who should have been grovelling at his knees offering to send him my first born child. Who knows what would have happened if Mr Kim hadn't saved me that night. I'd probably still be wandering around, getting on random buses, punching the drivers in the shoulder. As Mr Kim left he walked backwards, bowing the whole time until I couldn't see him any more. Possibly he's still bowing today. I walked inside and blessed the chance that had sent Mr Kim my way. I still don't know where he came from.

The next day, despite that act of kindness, I was again ready to flee Korea. When I tried calling Korean Airlines to ask about changing my ticket, the woman told me changing my ticket was completely impossible. I burst out crying and had to hang up on her. I seemed to do that a lot in Korea, burst into unruly tears. I hadn't cried so much since Grade 5 when Spencer Valley falsely accused me of throwing a nail at Miss Atkinson's glasses while she played a John Denver song on the piano. She loved John Denver. Anyway, I was determined to leave, no matter what Korean Airlines said. I had to replace Eric's food and then go to the airport.

On my way out of the dorm to the grocery store, I met another American teacher, Bob, who was muscled, built like a refrigerator, and possibly the friendliest person living in the eastern hemisphere. Bob talked me into giving it one more chance, the old college try, the old give-it-your-best-shot. He punched me on the arm and said there were so many jobs that it was crazy to leave. Maybe he was right.

It did seem a tad foolish to get all the way to Korea, then leave. Besides, things seemed to be working out for Bob. Perhaps I had just started this whole thing on the wrong foot. Perhaps if I had been greeted at the airport by someone and escorted directly to a school the way the other teachers had been, everything would be different. I wasn't a wimp. At least, I didn't think so.

Bob gave me the phone number of a small university in a suburb of Seoul where he thought there was a teaching job. I called immediately and talked to the head of the English department of Kwangwoon University, a Mr Kim. I wanted to ask Mr Kim if all men in Korea had the same name, but decided against it. Mr Kim said to come for an interview and he gave me directions for the subway, not very good directions, but I still made it there in two hours after taking a bus, then switching subways twice, then running fifteen minutes in the rain. From the train window I watched the drab city drenched in a cheerless drizzle and tried to imagine myself living there. Yes, I could do this. I could take this route every day. I could learn to appreciate bleakness, concrete. I just have to look at these visual offerings in a new light. It would be a challenge. I'd explore unknown territory, not only of a new city but of myself, myself living in an urban jungle. As we passed a particularly disagreeable section of industrial sprawl pumping foul fumes into the air, something sinister hit me: Seoul's major reason for existence must be to make every other place in the world look good in comparison.

Kwangwoon University resembled the rest of Seoul: ill-looking, grey East European-style buildings devoid of all character, devoid of grass and trees.

I was jubilant, however, because I was going to have an interview at a respectable teaching establishment, not one of those disgusting *hogwans* where they ask about short skirts. When I knocked on the door of the English department, a man, presumably Mr Kim, opened the door, looked at me blankly from his unfeeling face, and said two words: 'You late.' That's all he said. And I had left to take the bus and two subways five minutes after getting off the phone with him. I stood staring back at him in a state of suspension. Clearly, this Mr Kim wasn't nearly as nice as the previous two, and our short interview confirmed the fact that he would never hire someone who arrived late.

The next day I must have woken up and thought, hey, I haven't punished myself enough yet. I'm still not *that* miserable. So I went searching for one last opportunity, one more possibility of creating a wonderful life for myself in Seoul. Seoul. I can't believe they call it that. Seoul has to be the most soulless place in this world. Not that it means the same thing in Korean, but still. Wind and rain cut into me rudely that day. The faces I saw on the sidewalks revealed no emotion, no recognisable expression of any kind. I would have loved an insight into the thoughts behind those faces. I know Korea has had to endure dreadful Japanese imperialism over the years, not to mention deadly wars, but is that any reason to look so depressed? I never once saw a Korean laughing on the street. Along the sidewalks, caught in droves of human traffic, I watched young women with their hennaed highlights in their identical haircuts, all of them dressed in the same vogue fashions, petite size, all wearing the same vinyl black platform shoes, all staring straight ahead into a joyless tomorrow. Didn't even one of those girls ache to break away? Didn't one of them want to start screaming in the street that she was different? Didn't one of them want to kick off those stupid shoes and throw them at a bus? I passed among those faces, like a fleeting shadow over their existence.

It's amazing how quickly you crave connection, how you yearn for conversation in your own language. To think I've spent weeks on my own in the woods, not talking to anyone or anything but trees, and it has never bothered me. Yet in Korea, when I was surrounded by humanity in those congested, confused streets, as throngs of people carried on without me, I felt left out. I experienced a loneliness of spirit unequal to anything I had ever felt in my solitary wilderness. In the streets I searched for some sign of beauty, some pulse, some streak of light, some laughter, a hazed softness in the sky, petals, birds, anything to remind me that Seoul was part of the earth. But I saw no evidence. The Korea I witnessed was steel and asphalt, wet, cold and sad. I also saw a lot of cell phones.

The next day was Saturday and Eric was due back from Japan. Seeing him walk through the door was exactly like seeing an old friend. I couldn't believe how happy I was to see him standing there and had to remind myself I barely knew the guy to keep from knocking him over and licking his face to welcome him home. He seemed more tanned and relaxed than before, as if just over the water in Japan, the sun had been pouring down on a country of cheerful people, while here in Korea, everything was glum.

'I'm home!' He looked around the apartment. 'And my home's still here, and so is all my stuff! All weekend I was worried I'd given my keys to a Canadian redhead thief who pretends to be helpless at international airports.'

'Yeah, Canadians are like that,' I said. 'Especially redhead Canadians.' He threw his bags down. 'Oh, I ate some of your cookies. Did you mother send you those? I've been wearing your jacket too… as you can see.' I looked down at the bulky folds of soft brown leather, realising I was wearing his jacket inside the apartment. I'd hardly taken it off in the past four days.

'Oh, well… it suits you,' he said. He hesitated a moment looking around the small apartment. 'Christ, I've forgotten how small this place is. Wait till you hear about Japan. That's where we both should be.' He began telling me about his trip, about how every aspect of Japan is efficient, exquisite and clean, how they have parks there, trees and cherry blossoms. Grass grows in Japan. Everything is organised. People actually seem happy there. 'Japan,' he said, 'is opposite to Korea in almost all ways. 'Korea is a country where people hang dead dogs from trees in their front yards so the meat will dry in time for dinner. Korea is a country where you can get arrested for holding hands in public. Korea is a country where nobody makes eye contact on the street.'

'Korea is a country that makes you feel bad about life in general,' I added.

'Yeah, exactly, and Korea is a country which attracts all the freaks who couldn't fit into Western culture.'

'Oh, really? Like you and me?'

'Oh God, no. Well, I don't think so. But, like everyone else, anyway,' he said.

'Why are you here?' I asked.

'I've been stuck here.' Eric threw himself down on the couch. 'It happens to tons of foreign teachers. They do all kinds of things to make you stay, like withhold your pay. You stay because you believe they'll honour your contract. But this is Korea. It's lawless and corrupt. In my first year teaching in this country, in Pusan, in the south, the school I taught for gave me a brothel to live in. That was my free accommodation, a brothel. Every night I'd go to sleep to the sounds of groaning. Little drunk guys used to bang on my door at four in the morning when they couldn't find the right room. The woman who ran the place, the madam, used to try to sneak into my bed. She was sixty! Other than that part, we were friends. She taught me how to speak Korean. But she wanted to sleep with me, which made things a little awkward. About once a week I'd have to fight her off. I couldn't leave the school because they were always withholding my pay. They never did pay what they owed me. I lived in a room just big enough for a single bed. My mother sent cookies to the brothel every month. She thought I was living with Korean nuns.'

We went across the street where I got to try my first real Korean food: a delicious meal of rice and noodles in a big sizzling pot surrounded by little bowls filled with unidentifiable food, extraordinary condiments, like acorn jelly cubes, and delicious *kimchi* which is a garlicky, spicy pickled cabbage.

As we ate, Eric told me about his screwed-up childhood and teenage years moving all over the U.S. with his wacko parents, how he'd gone to the University of Oregon to study French, then to Paris where he'd had too many French girlfriends, all snobs, and came home to be an actor. He said he wanted to save a hundred thousand dollars teaching in Korea, then move to someplace beautiful on the West Coast and open his own theatre coffee shop and live in a solar panel house. A solar panel house and theatre coffee shop on the West Coast sounded like a dream to me, a dizzying golden dream from twirling around all afternoon in a meadow, a dream from a faraway lost world, a dream I could relate to.

'I can see you doing that,' I told him. 'I can.'

On the subway to see a movie we laughed for the entire ride because we kept taking the wrong subways. The subway is absurdly confusing, even to Koreans. This time it was fun to be lost. Suddenly Korea seemed like a different place since I had a friend. Everything is so difficult and frightening and lonely on your own. Now when people stared, I just stared back.

At one subway stop, we saw a Western guy from the subway window. In all my time there, except for the few English teachers at the schools, and Eric of course, I hadn't seen another Westerner among the crowds in Seoul, or any foreigner for that matter. Like Japan, Korea is mainly an ethnically homogenous nation. We rushed at the window and knocked at the guy. He saw us and ran over to our window, put his hands on the glass. Our subway was starting to move by then so all we could do was stare after him and wave and wonder who he was – some American or Canadian English teacher probably, alone in Seoul.

I was excited about seeing the movie *Shine*, but not surprisingly, going to a movie in Korea was just plain weird. We had to buy our tickets somewhere else, then walk down the street until we found the theatre which matched our ticket. Buying the ticket was like doing a drug deal, secretive and underground, like international espionage. Once we got to the theatre, which didn't look like a theatre to me – no marquee or advertising – we had to walk down a back alley and through a mechanic shop, then four floors up in an old-fashioned elevator. The theatre itself was like a high school gymnasium, cheap, with bad acoustics, fluorescent lights and silly little seats with numbered white hospital covers on their backs. The numbers were for the designated seats. Even though there were only twenty people in the theatre, they gave Eric and me seats separated by the aisle. I moved over to sit next to Eric, ignoring my assigned seat. Eric said we'd be arrested for that. The movie was good and I cried at the end and noticed Eric had also. I liked that.

We found a little pub in a university area of Seoul where they played Dolly Parton's 'Nine to Five' repeatedly. We ordered Black Russians, beer, and a plate of French fries. The fries were 10,000 won, which was $12.00 U.S. or $17.00 Canadian, and they were lousy and undercooked. The waiters kept screwing up the drinks and bringing us White Russians by mistake – they did this several times – then they would correct it and let us keep the original drinks also. I hadn't drunk in ages and I knocked back three drinks far too fast. I felt like it after all the harrowing times I'd been through. We laughed at the bad music, at our lives, at what we were doing in such a silly bar, in such a country in the closing years of the twentieth century. We talked about our generation, so jobless back in North America that we have to come to such an unusual place, so unlikely, so uninviting. At one point he said, 'What's this well-adjusted thing with you? Isn't that kind of odd?' An hour later, he took that back.

After they kicked us out of the American bar at closing time, we found an after-hours club down a dark stairwell where North American teachers and cool Koreans were dancing to Abba. We joined them. I loved it. It was like hell with a cover charge. My feet were killing me from the cheap shoes so I sat down at a table and met a guy from New Brunswick wearing a Che Guevara hat and goatee who told me about his hateful *hogwan* job, how they'd lied to him back in Canada about what his wages would be. His Elvis Costello-looking friend from New York came over and had a similar funny but tragic story of his job. Both of them had massive students loans to pay. When I told them I didn't have a massive debt but was just a teacher looking for a job to make money, they honestly didn't get it. What do you mean you're not in debt? Then why are you here? Are you nuts? We're all in exile here. Look around. Nobody is here who doesn't have to be. It's torture, haven't you noticed? I told them that actually I had noticed its Dante's *Inferno* qualities. 'Escape! Get out before it sucks you in,' they said. 'Flee, flee! Live for us in exile! Seoul is not for the soulful.'

We all danced after that. A Korean woman with a Rickie Lee Jones hat and a lollipop in her mouth kept wanting to hold my hand and practise English with me. She told me her name was So Young but I could call her So or Sue if I liked. She was wearing men's aftershave. The club was crazy and dark and wild, although smoky, and I loved it all.

We couldn't find a taxi to take us back. Most Seoul taxi drivers are rude and horrible people who rarely stop for foreigners and often can't be bothered going to a destination if they don't feel like it. Eventually we got some sort of ride at four in the morning. Back at Eric's dorm we ate frozen yogurt, watched a bad Julia Roberts movie, giggled, and told each other about crank calls we'd made as kids. I kept looking at Eric and thinking, I really *like* this guy. What a cruel joke that we had to meet in this godforsaken country where I didn't belong. Being in the dorm room with him was so comfortable and fun, but not real life. It was an escape, like hiding out in a bunker during a war. Even though we were incredibly attracted to each other, we knew we had no future together since Eric was planning on staying in Korea. So that night, instead of letting any passions fly, we had a massive tickle fight, which is surprisingly effective at releasing tension.

The next day it was time for me to leave Korea forever. I went to Korea because I thought it would be a new place to go in the spirit of adventure, and to make a pile of money. But I didn't like that particular adventure and I realised I should never do anything solely for the money. Life is too fleeting and valuable to make a few dollars if we're miserable doing it. I also realised this about myself: I simply cannot live in a place that lacking in the colour green, that lacking in spirit, and that lacking in friendly warmth, which showed me what I *do* want – just the opposite of what was there. I realised I wanted what I think everyone wants: connectedness to people and to a physical place. In any case, I knew I had to get out of Korea fast, before something really bad happened. Never had I been in a place where I didn't fit in more than in Korea. Just crossing the street felt dangerous to me.

Suddenly it was all coming to a close, the whole fantastically bizarre and frenzied trip. Eric came with me to the airport. On the subway, we talked to a sweet young Korean student who was studying to become a policeman. He was also practising English. Eric asked him what he would do if he caught some bank robbers. The student said he would give them a special talk and explain they were on the wrong road in life. The student asked why I was leaving Korea and Eric told him that I was like a wild mountain flower and I'd wilt if I stayed. Eric and I both laughed, but the student's face clouded over with sadness. He thought for a minute, then said, 'I'm sorry Korea hasn't been kind to you. I would have been.' I stopped laughing. I wondered if I had been terribly wrong about Korea after all, and I wondered how one small sentence uttered from a stranger could somehow make a difference to your soul.

But there was no going back. I felt so glad to be getting out, but sad too because I had met Eric who I might never see again. It made me wonder about the life I'd been leading, always moving on and leaving people behind. Maybe I just didn't see the right Korea, I thought. Maybe another Korea is just what someone else needs. It takes a lot to make a world. Eric walked with me all the way through the airport until they wouldn't let him walk any further, and then we kissed goodbye. I felt a pang in my chest at the sight of him standing there alone watching me leave and I had a sudden urge to run back to him and say, 'OK, I'll give it one more chance!' But I knew I'd given Korea enough chances, so walked toward my gate instead.

I flew from Korea to Vancouver, then took the ferry to Victoria, on Vancouver Island, where my parents happened to be staying that spring. On the bus from the airport to the ferry terminal, I could have fallen in mad love with the bus driver. He wasn't handsome in the least; in fact, he was probably in his mid-fifties, bald, with a substantial paunch, but it wasn't that sort of love. He was like no bus driver I'd come across in Asia, which is ironic because he actually had a very Buddhist way of looking at life. He was open, funny, philosophical, intellectual, bright, inspiring, *loving* – all qualities rather unusual for a bus driver to display on his route, I thought. He told me he'd spent three years in India studying kundalini yoga where he learned to tap into a powerful source of energy at the base of the spine that comes surging up and out the top of the head, at which point all thoughts and chatter stop to make way for pure bliss and peace of mind. Now he practises this driving from the airport to the ferry and back. I told him about Sumatra and Seoul and my nightmare bus rides there, how my trip didn't work out for me. He said that not everything's meant to work out in life, not the way you think it will. He said all people can do is follow their hearts. This seemed like the final irony to the end of my Sumatra–Korea trip – a trip dominated by horrendous bus rides – to have *this* guy as my last bus driver. I didn't want to get off the bus. I kept wondering, is this Canada, this ease with strangers, this openness, this exploring of new ideas, this friendliness? This must have been here all along and I'd never noticed. This is the culture that shaped me, I kept thinking, and this is why I'm so comfortable with it now on the bus, with this driver, with these fellow passengers all chipping in their views, laughing along at our conversation. Some of the other passengers were, like me, just off a plane from Asia, fellow backpackers, my tribe, and I felt such affinity and affection for them. I've never been so overjoyed and relieved to be Canadian, to be in my own country, to be home.

Spring lasts a long time on the West Coast. Giant blossoms were blooming everywhere in Victoria. Unexpectedly, I continued to be filled to the brim with a whole new appreciation for Canada. I could hardly contain myself. I went hiking in the woods, got a temporary job in a used book store in downtown Victoria, slept on my parent's pull-out couch in their rented condo, and talked to people on the streets, friendly people, helpful people, laughing people. They were all over the place.

I wanted to like Korea. I wanted it to be another place on the pathway of my life of exploration, my path of seeking out the beauty and wisdom in the world. But it wasn't my path at all. It was miles and miles off, as many miles as it takes to cross the deep and storied ocean to the West Coast of North America, and maybe even more than that.

Chapter 16

No please! Please no! Come on, Marcia. You can do it. Please, God, if you exist, and many times in my life I've felt you do, HELP ME! Please don't let my car break down out here. Not in the middle of the desert!'

'This too shall pass, this too shall pass...'

I'm driving across the state of Nevada in a state of panic while the desert darkens all around me. Up shadowy dangerous hills, hills which seem to be turning into mountains, Marcia is barely making it up at all. Every fibre of my being begs her to continue. I lean forward in my seat to propel her further into the night.

This isn't a time to become unhinged.

I'm listening to Joni Mitchell. California, I'm coming to kiss your sunset pink, or possibly, your sunset pig. Whichever it is, I'll kiss it when I get there. I just have to drive 425 miles through a desert first. That's like driving across the entire nation of France.

I have to occupy my mind with something other than Marcia. OK, if I'm really meant to live in California, then I won't break down out here. The forces of the universe will be with me, ferry me along on translucent wings far more powerful than any mechanical glitch. There. I'm becoming very Californian with that sort of thinking. I should fit in just fine. How interesting that the place I fit in the least, Korea, taught me the most valuable lesson of all my travels: always follow the pathway of the heart. Listen to life's inner callings at the expense of all else. I now know what I have to do. I have to break up with Andre for good this time. No matter how kind he is, how generous, agreeable and fun, no matter how effortlessly I could slip back into our old companionship, he's just not the one I've been waiting for. He's not the pathway of the heart, at least, not my heart. Just like Korea wasn't.

Breaking up. Breaking down. I don't think I've ever experienced this emotional combination before, being this sad, and this scared to death.

If I break up with him, does that mean I have a mechanical breakdown, instant karma? Breaking down out here in this black desert of utter emptiness tonight would border on a calamity. This desert would drink me down to the last drop and leave me too dry to continue. I've done some dangerous, naive and reckless things in my life – I was once drugged with mint tea and hypnotised into buying carpets in Morocco; I've hitchhiked thousands of miles by myself through fourteen countries; I've been lost in several mountain ranges, and was once stuck on the side of a treacherous icy slope where one wrong step would have led to my death; I hiked up a mountain one long terrifying night in the Alps with an Italian who planned on keeping me up there for good; and I raced across North America on the back of a speeding and fanatical souvenir hunter's motorcycle – but driving across the Nevada desert all night in a car that should have been scrap metal long ago has to be up there on my list of risky escapades. I think I've finally fully grasped what an incredibly stupid idea this is. What would I do if I broke down? Wait for a serial murderer to come by and give me a hand? Hitchhike to the nearest mechanic three hundred miles from here? Walk off into the desert to start my own cult?

It's now hours later and I'm coming to grips with my relationship breakup. Even though it seems cruel, it's the kindest thing I can do, to set him free. He deserves someone who'll love him wholeheartedly. He deserves so much better than what I can give him.

My car is continuing to move sluglike through the night as self-pity oozes through my soul. The same vehicle has been behind me for at least an hour, which seems a little creepy since I'm going so slowly. Still, I feel a Nancy Drew-like excitement at the thought of being followed. In my rear-view mirror, the sky is beginning to fill with tinted rose, and now that it's light enough, I see the driver behind me is an old guy in a beat-up pickup truck which probably doesn't go any faster than Marcia. So he's not following me. I guess it's for the best. All around me, grey mountains are taking shape after their slumber, the ground is growing into a soft violet carpet, and the sky is whispering into pure Ionian blue. Ahead of me on the highway a very fat man on a Harley Davidson is wearing a black T-shirt that says, 'If you can read this, the BITCH fell off.'

I've journeyed west in the depths of night and come to a strange land.

But maybe the West isn't so tough after all. I just remembered that John Wayne's real name was Marion Morrison, which might be a good metaphor for the West.

It's time to take a nap. I'd pull over to sleep somewhere but I don't want to stop until I'm well out of range of the maximum security federal prison I just passed. I keep passing signs telling me not to pick up hitchhikers. I can see that wouldn't be a good idea out here. If this state wasn't so full of dangerous looking vagrants and if it didn't have the highest crime rate in the country, not to mention the second highest rape rate, I'd be tempted to pick up a hitchhiker just so I could take a nap while the hitchhiker drove. That's one of the less commonly known reasons for picking up hitchhikers. The vast majority of drivers pick up hitchhikers because they're bored and want to talk to someone. Some do it because they're kind, decent people who want to make the world a more worthwhile place, and, of course, there are those who pick up hitchhikers so they can do something nasty, like expose themselves or scare you or worse.

On a trip I once took with Kevin before the Yukon, we were hitchhiking on a back road in West Virginia – I always liked to encourage my friends to travel to the U.S., so they could see it wasn't full of gun-toting maniacs and racists, but kind decent people usually very similar to us. On this particular road in West Virginia, however, a decrepit car pulled over for us and the driver looked slightly deranged. Actually, so did a lot of people in West Virginia. As soon as the door was shut with me in the back and Kevin in the front, the guy rammed his foot to the gas, turned his head around so he could show me his crazed eyes jutting out of their sockets while he yelled, 'You're in the car now!' He said this in a maniacal way, I might add, and he repeated it several times loudly, laughing after each declaration that we were now in a car with a psychopath who was probably going to take us to a backwoods river gully and make us squeal like pigs. 'You're in the car now, yep, in the car now, ha, ha, ha!' He drove faster than any piece of metal should be allowed to move across the surface of the earth while he held a half-empty beer bottle in one hand and a cigarette in the other. 'You're in the car now! Ha, ha, Wheeeee!' This was unnerving, but more unnerving was being stuck in the back seat of his two-door car. Kevin turned around and gave me a look that clearly said: 'Well, this is it. I guess we're going to die now. It's kind of thrilling, though, don't you think?' Next to me was a baby car seat. 'Oh, do you have a baby?' I thought inquiring about a child might remind him he had a family at home and it would be sensible for him to treat strangers nicely and not cut them up into tiny pieces to put in his freezer and eat in small portions over the next five years. He turned around and I saw insanity leap off his face. 'You could say I *used* to have a baby.' We drove on in silence for ten dreadful minutes. At one point we drove through a small town and I thought we should try waving frantically through the window at anyone we passed on the street. As I watched for someone, Kevin turned to the crazy man and, with surprising calm in his voice, said, 'Excuse me, but we'd like to get out now.'

'Like that's gonna work,' I mumbled from the back. This guy just killed his kid and maybe his wife and we're next and he's going to respond to politeness? But this is a lesson in life to remember: sometimes politeness works. The crazy man looked at Kevin and said, 'Oh really? Oh… all right. That's fine.' He seemed surprised, deflated, as if he thought the ride was going well for all of us. He slowed down to pull over, shook our hands and waved goodbye. 'Nice to meet you two,' he said as Kevin and I toppled ourselves out of the car in one fluid motion onto the grass. The crazy man beeped his horn a couple of times and drove off. It was a little anticlimactic, but at least we wouldn't end up in a basement freezer after all and we were very glad of that.

Even though it's 105 degrees, I can't let this Nevada desert pass by in a blur of hazy mirages. I want to explore at least some of this landscape, see how even small rocks cast giant shadows, and how if you look closely you see that the desert has colour after all, is filled with burnt pinks and a hundred variations of mauve.

I pull the car over to the side of the road and get out: no cars, no tourists, no escaped convicts. Through the heat

– at least it's a dry heat, as they say – I walk across the parched earth broken with cracks, and see small desert plants and cacti that miraculously survive, year after year, with the scantest of rains. As I look out across the vast earth in all directions, the desert's stark beauty begins strangely to glow, with the sun slashing in from the east. I feel the heat rising up from below, as if the earth were baking me, and everything starts to vibrate until I feel suspended, magically, between earth and sky. A shiny beetle – or is it a prehistoric cockroach? – rattles across the ground at my feet until it reaches a red flowering cactus, then plunges the top half of its body inside the desert bloom. Perhaps I'm feeling what this insect feels as it burrows deeper inside: free, removed from the world. A heady, wild joy.

Not wanting to get heatstroke, I rush back to the car and drive until I come to a rest stop. I'm in need of a rest after my long drive through the night. Luckily, this rest stop has shade I can pull my car under, a car shelter to block the sun. Where I come from, we have similar shelters to keep out the snow, like car ports and covered bus stops. After my nap, and Marcia's, we hit the road again, rattling along through a soft brown valley of dunes and tough desert scrub.

There is a God! Thank you! I didn't die in the Nevada desert. I see civilisation just ahead in the form of a coffee-stained cloud of smog hovering over skyscrapers.

I'm entering the intense heat of Reno, a neon and tacky sun-punished place that I can't imagine I'll like very much. But after driving through the desert for what feels like a month, I could use some distraction. Reno comes on so fast. A moment ago I was in an empty, stark no man's land, and now I'm in Disney World, sort of. As I drive down the colourful strip full of giant signs advertising casinos, Reno begins to seem a little rough around the edges with its glaring black, mirrored casino hotels that look as if they've seen better days. I'm starving and plan on finding one of those all-you-can-eat buffets that are so famous here.

I feel like a stuffed walrus. I'll never eat again. I've just waddled out of the buffet with all the other gluttonous people, mostly middle-aged tourists who are on their way to the gaming rooms of Reno like kids at a funhouse fair. I've just built my own chocolate sundae for the first and last time of my life. Taped sounds of squawking cockatoos and parrots blared out of the speakers for a wild jungle theme, but the nature effect was somewhat undermined by the presence of the fake plastic flowers and all the really fat, pasty people lined up to mound obscene piles of saucy chicken breasts, creamy seafoods, jellied mayonnaise marshmallow dishes called salads, and caramel pudding on their plates.

A man eating at the table next to mine told me about a new casino they're planning to build in Las Vegas. It's to be called Titanic – not *The* Titanic, just Titanic, like the movie – and the entire hotel will actually sink into a huge body of water every night. The guests will have portholes in their rooms so they can see the water level rising to get that really cool near-death experience. The meals served will be exactly the same as those served on the actual Titanic, which I imagine consisted of a lot of bland, overcooked English food with mushy peas on the side. The man told me about this as he was eating plasticky cherry cream pie and he said he thought the Titanic casino was the best idea he'd ever heard. I didn't know what to say, so kept repeating, 'Are you serious?' over and over. He kept saying, 'Yep. It's true. That's what I heard anyway.' A Titanic casino would probably make millions. Americans love to Disney-fy things. They also have a morbid fascination for tragedy. I wonder if the people with the cheaper rooms will be stuck down in steerage. Maybe they'll be blocked by the rich people up top if they try to escape. Maybe the casino could hire Leonardo DiCaprio to do a lounge act, which could be some kind of tragedy in itself.

I think I've had enough of Reno. I need more trees. I don't know why they need to make so many cities ugly, like Reno, like Seoul. Some cities seem to be running a competition trying to redefine the lower limits of bad taste. I'm tired of passing the same stores and fast food chains all strung together along the strips like the background of a Road Runner cartoon where the scenery never changes. But I suppose people have always complained about the aesthetic qualities of their society. I read a 1912 hobo's account of the West, of how the hobo and his friends laughed at the false-front architecture of the buildings.

California, I'm not coming to see that side of you, although I know it's there. I'm coming to see your natural wild side and to meet your people.

I drive down the main drag to the highway out of town, leaving Reno and its strip malls behind me in the dust.

Chapter 17

This is it. The other side of my life, the other side of the rainbow, is a mile away, according to the road sign. Marcia, we're almost in the land of milk and honey, or really, the land of enriched vanilla soymilk and bee-friendly organic honey, with maybe some sushi on the side. Just the name *California* inspires amazement around the world. The name sizzles, holds magic, makes people think *this is where my life should be taking place*. I want to see all of this thousand-mile empire's wildly disparate sites: the mountains, the desert, the small coastal and valley towns, the sea pounding the ochre sandstone cliffs, the fog floating through redwood rifts, the lonely twisting Joshua trees, the artichoke farmers in their fields, the Chamber of Horror rides at beach amusement parks, the movie stars wandering aisles of gourmet food stores, the crazy people, the creative people, the extraterrestrial and regular people – the many worlds within California. California, where the intensity of the environment matches that of the people.

I can't believe we've made it. If I made it here in a car, even Marcia, I can't imagine how the pioneers, gold-seekers, drifters and the Okies must have felt, trudging by foot and wagon through hundreds of hot and muddy miles, finally arriving here often a year after they left home. The pioneers must have been out of their minds with relief when they got to California, which, until 1848, was a far-off Mexican province rumoured to be an earthly paradise where the sun always shone and fruit grew wild. To those early pioneers just arriving here, California must have felt wide open for anything, like perfection verging on chaos, like a twelve-year-old girl. I wonder how many of those settlers found the California they were looking for. I wonder if I will.

I'm at the California border check and a cute guy is asking if I have any fruit with me. Californians don't want diseased fruit entering their state. I just happen to be eating a mango which I got from the buffet in Reno and mango juice is all over my hands. 'Nope, no fruit.' I throw back my head and laugh at my obvious lie, feeling like a 1940s movie star, like Lana Turner in a convertible instead of a sunburned Canadian in a busted Bronco. He laughs too, in a California kind of way, and we decide I should finish the mango right there.

Already the view has changed. I'm in the mountains again and they're green and majestic, like a digitally enhanced postcard. As I drive north on Route 89, everything seems to be a glorious dream. Even Marcia has perked up. She's actually sailing.

It's all coming back to me now, how I felt the very first time I stepped foot in California. I always seem to get this same feeling whenever I return here, no matter from which direction I enter. After the rainy night at the East Indian man's place in southern Oregon, I got a ride with two women and a little boy – the first women ever to pick me up – and they were on their way to Eureka, California. I told them I'd never been to California before and they said I had to see the redwoods. We drove through the rain into Jedediah Smith Redwood State Park, deeper and deeper through thick, moist, old growth coastal forest with the tallest trees in the world. I'd never seen trees anything like that, except in pictures, but photographs and paintings can never do justice to redwoods since the impression they make on your psyche simply cannot be transferred. We drove slowly along winding narrow dirt roads in an old Dodge Dart that felt like a toy compared to the girth of the trees. The women and boy seemed as awestruck as I even though this was not their first time among the redwoods. The damp undergrowth contained honeyed scents of life and decay, a dense variety of mosses, ferns, flowers, wild berries, lichens and shrubs. Far above, an unbroken canopy of dark green needles filtered the light. It's difficult to describe the feeling of being dwarfed by those two-thousand-year-old tree giants, ambassadors from another time, but it feels other-worldly, enchanted, as if elves might pop up from a hole at any time and ask why you're there. Even though the campground was closed – it was too early in the season – I asked the women to let me out. I had my cheap little Canadian Tire tent. The women and boy dropped me off and wished me luck, leaving me alone with the staggering silence of the trees.

I don't know how long I just stood there letting the soft rain fall on me but very soon I felt absorbed into the forest's cathedral hush. Looking around the woods empty of people but so full of life, I was struck with the knowledge that I belonged in this powerful land, that somehow, I'd found my place. I no longer felt like a hobo, or a student, or a Canadian or any other defining label: it was simply that I felt I fit into the landscape, that it could envelop me whole into its earthy, dank, ancient arms. Perhaps I've always responded passionately to a geography unburdened with human interference, for this same overwhelming sensation would happen to me again years later on a remote Fijian island, but never so profoundly as that rainy day in the redwoods of northern California where, inexplicably, I felt I'd come home to a place I'd only just arrived.

And here I am entering California again, feeling once more a different order of things here in nature's grace, something quiet in the air as the evening hand of summer cups the earth and a few far off clouds curdle the blue sky.

So far, I can only get one radio station in the Sierra Nevada. A California talk show host is speaking with a college student named Jenny who has a permanent webcam set up in her dorm room for anyone to watch her any time of the day or night. People from all over the state are calling in to cheer her on, ask her to have more sex, tell her she should be ashamed of herself, to sleep naked, or to stop snoring. I couldn't get this kind of radio in Kansas. I feel as if I'm driving off a flat black and white map and entering Oz.

I'm heading first to the High Sierra Music Festival in the Bear Valley where I'm meeting Ann and Lawrence, friends I met in Fiji six years ago. I've already been to visit them a couple of times at their home near the coast, in a town called Sebastopol, an hour north of San Francisco. We decided we'd meet this time in the mountains at the music festival, and after the weekend, travel together back to their place. Ann and Lawrence are organic farmers, among other things. Lawrence is studying to be a lawyer with ethics and Ann is a yoga teacher. Ann also works at a Japanese spa called Osmosis where, she jokes, she composts people by shovelling piles of steaming fermented wood chip matter on their naked bodies while they lie in a giant tub surrounded by a Japanese garden. How very Californian.

I've arrived a night before the music festival and am about to sleep in the back of Marcia. The moon is rising above the trees and I'm parked beside a babbling mountain brook where I've just taken a ludicrously cold bath. I met a woman sitting on a rock in the brook, a woman with wild woodsy hair, bleached blue eyes and strong wiry arms. She hasn't decided if she'll go to the music festival or not because she says she's not in the mood for society, but she invited me to eat dinner with her. Together, we have the combined makings of burritos.

I feel so refreshed, not at all as if I've just driven across a continent. Everything has taken on an added depth and brightness, a clarity that feels infused with anticipation, with the colours richer, the smells more pungent. Could I be tuning into some kind of amassed collective consciousness of how it feels finally to have arrived at this place? Perhaps memories were left scattered here, memories from people who had travelled far and were about to step further into the stream of the unknown. This place feels surrounded by a sense of adventure, by tomorrow and the day after that.

I'm at the music festival and already have at least twenty new friends. Ann and I were doing gymnastics earlier today on the grass, just as we did in Fiji on the beach. Last night we saw a band called The String Cheese Incident, an energetic electro-bluegrass-funk band from Boulder. The best part of the night was back at the campsite where we had a fire and lots of guitars. We ate Trader Joe's chocolate-mint chip cookies, drank kiwi-lime margaritas, and sang until the stars blinked out and birds began to sing. At one point someone started singing an old disco song, 'That's the Way I Like It' which went on for half an hour with all of us singing, joined arm-in-arm, circling the fire. Some people on mushrooms stumbled by to join us and kept falling down to laugh. Later, they said singing that song had been the highlight of their summer so far. I think it was mine too.

This is a small and cosy musical festival surrounded on all sides by mountain peaks. I hope the High Sierra Music Festival doesn't become too big and popular, lose its charm, something that inevitably happens all over the world to certain towns, cities, festivals, even tropical islands. People have to keep finding new places, new festivals, ever reaching out into the world to replace what were once happy little secrets. I wonder how much of California has suffered this fate already.

Ann and I are driving across the sizzling central valley towards the coast in Marcia, while Lawrence is driving his truck behind us. We're reeling from our marathon weekend of dancing, starry crisp nights around the fire, and too many margaritas.

Sputter, sputter, lurch, squeal, groan. So much for Marcia's California joy ride. I guess she was excited to be here and got a little carried away. Now she's back to her old cranky ways. Lawrence just stopped us to say that every time we go uphill, black smoke streams out of the exhaust pipe. California has the toughest anti-pollution vehicle emission laws in the world, which is great, except it may mean I'll be pulled over any minute. I really have to get this heap of junk fixed once and for all. Either that or drive her off a cliff into the ocean. I'd make my escape right before the plunge, just like in *Harold and Maude*. Then I'd sing a Cat Stevens song and be on my way.

When we arrive in Sebastopol it's even lovelier than I remember. On previous visits, I've always flown from Ontario to San Francisco and driven with Ann up to Sebastopol, but arriving in Sebastopol this way, driving from the hot central valley, gives me a new perspective on how temperate and fresh this place feels, like coming across a cool blossomy garden after a desert. The ocean is less than half an hour away by car and I can almost feel its breezes. On the porch of Ann and Lawrence's blue cottage-like house just outside of town, their Australian sheepdog Charlie is waiting for us on the porch. Inside, they offer me their favourite indulgences, sourdough bread baked in a French wood-fired oven from a local bakery, and some deliciously dark, freshly roasted gourmet coffee called Peet's. Lawrence shows me the office at the back of the house where I'll be staying while I explore the idea of moving here. It's a small room with a futon on the floor, a book shelf, and a view outside of an apricot tree. I love it.

I take Ann and Lawrence out to their favourite Mexican restaurant in town where for the first time I drink *horchata*, an icy Mexican beverage made of rice, almonds, cinnamon and sugar. The enchiladas with guacamole are so good I make a vow to eat every meal here for the rest of my life.

That night, Ann goes to bed early so she can teach yoga at dawn, and Lawrence and I stay up late talking about Fiji where we first met, how much our lives have changed since those carefree days on our little island campground, how much fun we had laughing and playing music with the Fijians. But life can still be fun now, we agree, just not on an extended basis like back then. And even back then, we recall, travelling wasn't always easy, not at all.

In the morning I borrow Ann's bike to go exploring. I ride by rolling hills, apple orchards, a vineyard, and a steep hill leading into a redwood forest. When I'm in Sebastopol, I see it hasn't changed since my last visit. It's one of those perfect little American towns which might have inspired Norman Rockwell. I'm envious of the 7,000 or so people who can afford to buy a house here, who get to enjoy spring-summer weather all year round, an eclectic array of arts, world-class wine, and fresh produce from the surrounding farms. There's a Sunday morning market in the town square where people buy organic and discuss the week's events while their children play in the fountain. Almost all the women in town wear the same Danish leather clogs and everyone practises asthanga yoga, or at least look like they do. The most popular grocery store is a giant wholefood market right in the town square. There are no malls, no urban sprawl, and the thriving downtown's shops are locally run. The only downside I see is too much traffic. Some of the cars are old classics, though, cars that stay pristine since they don't have to salt the roads in the winter: 1963 Ford Galaxies, 1956 T-birds with porthole windows in the back, 1949 Fords with their rocket-inspired front bumpers, El Caminos (the mullets of the car world), 1955 Corvette Stingrays, early Mustangs and Chevy Novas. Today, I even spot a sky-blue 1965 Ford Falcon station wagon, exactly the car my parents had when I was a kid. A Road Runner from the late sixties ahead of me on the main street has this bumper sticker: 'I'm pro-accordion and I vote.' Unfortunately, I don't get a look at the driver.

I like Sebastopol, but after a few days of driving around other parts of Sonoma County, I'm drawn towards the land just west of here, near a village called Occidental, closer to the ocean. The hills are bigger, the forests more imposing, and there aren't as many people, although all the people I do meet, I like. I take drives to the tiny towns of Bodega, Freestone, Valley Ford and Tomales. I find out-of-the-way libraries where I chat with the solitary librarians working there. I come across extraordinary bakeries selling raspberry chocolate French pastries, and hear how in one bakery, John Belushi used to come in for their pain au chocolat. I wind down roads where I'm suddenly driving under the woven dark canopy of a redwood forest. For miles I inhale the cool breath of eucalyptus trees from Australia, or occasionally look up to see a stand of palm trees, not native to northern California, spray their branches like a fountain to the sky. From out of the green hills, I turn a corner and find myself facing the turquoise folds of the Pacific. I discover remote beaches with smooth blue rocks, run down a shore and trip over driftwood. Yesterday I passed the farmhouse of Tom Waits, the gravel-voiced poet laureate of the down and out, who once happened to sit next to me in a country café around here.

As I drive along the narrow twisting roads on these wistful summery days, beside the ocean or up high on the cliffs, I feel as if I'm expanding into the very beauty of the land itself, and I sense something opening up inside me, a gradual awakening of a foreign pulse. I heard recently of a study where scientists measured brain activity while people engaged in different actions. Not surprisingly, they found the lowest activity while people watched TV. However, they found the most activity when people walked in a new city, as people not only adjusted spatially to a new environment, but strove to make sense of their new surroundings. This is how I always feel when I travel, like a kid wandering through a magical, ever fascinating world where every turn reveals something new and incomprehensible.

After years of searching I may have finally found the perfect place to live, although I haven't moved in yet so I can't be entirely sure. An hour and a half north of San Francisco, in Sonoma county, in a town with the gumption to call itself Camp Meeker, I'm going to rent a room in a house entirely surrounded by redwoods. My bed will be in a glass-encased loft so all around me will be thousand-year-old giants. Faith Fauna is the name of the woman who owns the house, although I'm sure that can't be her real name. I saw her ad yesterday on a bulletin board in Occidental:

> LOOKING FOR VEGAN HOUSEMATE TO SHARE LOVELY HOUSE IN TREES, NON-SMOKER, MUST LOVE ANIMALS, NO PETS (SINCE I HAVE CATS), $350/MONTH.

The ad also had a map showing where the house was and a phone number for a health food store in Santa Rosa where

Faith Fauna works. Faith Fauna sounded very cheerful on the phone and thought I did too. When she asked if I was vegan, I told her honestly that I eat cheese sometimes but have been planning to cut it out anyway. Also, I occasionally have a weakness for ice cream, although it usually makes me feel terrible afterwards, so I'd definitely cut that out too. I drove a mile down the winding, forested Bohemian Highway from Occidental until I came to an old wooden sign that stretched above the road saying CAMP MEEKER painted in white. I had trouble getting Marcia up the steep narrow roads into Camp Meeker, and since I was early in meeting Faith Fauna, parked, and walked around the place. Camp Meeker isn't really a camp, although it was when it was founded in the nineteenth century as a lumber camp, but it isn't really a town either. It's a cluster of about three hundred houses hidden beneath a dark forest where a few roads roller-coaster through it like an accident waiting to happen. Most of the houses are small and appear even smaller since they're dwarfed by three-hundred-foot redwoods. Most of the houses are made of wood, don't get a lot of sunlight, and look as if gnomes live in them. I saw kids playing in a big creek which snakes through the settlement and they wanted me to join them. The place isn't big enough to have its own general store, but a post office sits beneath the trees, in a trailer. When it was time to meet Faith Fauna, I walked up about fifty steps to get to her house and once inside, knew immediately it was where I wanted to live. Luckily, she felt I belonged there too and said I could move in immediately.

When I wake up this morning, I do yoga with Ann, pack my things, and take off in Marcia for my new home. I love the drive from Sebastopol to Camp Meeker, first passing rolling meadows of California poppies and apple orchards, then winding higher through a dark forest beside a brook, then passing through Occidental, an historic village surrounded by towering trees and full of old Italian restaurants and art galleries. When I get to Faith Fauna's, she's waiting to help me unpack, not that I have any furniture. In fact, that's our project for today, to buy a futon mattress for my room, and a used couch for her living room. In Faith's truck, we drive over hilly country roads lined with vineyards to Santa Rosa and find a used, slightly weathered couch, which Faith says she'll cover with a Guatemalan blanket; and in a futon store, I buy a bed for myself. Faith also takes me to the Santa Rosa health food store where she's a manager, and introduces me to her friends working there, all vibrant student types, full of bubbly enthusiasm, wheatgrass juice, and detailed plans to change the world.

We carry the furniture up all the steps to the house with the help of a friendly neighbour, Jack, who seems to have a crush on Faith, although with his extensive beer gut and the licorice hanging out of his mouth, he hardly seems to be her type. Jack tells me he used to be a logger further north and is now trying to make a living selling used books on the Internet. 'Oh, so that means you get to read a lot of books,' I say. No, he tells me. He gets his mother to read them, rate them, and write a review for the Internet. 'That way,' he says, 'my mother has something to do, and I get free quality control for my product.' I laugh, although I'm not sure he's kidding. In any case, Jack seems like a jovial, bighearted guy and offers to show me his book collection some day.

Inside, Faith says she's going to cook us a specialty of hers. Most vegan food is delicious and I wonder what she'll make. It turns out her specialty tonight is wholewheat pasta with beet sauce. 'This will transport you to another place,' she tells me. I take a bite and sure enough, it does: a Siberian labour camp. However, the vegan brownies we have for dessert are scrumptious. As we drink blueberry tea, Faith tells me about growing up in Florida, how she used to follow the Grateful Dead across the continent in a van, and how she was able to buy this house when her father left her money he'd gone to jail for in the Savings and Loans Scandal. After dinner, we continue talking on the new couch in the living room, sharing bad date stories, and laughing about how hard it is for women in their thirties to find the perfect guy. I like Faith.

I go to bed thrilled with my new surroundings among the redwoods, and sink into my new cushy futon in the glass-enclosed loft. Rain falls gently all night, splashing through the leaves off the mighty dark branches just outside my open window. I inhale misty cool air, taking deep breaths of California, and feel a familiar, wild happiness.

After four days, I'm already starting to have a life here. I've found a paying job editing a manuscript written by an incredible woman named Arlene Blum who has led teams of mountains climbers up some of the world's tallest peaks and has hiked a 2,000 mile, nine-month trek across the mountains of Bhutan, Nepal and India. Her autobiographical manuscript is fascinating, and so is she. We just met yesterday at her home in Berkeley where we talked for over two hours about travelling and travel writing. Today, I substitute taught for a friend of Ann's, a guy named Arnold, who teaches at an alternative school called Nonesuch where they run summer classes. The school is in the middle of nowhere, set back deep in the woods, and I got lost trying to find it. When I arrived ten minutes late, nobody seemed to notice since the school's five teachers and 25 students were sprawled on couches, eating oatmeal and telling jokes. Apparently, school starts whenever people feel up to it. Nonetheless, I loved teaching the kids geography all day and told them about my travels, pointed out places on maps, and related cultural oddities of various island societies. I don't think much learning goes on at that school, but at least the kids are among the trees. I'd like to teach there again, although it doesn't pay very well. I'll have to find a real job soon. In the meantime, I'm becoming intimate with Camp Meeker. I've met some more neighbours and their dogs, and have talked to the kids who play in the brook. The babble of this brook outside my glass loft lulls me to sleep at night and every morning I go for walks to look at all the other little glassed-in houses set back in the woods and I wonder about the people inside.

I'm learning a lot about Faith Fauna too. Faith Fauna is an animal rights activist, strict vegan and an Earth First! member. She has secret meetings in her home she thinks are monitored by the FBI and she owns six cats, most of them vicious bird killers which seems to counter her animal rights stance since every day one of the cats deposits a dead bird on the kitchen floor. As she's a vegan, she doesn't want any animal products in her home, except dead birds I guess, so I'm not allowed to bring any ice cream into the house, or butter, or even my old suede jacket. I don't mind actually. I'm feeling very healthy.

Faith Fauna has many interesting friends: Egrett, who likes to come by on the full moon; Saffron, who looks like one of Charlie's Angels; Feral, who lives in a teepee; Cool Mama; a guy named Jenny; Sha-na-na; and Anarchy. Anarchy lives in redwood trees to keep them from being chopped down. She needs a bath. Anarchy stinks.

Last night, I burned one of Faith Fauna's cats. I've never been a cat lover – the hair, the dander, the bird killing, the litter, the unspoken demands, the attitude. But I certainly didn't mean to harm this cat. The cat was on top of the stove when I wanted to turn on an element. Faith Fauna lets her cats go wherever they please. The cat was bugging me up there looking exactly like it didn't give a crap so I turned the gas stove to high, thinking I was turning on the front element when it actually turned out to be the back one. I only wanted to startle the cat. When the back burner flared up, a yellow flame immediately transferred to the cat and a good chunk of the cat's fur went into flames for a few seconds. The curious thing was, the cat didn't care. It just stood up, stretched, and jumped off the stove. Ten minutes later I was watching a video – *Tootsie*, which I haven't seen in years – and the cat curled up on my lap. I noticed a substantial patch of missing hair along its side.

It's two days later and Faith Fauna is taking me on one of her political protests with her political friends, a highly-impressionable-to-conspiracy-theories bunch with good hearts and dishevelled bird-nesty hair. We're participating in a demonstration against biogenetic engineering by performing street theatre in front of Safeway, with people dressing as giant tomatoes who run away from a mad scientist with a bovine growth hormone injection. Other people are dressed as pigs with fish fins coming out of their heads, or vegetables with animal noses. My job is to video all of this, which means I get to enjoy myself without dressing as a mutant turnip. When some of Faith's friends run into the store to attach stickers on baby food saying, GMO CONTAMINATED!, the manager chases them outside. We make the local news.

Tonight, I'm in my bedroom writing when there's a knock at the door. Faith isn't home so I get up to answer it and even before I get there, I hear, 'Anyone home? Anyone home?' coming from a high-pitched voice fraught with tension. When I open the door, a woman, looking to be in her mid-forties with long black and white frizzy hair floating down her back like a wild mane, is stroking a cat, perhaps one of Faith Fauna's cats – I haven't got these cats sorted out yet. I invite her in and she asks what kind of tea we have. We go into the kitchen. 'Well, let's see. There seems to be all the regular herbal ones, and Chinese sorts of things. How about jasmine?' I say, thinking it might calm her nerves. Or maybe that's chamomile.

'I want to try to get pregnant, but not until January,' she says out of the blue.

I look at her, this woman whose adolescence seems to have congealed beneath the wrinkles of middle age, then I look down at the boxes of teas in my hand. 'Then do you need a special tea for that? For fertility or something?'

'Yeah, probably, but I told you I don't want to get pregnant until January. If I wait 'til January to get pregnant, then I'll give birth to a Virgo Rabbit. I want a Rabbit to get along with a Pig. I'm a Pig and so is my son. Chinese astrology.'

'Oh, right.'

'I definitely don't want to give birth to a Rooster. I hate Roosters. My ex-husband's a Rooster. Roosters are assholes.'

'Oh, so who do you want to have the baby with?'

'My ex-husband.'

'The Rooster?'

'Yeah,' she says, as if it's obvious.

I stare at her hair, how it looks like an unruly multidirectional headdress. 'Well, why are you telling me this?'

'I tell everybody this.' She speaks in a tone which tells of ongoing bitterness, a tone which discourages further questions. I boil water for the tea. Luckily, just then, Faith returns home with a guy named Earle who works with her at the health food store. Earle is a poet and I suspect that's not his real name since he's only 24. While we're drinking green tea and eating hemp carob muffins, Earle, the Chinese astrology woman and Faith get into a conversation about how the FBI introduced crack cocaine and guns into the ghettos of New York City to get rid of all the nonwhites. It seems a little far-fetched to me, but under the circumstances, all I can do is go with the flow.

I've now escaped back into my room. OK, so it's a little flakey here, but it can be flakey anywhere. Just two years ago in Guelph, I lived with three friends in an old Victorian house where the vegetarian landlady downstairs came upstairs once a week, ostensibly to vacuum, but really to sift through our trash for evidence we'd eaten meat – frozen chicken wrappers, old torn-up recipes. She wanted a vegetarian household since she claimed dead animal flesh upset the energy balance of the house, disturbed her dreams, and stunk up the kitchen. We never did eat meat while living there but she didn't believe us, insisting she kept feeling a suspicious vibe of carnage coming down through the ceiling. Her husband, an anaemic-looking waif of a man who hardly spoke, placed copies of the appallingly-written *Celestine Prophecy* on each of our beds when we moved in, explaining it was required reading for anyone living there. Our beds, incidentally, all had to be facing north, something to do with the magnetic pull of the earth. The landlady eventually evicted us because she 'couldn't handle' the negative energy seeping down into her 'living space', negative energy aimed at her. Come to think of it, she was probably right about that part.

No, California doesn't hold a monopoly on flakiness. And besides, not everyone in this state is like these people I've met at Camp Meeker. It's just one Californian world within many. I just have to meet more people.

I'm now meeting more people, at a dinner party in Sebastopol at the home of a botanist named Gerry Green. (Does everyone invent a name for himself around here?) When each guest arrives, Gerry Green tapes the Latin name and common name of a plant on our foreheads and we try to guess which plant we are by going around to each other saying things like, 'Do I flower?' 'Am I deciduous?' 'Do I attract spruce bud worm?' I keep saying, 'Can you smoke me?' which people only laugh politely at, so I start saying, 'Do I smell nice?' and people sniff me. It's actually kind of fun in a nerdy kind of way. It turns out I'm a sugar maple, which I think Gerry Green chose for me on purpose, thoughtfully. I have to ask about 45 questions before I get it, which is strange since I grew up with a giant old sugar maple right in our front yard, a maple that was like a best friend, that I did handstands against, climbed and even, when I was eleven, gave a special name to – Lady Louise of D'Austriana – a maple that crashed down in a tornado five years ago right in front of my eyes, a loss that was like a death in the family. Maybe I fail to guess a sugar maple because there aren't any out here. I'm sure I must be a sequoia or a California sycamore or a juniper or cypress or something. When it finally hits me to say, 'Do I turn red?' everyone shouts out, 'Yes!' as if they can't believe it has taken me this long to guess, making me actually turn red myself. The whole experience has a strange effect on me, saddens me a little being so far away from sugar maples and knowing that if I lived here, I wouldn't see them any more.

The people at the party are all friendly, fun and intelligent and I keep thinking that they could be my new friends. At the same time, I keep thinking that I already have friends back home and in making new ones, would I be replacing the old? I don't want to lose my old friends, but in moving here, I know that gradually over time, I'd drift away from friends I once knew. Also, how long would it take to break into this new group of friends? Could I really do that? I feel like such an outsider to them. I don't have the clues and codes for this culture. It's hard to know what questions to ask, where to even begin. On the other hand, I'm still a traveller here and being a traveller, I'm out of context so I relate to people in a way

I'd never relate to people back home. These Californians are as much a curiosity to me as I am to them. Over time, we'd become real people to each other. For now, our encounters are like travel encounters, inspiring and entertaining, but limited in that we only see the glossy outside.

As I'm thinking about all this, a woman named Cheron sits next to me and tells me she's also just moved here, from upstate New York. She's an artist who turns cutlery into sculptures and wants to open her own studio. She's also very hygienic. She tells me that if a tall man ever comes to visit me, I should ask him to sit down on the toilet to urinate rather than stand, because tall men always splash and get their pee all over the bathroom which is dangerously unsanitary. She's even seen this on *Oprah*.

I'm not sure I could be friends with Cheron.

Even though some of the people I've met can be a little extreme, I do like it here. I've always dreamed of living by the ocean and here I am – it's just over a mountain, twenty minutes away. I've always wanted to be in a place where nature is enormous, magnificent, lushly green, and doesn't include winter. I've always wanted to live in a remote wilderness but be close enough to buy Ben and Jerry's chocolate peanut butter ice cream down the road. I've found all this here. This really is the perfect place.

If only I could wake up in the morning and tumble into the easy current of California. If only I didn't have to sneak out to my car to eat ice cream. Not that I've actually done that yet, but still.

Maybe I'm just a little homesick right now. I broke up with Andre over the phone tonight, a horrible way to break someone's heart. Understandably, Andre is anguished and furious and says he doesn't want to talk to me for at least six years, unless I wake up tomorrow and change my mind.

Dawn is breaking into my foggy shrouded stand of trees, and I still haven't changed my mind. I haven't slept much either. My heart feels like lead and it takes all my will not to pick up the phone and tell Andre I'm coming back home. Yet I know absolutely, no matter what happens to me here in California, I don't belong with him. I'll probably never meet anyone as kind and supportive as he is again. Logically, I should go back to him, but this has nothing to do with logic, and everything to do with a feeling in a much deeper place than where logic resides.

I go for a walk through the woods along a trail to Occidental, which takes about an hour. My heart is aching, but being in this muted cathedral forest helps tremendously. I've never gone for a walk in the woods and not felt better for it.

In Occidental, a village of just two small roads, I'll go to a natural gourmet food store where I'll be able to buy things that I could never find in Guelph, population 120,000. That's a crazy thing about California. Everything is the best quality imaginable. Almost every little town, sometimes even a country crossroads, has a fully equipped espresso stand or Mexican food to die for, a funky used book store, or an artsy movie house, or perhaps a world-class bakery gleaming with pies and astonishing bread selections – multigrain orange macadamia nut, oatmeal apricot chocolate chip, rosemary sea salt rye. Sometimes I enter stores and feel overwhelmed. There are seven kinds of organic pears, six varieties of melons in varying shades of pastel, a stunning selection of avocados, barrels of exotic fruit – fresh dates, calimyrna figs, star fruit, kumquats, lychee fruit, persimmon, feijoa fruit – and mounds of just-picked local spring salad mixtures. Everything is bright, burnished and in season. There are rows upon rows of the best quality, organic, exotic edible delicacies, like chocolate espresso cheesecake muffins, fruit sweetened carob-covered roasted almonds swirled into soy vanilla ice cream, marinated portobello mushroom and sun-dried tomato wraps to go, eighteen flavours of organic coffee, and fresh juices one could live on exclusively for a solid year. And all this just at the corner variety store. Sometimes I wonder what one is to do with all this choice, this excess of health, consciousness and vitality brimming out of every passing man, woman, child and pet. The other day, I went to a restaurant in Sebastopol for lunch. The waiter took a break to step outside for what should be called a 'California cigarette break'. When I saw him through the door, he wasn't smoking a cigarette like nearly every waiter in the rest of the world would do; he was striking a yoga pose, the Eagle Pose to be exact, and he held it for his entire ten-minute break. I figure this is as Californian as it gets.

Everyone is after the same dream in California, all wanting to live the good life. Many of the people I meet are like me times ten, which I find disconcerting. I actually feel kind of conservative in this place. Everyone has a cause and all the causes are worthy. Maybe only a special few can make it in California because the place is so blinding in its excess, its super consciousness, its vitality, its UV index.

Nonetheless, I'm getting used to Faith Fauna's diet of never consuming animal products. In fact, I like being a vegan. It's not a huge leap since I've been mainly vegetarian since I was fifteen. But I'm not a cat lover the way Faith is. Her cats are still driving me crazy. Just this morning I found out there are seven cats living here, not six. What I thought was one big fat slob of a black cat has turned out to be two big fat cat slobs who look and behave exactly alike. The only thing I like about these two particular cats is they're too lazy to kill birds.

A week later I'm beginning to realise that all journeys are strewn with unlikely and small events that strike a resonant chord if only listened for, a chord that could easily be missed. When I travel I always seem to relearn that sometimes it's the seemingly insignificant events which teach the most, their lessons often too fragile to capture.

The other day I got a call from a guy who invited me to the beach. His name is Greg and I'd never met him before but he's an old friend of a friend of mine back home. Greg said he lives in Berkeley and was going camping at a beach just west of here, and he asked if I'd like to join him. I said yes. He is, after all, a good friend of my friend back home. After I drove over my favourite road in the world, Coleman Valley Road, which leads west from Occidental to the ocean, passing first through the redwoods, then over a mountain and past a lonely looking commune called Wind Song, and then past several roaming red cows on a windswept cliff, I arrived at the beach where I was to look for a guy in a large blue van. Greg forgot to describe himself on the phone, so all I had to go on was the blue van. Luckily there weren't many people around. When I saw a guy with tousled brown hair and brawny legs running along the shore with his golden retriever, my heart leapt. As I was contemplating calling out, 'Greg! Over here! The one you've been looking for all your life,' a voice called out behind me. I turned around to see a man with a long grey ponytail and unreasonably large beer gut standing next to a blue van and waving at me. The guy running on the shore began throwing sticks into the ocean for his dog. I watched the scene for a moment longer and let die the fantasy of my new life with that guy and his dog and all those evening jogs along the sand at sunset. It was a little hard to let it go because a goofy golden retriever is one of the things I've always wanted in life eventually and, of course, a guy to go with it. I turned around to walk towards the blue van, which the man with the ponytail, who didn't really look like a Greg, was rummaging through to pull out a case of beer. We shook hands and when he revealed his imperfect teeth to say, 'Hi there!' I was suddenly overcome with a wash of happiness. It seemed at that moment that nothing in this world is as remarkable as a single 'Hi there' from a fellow human, perhaps because I've been feeling a little lonely lately. We had an instantly friendly connection, chatting affably about our old friend back home and how the two of them had met when their bus had broken down in the Andes and how they'd had to walk down a mountain at midnight. Greg and I made a campfire, ate sandwiches and drank red wine. He told me his life story but forgot to ask about mine, and we discussed the Middle East. He told engaging stories of his love life: how once a woman tried to bill him for her counselling after they broke up. He said he'd been married already and was now between girlfriends. It was an unusually cold night, as it sometimes is right on the coast in the summer, and when it came time to sleep, I realised my sleeping bag wouldn't be warm enough. I was going to sleep in my tent and Greg casually suggested I sleep on the bed in his van since there was lots of room and it would be much warmer in there. This all seemed fine until about twenty seconds after we went to bed and he started snoring at 300 decibels. The noise was fearful, a thunderous crashing much louder than the nearby waves. He seemed to have that condition, sleep apnoea, where people don't breathe for a long time, like ten seconds, and you think they've either finally stopped snoring or are dead, but then they suddenly suck in the equivalent of a whole van-load of oxygen and seem to be warning you that the world is about to end. It was truly awful, possibly the worst event I've participated in since Grade 7, and I couldn't sleep for more than ten seconds at a time. I couldn't see how he could get a restful sleep either, practically having a thousand heart attacks all night like that. The poor guy. I doubt robust snoring is one of the seven habits of highly effective people. Eventually I bolted up to say, 'Oh my God. I have to go now. I really can't sleep here.' I was ready to get in my car and drive back home at three in the morning. Greg was quite offended, as people who snore often are when accused, and he slammed the door to set his tent up outside, swearing and muttering to himself throughout the whole tent erecting ordeal. I felt bad, but at least I could sleep after that. It was awkward in the morning. We took a walk on the beach and parted with one of those let's-never-see-each-other-again goodbyes. As I drove back home I thought of how it was all kind of sad, for both of us really, another aborted attempt at making a new friend, and I thought of how I'd already been through far too many similar nights like that in my life. What was I doing wrong? Hadn't I learned, at one time or another, everything I needed to know to make my way as a single woman? It should be enough already. I should be able to piece all the years of my life together, all the things I must have learned along the way, and have it figured out by now. I have enough stories. I once scared a guy away because I had too many stories, scared him with my life's adventures, every story dating me, ageing me, making him wonder if I was too eccentric. After a while, the stories aren't so funny. They're just a series of bad nights when snoring keeps you awake, or the bus breaks down. The months and years keep blowing along by that calendar-ripping wind from old movies. I sometimes wonder if going from one place to the next, free and easy, is all it's cracked up to be.

It's a few days later and I'm at a famous bookstore in Berkeley called Cody's because Suzy Bright is reading her latest anthology of erotica. She's really funny, and I love it that there are so many book events in the Bay area, a different one every night. Afterwards, I take a walk to buy a juice, but all the shops in this trendy neighbourhood are closed, so I find a corner gas station variety store. Once inside, I get into a conversation with the guy behind the counter. He's from Bhutan and has only been here ten months. I've never met anyone from Bhutan. It's one of the places I've always wanted to go, a closed kingdom in the Himalayas which few people ever leave and even fewer visit. This endearing little guy tells me that when he first landed in the San Francisco airport he didn't know how to use the phone because he'd never *seen* a phone before. He tells me his country is truly ancient, nothing modern at all. While we're talking, a policeman comes in and asks us if we've seen a big Samoan guy. Apparently, as the Bhutanese guy and I were talking, a big Samoan guy had stolen a car from a couple buying gas, just outside the store. We're a little bewildered, yet feel strangely removed from the situation because it seems so unreal, both of us being from places where robbery isn't a daily occurrence. I ask him about theft in Bhutan and he says when he was a kid, someone stole one of his father's yaks. The whole village was up in arms about it.

I sense he's a little homesick, as is to be expected in a place where there aren't any yaks around. I miss yaks too, even though I've never seen a yak. I guess it's something else I miss. I'm just not sure what.

Cave Journal

Another failed attempt at making a fire! It's too damp here, the driftwood is moist, and I don't have any kindling or paper to burn. I really want to try cooking those mussels, but more than that, I want a fire for warmth in the evening. And for company too. I think I might finally be getting lonely here, or at least pensive. I'm wondering what to do next, where to go, and when. I can't exactly live in a cave forever.

Here, my life is pared down to its barest bones. With no distractions, far from the world of people, I get to see a part of myself that I don't often see. Only what is significant rises to the surface of my mind. For instance, more and more lately, I've come to realise that one must care deeply about something to make life truly fulfilling. I don't want to continue living day to day, moment to moment, as a hobo on the road. I need to care about something large and important, but what?

As each day passes into the next I'm marking myself with this place, with its dark sand, eternal surf and seclusion. If I stay long enough I'll have marked myself to the point of no return. I'll turn into a wild woman who has forgotten how to speak. Every day the sand grinds deeper into my skin like a gauge of how far I've come from my old self. Occasionally I check for signs of how I might be different. Under these Pacific skies I'm becoming whatever I can find out about myself. What do I want to do in the world? I'm certainly not good at making fires, that's obvious. (I guess that rules out being a camp director.) I love reading, contemplating life and travelling – except, like fire building, travelling is a lot harder work than I ever thought it would be, something I learned earlier this year, hitchhiking in Oregon. I'll just have to keep thinking about it. I suppose that all of us, in our own way, ventures as far as we have to in search of ourselves, even if we happen to be in a cave at the time.

I wonder when I'll return to this place, if ever. Maybe it won't be until after I die. I'll come back here on my old woman wings, fly here like the gulls and look down on who I used to be. The sky is turning a dark shadowy blue. Will I leave here tomorrow or stay another day?

I don't remember feeling lonely in the cave, but reading this entry I guess I did. Perhaps loneliness isn't a memory we recall easily. It slips away, surges forward and recedes like the tides, overcoming us one moment and edging back the next, always a little mysteriously. My memories of that place are so sublime. I know I was never bored on that beach for a second and always felt as if there was so much to do. But how could there have been? For a lot of the day I tried to find and dry firewood and I collected things on the beach – I still have a collection of blue rocks and shells from there. Every morning I'd lay out my cold damp sleeping bag and clothes on a big flat rock in the sun. I read lots of books, walked along the shore, ran in and out of the feet-chilling waves. I remember drinking cool fresh water from the stream which thankfully never made me sick. I didn't have much food with me, just a bag of granola and dried fruit from San Francisco, which wasn't very good planning. My most vivid memories are of tracking the sun, climbing up in my cave every evening to watch the sun slip into the sea, trying to memorise the red violet scars left in the sky. I'd notice the beach's change in mood after the sun dropped away, how the gulls' calls rose higher, became almost frantic, as if they were wary of the coming darkness. And afterwards, all that starlight. No sight our eyes can look on is more inspiring than the night sky flamboyant with stars. The stars wouldn't let me sleep. I'd dream of my whole future under those stars, a different future every night.

I wonder what happened to those futures dreamt by the cave girl? Did they make their way up to the stars, or burn up like stray aimless meteorites on their way?

Today I'm driving north from Bodega Bay along Route 1, which, on this part of the coast, is always within view of the ocean. It never gets too hot or too cold on the coast here in California. The ocean acts like a giant air conditioner in the summer and keeps the air relatively warm in the winter, producing a Mediterranean climate. I'm envious of the people who grew up in this scenically magnificent place and would always feel at home here. I just don't feel at home here.

As I drive I keep thinking that there are so many things I love about this place, but I can't help missing the familiarity of home. I miss just walking down the street in Guelph and knowing half the people I see. I miss the market and going to my favourite coffee house. There are so many better coffee houses out here, with better food, better coffees, more interesting magazines to read, but I don't know the people inside them. That seems to matter. I guess something about familiarity is important to me: being in a place where you know intimately every house in your neighbourhood and who used to live there and you know all the shortcuts to get anywhere in town and you know which dogs are friendly and which neighbourhoods are too; you know all the hills and curves in a road and where to slow down on your bike; you know the scents in the air in the different seasons and you understand the architecture and the vegetation. The thing is, I can still move to a new place like this and learn all these things, but how long will it take? Or maybe I'd never really learn these things. Maybe, some of these things you can only absorb when you're young and rarely when you're an adult, just like speech. Maybe I can never feel truly at home anywhere but in my hometown. When I think of Guelph I think of riding my bike all over the place, my green ten-speed I had for years. I knew every inch of road. I still do. Could I ever really get that feeling of familiarity riding a bike somewhere else? Does it matter? What do I lose moving here and what do I gain? There are so many ideal places in the world with mountains and oceans and rivers and interesting people, but the place where we were raised must be imprinted on our psyches like a brand. The fact that my home lacks scenic drama is an aesthetic misfortune, but comfort is an emotion. It's emotionally comfortable for me in Ontario. When I lived in Colorado at 17, I was surrounded by snow-capped mountains, green meadows and sweet-smelling conifers, but I missed maple trees. The mountains, in their towering magnificence, never felt like home.

But perhaps one always feels like an outsider in a new place, an outsider to the community and to the landscape, and then eventually the feeling passes. And I know that sometimes I've felt intimately at home in places I'd only just arrived, places where the spirit of the earth is too strong not to feel at home, like right here in the redwoods when I first came to this state. So maybe it's the people. I see people all over the place here in California that I could be friends with – and I've actually already made quite a few new friends – writers and travellers, outdoorsy environmentalists, fun-loving and like-minded outcasts of normal. Yet other than Ann and Lawrence who I've known since Fiji, I don't have a history with these people, although I could if I stayed.

These are my thoughts as I drive high on this meandering road along a cliff and beside a creek gushing into the Pacific below, as the sun melts the sky and water and my memories together on the horizon. Higher up I drive, around a bend where I look out to find exactly the blue and green colour combination I've always dreamed of, like a tropical parrot flying free, and what lies beyond the ocean on the other side, Asia in all its aching beauty – so far gone from me now – and the sea birds so close I could reach out and touch the sky reflecting off their white wings.

It's all so damn perfect, California, and I wonder, why don't I want to stay here?

Chapter 18

It's a few days later and Ann and Lawrence and I are on our way to the annual Straus farm party in West Marin, near a place called Marshall. It's to be a giant 'potluck' on an organic dairy farm, an all day party by the ocean with live music and dancing and people from as far away as San Francisco. Parties are a regular occurrence here in California. We stop on our way at the five-star Tomales Bakery and the owners tell us they're moving their business north where it's quieter, since here they're bombarded daily with bicyclists who pile into the bakery wanting specialty coffees and buying up all the pastries. Even though business is good, they say, it's too hectic. We continue south along coastal Highway 1 where we pass droves of bicyclists heading for the bakery, and feathery pampas blowing in the breeze. It's a perfect day for a party. Even Ben and Jerry, the ice cream makers, are supposed to be there since they use the Straus's organic cream in their products.

When we arrive, there are already at least a hundred people at the party, standing around talking, playing mandolins and singing, gazing out at the ocean. Long tables are crammed with fresh food: home-made breads and mocha cream tarts, local wines and cheeses, soufflés, quiches, candied yam tortes and gigantic exotic salads. There's also a chocolate fondue with organic strawberries and mangoes for dipping. Where I come from, people bring nachos to a potluck. Ann and Lawrence introduce me to the host, Michael, who tells me he's visiting Europe soon, but stopping first in Guelph of all places, to meet another organic dairy farmer.

It's now dark and we've made a bonfire. I go inside to borrow a jacket and get into a conversation with a Chinese-American woman law student who is the lead guitar player in a band. She and I decide to explore the rambling nineteenth-century house, and come across an old record collection which we rifle through with glee. I love old records. There's Neil Young's *Harvest* album, a favourite of mine in my twenties, lots of Bob Dylan, Billie Holiday, John Prine, U2, even Bruce Cockburn from Canada, and, I'm thrilled to see, all of Bruce Springsteen's albums, even his early ones. Then I find a record without its cover, a little scratched, and when I look at the label, I see it's Joni Mitchell's *Blue* album. I put it on the stereo and we turn up the speakers so they can hear it outside. When the song 'California' comes on, I go out to the fire and ask the people toasting marshmallows what Joni Mitchell is saying: is she willing to kiss a sunset pink or a sunset pig? We have to play that part of the song back a couple times to discover what I already know, that it's impossible to tell what she's saying. One guy claims she's saying 'pig', what the hippies called policemen in the sixties. He says Joni Mitchell was singing she'd come back to California even if she had to kiss a cop on Sunset Boulevard, but Joni Mitchell herself has never confirmed this. Someone else has a more poetic explanation. At first all I hear is a voice across the roaring tall fire, a voice saying something about kissing a sunset pig being an old Greek superstition. I look through the flames to see a man looking back at me, and I wonder where he came from. I haven't seen him at the party until now and I marvel at how I could have missed him. He seems to be about my age or possibly older – I've lost the ability to gauge people's ages – and he has windswept blondish hair and hazel eyes alit with the perfect blend of calm and trouble. He's wearing a lived-in Levi jean jacket and when we move closer I see that his entire personality is caught up in the shyness of his smile. His name is Gabe. He isn't clear on the details of the Greek superstition, but he thinks that when someone was lost, like a Greek sailor, and washed up on a Greek island and wanting to find home, the islanders would dare that person to kiss a pig so they could find their way home. Those who kissed a pig at sunset would be sure to find what they were looking for. As he's speaking, I wonder if I've just found what I'm looking for right beside me. Except there's no pig around – it seems to be a vegetarian potluck – and the sunset is long gone. I have to remind myself this isn't the first time I've thought I've just found Mr Right.

The party goes on for hours. I sit next to Gabe and sing along with Ann and Lawrence songs we sang at campfires in Fiji, which makes me nostalgic for those soft languorous nights with bowls of kava and stories and South Pacific waves washing ashore. Later, Gabe and I take a walk along the beach with his friend Malcolm Chase. Malcolm Chase's father is Hal Chase, the character named Chad King in Jack Kerouac's *On the Road*. It was Hal Chase who brought Kerouac, Neal Cassidy and Allen Ginsberg together. I'm fascinated by Malcolm's stories of his father and his friendship with the famous Beatnik whose books I've read so many times. The three of us take a drive in Malcolm's '52 Chevy panel truck down the winding road to Gabe's place and sit on his deck. Gabe's deck is right over the ocean, or, actually, right over Tomales Bay and the San Andreas fault line, and on the other side of the bay is Point Reyes National Seashore and my cave. My cave. I can hardly believe I'm standing so close. As I contemplate this, Gabe and Malcolm tell me they're building remote control sharks to scare away the hoards of kayakers who paddle down the bay every day. I've never thought of kayakers as being annoying, certainly not like snowmobilers, or those obnoxious brats on jet skis. Maybe the kayakers are like the Highway 1 bicyclists, too many of them taking up a small space with a nice view. This seems to be a recurring theme here in California: too many people knowing it's beautiful and wanting the beauty only for themselves.

When dawn begins to fill the sky, Gabe and Malcolm drive me back to the party, where Ann, Lawrence and about six of their friends are still singing at a dwindling fire. Gabe invites me to come back and visit him. I think I will. Anyone who claims to know about Greek superstitions, can build a fake shark, and whose best friend's father was an old friend of Jack Kerouac, must have a few things to say.

It's a few days later and I'm driving down to Point Reyes to find my cave, taking narrow back roads that amble through the woods and then come out onto grassy hill country by the ocean. I've tried finding my cave before and it's as if the place never existed. But of course it did. I have the journal and pictures, along with a collection of memories, shells and blue rocks I gathered there.

I'm broken down in Tomales. Only halfway to Point Reyes, halfway to my cave, and Marcia has decided this is finally it for her. She barely rolls into the Tomales mechanic shop, a place called Dan's Automotive, where Dan is away on vacation. Dan's brother, however, a mechanic in training, tells me he'll fix the car. Although I've heard this before all across the country, I believe Dan's brother. This time feels different. After spilling my situation to him, Dan's brother looks sympathetic, determined, and entirely innocent. He tells me to come back in two hours.

I've explored all of Tomales, have taken a walk, have had peppermint tea at Angel's Café, have eaten a spinach feta turnover at the bakery, and have sat on a bar stool drinking beer with some locals at the William Tell tavern. After two hours, Marcia still isn't ready so I wait another hour, then another. Finally, Dan's brother tells me to come back tomorrow.

Fortunately, Gabe just happens to live twenty minutes down the road.

He comes to pick me up and the drive back to his place is a winding blur of golden grasses in the late afternoon sun, old farms, the Pacific Ocean, wild flowers, deer galloping across the road, and two people pretending to have a light conversation about the nice weather we've been having lately, when really, the two people are trying to ascertain if the other person is 1) smart enough, 2) good-looking enough, 3) interesting enough, 4) open to the idea of a meaningful-yet-fun and deep long-lasting relationship. Children aren't mentioned since the ride is only twenty minutes.

Back at Gabe's place, he shows me his workshop off the deck where he makes intricate metal designs for rich people in the area, and a clever poster he has just painted about dogs which I tell him could sell nationwide. We drive east in his truck over the mountain to the town of Petaluma where we play a pickup volleyball game with his friends, and afterwards, all go out to eat and drink at the lively McNear Restaurant and Mystic Theatre. I laugh most of the night because Gabe is so funny. At midnight when we drive back, a deer leaps out in front of the truck and Gabe has to slam his brakes. When we return, we watch shooting stars from his deck, and then, as I begin to fall asleep on his couch – although he's offered to share his bed – I listen to the lapping waters of Tomales Bay and think, tomorrow, I'll find my cave.

It's now 'tomorrow' and I won't be finding my cave just yet. Dan's brother still hasn't figured out Marcia's problem, but he tells me he's trying different ideas and says to call back later today. Gabe and I go for a ride in his boat and find a colony of seals playing on some rocks. When we reach an island, we get out for a picnic. Gabe tells me about his last girlfriend who wanted to get married for years, but then mysteriously left him, and he never found out why. I wonder why too. He's so creative and fun. Still, I sense something guarded about him.

Another day has passed and still Marcia isn't fixed. Dan's brother seems to be doing a full autopsy on her, taking all her insides out, putting them back in. Poor Marcia. Gabe has to build someone an outdoor staircase, so I spend the day on his deck reading. I'm starting to feel kind of stranded here, even though I like Gabe's company. But something doesn't feel quite right. Even though all the ingredients are inside him for the perfect guy, I don't think I'm falling in love with him. When he speaks of his past there's a sadness around his eyes which I'm not sure I can bear. What's strange is he's not saying a single sad thing.

Why is finding the right person so difficult for me? I've read that once a woman reaches 30, her chances of finding a mate decrease by 10 per cent every year, which isn't good news for single women in their forties. But what a ridiculous claim, as if love can be measured statistically. Still, among my girlfriends in Guelph, the city of women, this seems to be true. I sometimes feel that with every year that goes by, I become more independent, more self-reliant, maybe more unique, and finding someone to match my personality becomes harder and harder.

What I want is for my car to be fixed so I can go to Point Reyes. Sometimes I look across Tomales Bay from Gabe's deck and know that somewhere on the other side of the water lies a sunset cove with a cave and the footprints of a girl who believed that among all the struggle and beauty of the world, life would work out exactly how she dreamt it would.

On my fourth day here, Dan's brother is extremely proud of himself when he tells me what Marcia's trouble has been all along: a tiny computer chip. The tiny computer chip was confusing the car, making Marcia 'run rich' with gas, surge, and then mysteriously slow down. To think I had to drive across a continent to find this out. Dan's brother doesn't even charge me much since he's still in training and says it shouldn't have taken him so long to figure out something so basic. I tell him he figured out what no other mechanic on a 2,500 mile drive could.

I leave Gabe's place after lunch and continue south to Point Reyes in what feels like an entirely different car. In the Point Reyes visitor centre, I learn that in 1962, Congress approved the establishment of Point Reyes National Seashore, a pristine area of beach, dune and forest, 53,000 acres in size, to be kept in splendid isolation. Then I find a map I've never seen before. Touching the drawings of its many beaches, I feel exhilaration shoot up my arm like an electric shock. One of these beaches is where I spent six days.

I drive north from Point Reyes Station, then west, towards a lighthouse. Occasionally the road reaches a high place where I catch glimpses of the Pacific stretching out to the sky, a giant liquid mirror to a sun that scatters stars across the water. At the lighthouse, a few people are gathered to look for whales but it's not the right season for their migration. I stop at a beach near the lighthouse and walk towards the shore. Nobody is around and I try to recall something of the place, try to squeeze a memory out of its parched driftwood. A lone pelican swoops its wings towards the sea at breakneck speed and it's like something out of the world's dawn. I don't recall seeing pelicans all those years ago, only hawks and gulls. I don't see where a cave could have been here either. In fact, nothing about this beach is familiar.

I try another beach, this one with some trees on it. Trees don't seem to belong out here, certainly not to the memory of my cove, and I wonder how much a place could have changed in thirteen years. No, I'm sure this isn't the right beach either.

The next beach is long, narrow and not secluded like mine was. I begin to wonder if I should give up the search. It's not as if this is the first time I've tried to find the place again. I always seem to decide that maybe the cave is best left to my memories and journal anyway. As I continue my drive, an elk dashes in front of my car and we almost collide. That would be ironic, to crash my car after finally getting it fixed. On the main road back I see a smaller road turning north. I take the road even though I doubt it will lead to the cave, then take another road off that one, now just driving for the hell of it and not even looking at the map. The sky is a piercing blue, bluer perhaps since the ocean is so close, and above the blue of the sky I sense the whole of outer space: a field of stars and youthful dreams and time standing still, or maybe, moving so fast we don't even see it. I continue north on the narrow road through rolling hills and gradually, everything around me begins to feel like a vaguely remembered dream. I recognise the meadow of cows, the surprising pastoral feel to the place – cows way out here so close to the ocean, so far from any visible farm. I remember commenting on that to the Quaker couple on their first date. 'What are cows doing out here? This feels like Wales!' I stop at Kehoe Beach and it's gleaming and remote and full of unusual rocks, but it's not my beach. I get back in the car and keep going. I drive all the way to the end of the road, to McClures Beach, not a familiar name, but maybe I never even noticed the name. I was after all, just hitchhiking that day and hadn't intended to stay so long. I park Marcia at the little parking lot gripped by wind, and that's when I see it: the little path in the corner of the parking lot leading down to the shore. I grab my cave journal and camera from the backseat and run for the path. I run all the way down, past the brook where I drank the water, until I arrive at the beach. The beach lies naked, not a soul around, just as it was then. The sun is a sharp glare on the ocean. I look down at Rocky Point, Mystery Cove, Jagged Beach. I turn around to scan the red cliffs. I run further down the shore. I see the place where I collected stones, where I used to read, where I dried my clothes on the big flat rock. I see my familiar view out to sea, but I don't see a cave. The cliffs look different, eroded, and for a moment, I'm stunned. But there, near the brook and halfway up one of the cliffs, I see where a cave could have been. There's an indentation along the cliff wall where the cave must have been washed away, perhaps by the 1989 earthquake or by the torrential rains of El Nino. Everything is coming back to me. I remember where I used to walk to the right of the brook along a cliff-side path to get up to the cave. I can't believe the cave is gone. I can't believe the cave ever was there. A cave that I stayed in, where I slept six nights, and where every one of those nights I watched the collapse of the sun into the sea, the first stars lighting up the cold nights and their slow steady passage through the darkness. Standing here after thirteen years I feel the tide of the ocean sweeping through me all over again. I thought I might never get back here, or at least not until after I died when I'd fly over here with long white hair flowing, looking down. But I haven't died. I'm just starting new. The briny air is full of memory and I'm breathing it in as though I can never have enough of it. There's no sense in trying to describe such a moment. I feel an old wildness again. I want to run up and down the shore. I want to stay here until the stars come out and dance across the sky. I'd forgotten. I'd forgotten so much of her.

The big rock down at Rocky Point is still black with mussels. The roar of the ocean is deafening, the waves thunderous. I wonder how I slept with those waves. I wonder how I slept with them gone. What did I do when I left this place? I remember walking away from here, walking along that winding road and wondering if I really should be leaving, and then, hitchhiking with a Frenchman who told me he'd been staying at a lighthouse hostel where he'd heard people talking about a cave girl, and now here he was meeting that girl. He had doubted the story before that. He was an artist, drove a breezy little rented car, and wanted to visit Alcatraz that afternoon. I remember getting to a bus station in San Francisco that evening where I bought a Trailways bus pass which would allow me to go anywhere in the continental U.S. in ten days. In the bus station restroom, I washed my hair and saw myself for the first time in a week. The cheap fluorescent lights on either side of the mirror above the sink revealed a startling sight: a face grown thin with strangely deep-set eyes, a sunburned face, streaked with dirt and some scrapes across the cheeks, a face that anyone who happened to notice would see was clearly, and irrepressibly, radiant with life.

Cave Journal

I finally made a fire!! I had to tear tons of blank pages out of this journal to do it, pages that could have been filled with more ramblings, but I really needed this fire. This is the first fire I've ever made all on my own and I was down to my third last soggy match when it finally took. After getting the fire going, which the gulls seemed to celebrate as much as I did, I ran with my cooking pot down to Rocky Point where that big black rock is covered in mussels. The tide was coming in and it was dangerous as hell making my way out there – it would have been better an hour ago. I slipped on one of the rocks when a wave crashed in and I fell right down, scraping my knees, hands, and even my face a little. I almost turned around and gave up, but am so glad I didn't. I cooked the mussels, which were exquisite, sort of, and am now letting the fire burn down as the sun touches the horizon. Making this fire has energised me, made me see things more clearly. I feel so full of my future. I have so much to do in this life. How can I grasp it all? Where do I even begin?

I begin by leaving here, by riding this wind that has been blowing through me all week, because I finally know where I want to go, what I want to do, my direction: I want to return to university. I want to be a teacher and a writer. And then I want to travel the world, not as an aimless wanderer, but as a writer and a teacher. I want to explore this planet, meet interesting and unusual people, teach overseas, in different cultures, have adventures, international intrigues. I want so much. These sleepless nights under the stars have distilled this understanding in me, of who I am and what I want. I'll return to university next semester and learn as much as I can. There's a lot to learn and to care about deeply, and it can't all be done on the road. I'll keep travelling, of course, but I want to travel with more of a purpose, at least, some of the time.

I'd love to live in a place like this, but there's so much to do first. For now, all I can do is close my eyes, face the ocean, and breathe in a promise that I'll come back some day.

It's now past the pink time of night and sunlight has faded over the world. I know I have to leave here tomorrow. I've run out of food – unless I want to live solely off mussels – and I'm worried about drinking water from the brook when cows are up in the hills. The idea of leaving here gets harder by the hour. It could be easy to stay another six days, another six days after that, letting the pulse of the sea keep alive my heartbeat, while day by day, language grows more scarce and I more distant from the other world, falling further and deeper into a cove uncomplicated by human intervention.

But how could I keep creating my life if I stayed? There's only so much this place can teach me. The other day I found a quotation from Plato scrawled into one of my second-hand books. Now I think I understand what he meant: 'And the climb upward out of the cave into the upper world is the ascent of the mind into the domain of true knowledge.'

I'll leave my cave tomorrow. Other world, here I come…

The words have been written all along in this notebook, words I wrote years ago right on this beach. How could I have forgotten? This is what happens with this kind of thing. You have a youthful idea or notion or revelation and you put it away, like putting something in the back of a dark closet, and gradually you stop thinking about it. Other things begin to crowd it out as the years go by, until you've forgotten completely that what was in your dark closet was your treasure. This is the place I dreamed up my life, right here. This is my treasure. It's my treasure because I've lived the life I wrote about in this notebook. I did return to university that next semester, studied international development and read hundreds of books about history, politics and anthropology. I went to teachers' college a year after graduating from university, after my trips to Europe, Jamaica and the Yukon. I taught school on the native reserve, in Fiji and Malaysia, taught English as a second language to immigrants in Guelph, taught English Literature in high schools, loved and lost, lived in remote and exotic places, became a writer, and had several adventures along the way. The cave was just the beginning, the place I needed to go first to decide how to live, to draw the map of my life. I see now that I haven't been living the wrong life after all, that my travelling and writing and teaching and relationships have evolved past some string of adventures into my life itself. I guess I've grown up since leaving the cave.

It's so strange to look back across all these years and journeys to arrive at the edge of my own continent, back to the girl I once was. I'm coming home to my beginnings, unleashing that girl. A whole hidden life is flooding back to my consciousness. It hasn't been a home in California I've been looking for all this time, but the girl who spent six days in a cave, running up and down the shore calling out to the cliffs and gulls and staying awake to watch the stars swirl through the sky, the girl who knew finding a permanent home would never be her nature and who knew exploring the world was. Like these odd little rocks and shells strewn along the shore, I'm picking up pieces of myself I left here years ago. I can still polish her off. I can still let her shine as she did then.

Gazing up to where the cave was, I wonder if I could stay here again for another six nights. Would I want to? The ground couldn't have been anything but hard, cold and damp. No, I don't think I could do that again. Nor do I want to live in a teepee. Is it because, as Wordsworth wrote, reflecting on leaving his childhood, that 'there hath pass'd away a glory from the earth'? Maybe none of us, once we reach a certain age, can go back and see the world the way we used to, through youthful eyes. For now it's enough to know I can still see the world this way sometimes, catch glimpses of it, like right now, or occasionally in a foreign land. It's enough to know that I slept on Greek beaches, in trees and caves and inside hollowed-out logs and on tops of picnic tables so I could watch the stars all night. It's enough. I still like sleeping outside. I just can't work up the enthusiasm for these hard, cold grounds any more.

I walk towards Mystery Cove. I don't recall the exact view from Mystery Cove, but am starting to realise I may be at the end of this particular journey, a journey where I've learned that out of all the confusion comes the answer to the question I didn't ask, but should have: not where should I live, or even, where do I belong, but how do I recapture the old me? I've been right here all along. I never left.

I had the whole world ahead of me when I left this cove. I suppose that's a gift of youth: we never knew what would happen next. That's what's missing as we get older. We lose that thrilling sense of not knowing, the gift of a possible turn in the road, of anything might happen. We had no idea what life had in store for us, but we longed for things. But being back here today, I feel that again, not knowing where the road will lead, and I like it as much as I did then. The notion of having a home in California doesn't seem necessary to me right now. It has been devoured by the immensity of this brilliant beach where I imagined my life into being, by the influence of the sky, the sun, the water, on my inner landscape, by the place near the shore where I once built a fire, where I was truly happy. I'm feeling an inexplicable pull back to Ontario and I have to follow it. Perhaps I'll try living in California again when the time is right, and perhaps it's true that home isn't a place after all, but something we carry inside us. I knew this once and am only now recalling that there's a profound world of discovery in the familiar.

The sun, getting low on the horizon, warms my face as I look out to sea. A gull cries out over the waves. Nobody can see very deeply into the ocean and who really knows what will happen next? As the sun shoots its rays all this way across time and space, our hearts are pierced by memories of something like paradise. We're seekers then, if we choose, and the vast blue skies are full of endless possibility.

In the sand I begin to draw a giant pig, a pig with an enormous grin and looking more handsome than any pig I've ever seen.

Epilogue

Shortly after re-finding my cave, I flew home to Canada, deciding that driving back across the scorching desert in September bordered on insanity. I left Marcia with friends in San Francisco, parked high on a hill with a spectacular view of the Golden Gate Bridge. The next winter, I returned to California where once again I tried to make it my promised land, but after four months, felt the same overpowering magnetic draw back to Ontario. That spring, in my hometown of Guelph, I met the man who would become my husband. The next year, we travelled together for six months in a camper van, mostly in California, up and down the coast, in the deserts, under Joshua trees, and in a place I didn't know about in my early California days, San Luis Obispo, the perfect town. After our trip, we returned to Guelph to live in a farmhouse outside of town where we got married beside a river, surrounded by a lively wealth of friends and family. We now have a baby son, Quinn Orion (a very Californian name, someone recently mentioned), and live part time in a Quebec village overlooking a river on the Canadian Shield, and part time in Guelph. I often still dream of living in California, but now that I'm no longer an entity on my own in this world, logistics get in the way. I like to think that on the other side of the continent may be another life, one I didn't live, one I imagined, or one still to be lived some day.

As for Marcia, I like to think she's still cruising around California living the good life.

About the Author

Lauded by *TIME* magazine as 'one of the new generation of intrepid young female travel writers', Laurie Gough is author of *Kite Strings of the Southern Cross: A Woman's Travel Odyssey*, shortlisted for the Thomas Cook Travel Book Award, and silver medal winner of *Foreword* magazine's Travel Book of the Year in the U.S. Seventeen of her stories have been anthologised in various literary travel books, including Salon.com's *Wanderlust: Real-Life Tales of Adventure and Romance*; *AWOL: Tales for Travel-Inspired Minds*; *Sand in My Bra: Funny Women Write from the Road*; *Hyenas Laughed at Me and Now I Know Why: The Best of Travel Humor and Misadventure*; and *A Woman's World*. She has written for Salon.com, the *LA Times*, the *Globe and Mail*, the *National Post*, *Outpost*, *Canadian Geographic*, numerous literary journals, and has got lost on buses in so many countries that she has decided to take up hitch-hiking again when she's 72.

www.lauriegough.com

Photo by: Laura Taylor